Enter the Mouth of the Dragon

For hundreds of years, the imagination of humankind has been captured by the vision of the mythical dragon—an archetype which resonates deeply within the human psyche as a symbol of knowledge and wisdom beyond the reach of mortal humans.

However, dragons are far more than imaginary creatures in fairy tales. *Dragons are as real as we are*—but they live on the astral plane, which coexists with and intersects our physical plane. Dragons have control of deeper currents of elemental energies than are usually felt by humans—and once befriended, dragons make excellent protectors and powerful fellow magicians. *Dancing with Dragons* will tell you not only how you can make contact with these ancient astral powers, but how you can work with them to protect your home … tap into a vast reserve of energy … gaze into the future … and aid all of your magickal workings.

Until now there has been little of practical value written on dragons, especially dragon magick. This is the first book ever to provide complete dragon rituals—for initiation, blessing your tools, calling your chosen dragon and more—as well as information on appropriate music, dance, and tools to use with your rituals.

Because you need to learn as much as possible about the many types of dragons and their habits in order to make contact with them, this book has chapter after chapter packed with dragon lore to help you contact the appropriate power, depending on your need.

Early mapmakers drew dragons at the edges of their maps to denote unknown territory. Some explorers ventured no further than what was known—but others looked upon this venture into dragon territory as an opportunity for amazing discoveries.

This book is your invitation to open the door between realms—and dance with the dragons to lift all areas of your life into a powerful new plane.

About the Author

D.J. Conway was born in Hood River, Oregon, to a family of Irish-North Germanic-Native North American descent. She began her quest for knowledge of the occult more than 25 years ago, and has been involved in many aspects of New Age religion from the teachings of Yogananda to study of the Qabala, healing, herbs, and Wicca. Although an ordained minister in two New Age churches and holder of a Doctor of Divinity degree, Conway claims that her heart lies within the Pagan cultures. No longer actively lecturing and teaching as she did for years, Conway has centered her energies on writing. Several of her stories have been published in magazines, such as *Encounters*, which pertain to the field of science fantasy.

To Write to the Author

If you wish to contact the author or would like more information about this book, please write to the author in care of Llewellyn Worldwide and we will forward your request. Both the author and publisher appreciate hearing from you and learning of your enjoyment of this book and how it has helped you. Llewellyn Worldwide cannot guarantee that every letter written to the author can be answered, but all will be forwarded. Please write to:

D.J. Conway
c/o Llewellyn Worldwide
P.O. Box 64383, Dept. L165-1,
St. Paul, MN 55164-0383, U.S.A.

Please enclose a self-addressed, stamped envelope for reply, or $1.00 to cover costs.
If outside U.S.A., enclose international postal reply coupon.

Dancing With Dragons

Invoke Their Ageless Wisdom & Power

D.J. Conway

1998
Llewellyn Publications
St. Paul, Minnesota 55164-0383, U.S.A.

FIRST EDITION
Sixth Printing, 1998

Cover by Lissanne Lake
Illustrations on pages 54, 59, 67, 70, 72, 73, 74, 75, 76, 77, 78, 81, 94, 142, 145, 147, 149, 151, and 195 by Jim Garrison from sketches by D.J. Conway
Illustrations on pages 9, 12, 15, 17, 21, 27, 29, 32, 35, 37, 41, 45, 51, 101, 103, 107, 123, 157, 161, 165, 169, 171, 175, 177, 180, 181, 191, 201, 220, and 230 from *Treasury of Fantastic and Mythological Creatures* by Richard Huber (New York: Dover Publications, Inc., 1981. Used by permission.
Drawing on page 23 by Linda Norton
Chapter motif from *Pugin's Gothic Ornament* by Augustus Charles Pugin (New York: Dover Publications, Inc., 1987), originally published as *Gothic Ornaments Selected from Various Buildings in England and France* (London: 1828–31)

Library of Congress Cataloging in Publication Data
Conway, D.J. (Deanna J.)
Dancing with dragons : invoke their ageless wisdom & power / D.J. Conway.
p. cm.
Includes bibliographical references and index.
ISBN 1–56718–165–1 : $14.95 ($20.50 Can.)
1. Dragons. I. Title.
GR830.D7C66   1994
299'.93—dc20   94–28370
                                                                        CIP

Publisher's note:
Llewellyn Worldwide does not participate in, endorse, or have any authority or responsibility concerning private business transactions between our authors and the public.
  All mail addressed to the author is forwarded but the publisher cannot, unless specifically instructed by the author, give out an address or phone number.

Printed in the United States of America

Llewellyn Publications
A Division of Llewellyn Worldwide, Ltd.
P.O. Box 64383, St. Paul, MN 55164-0383

To my close friends who are confirmed dragon believers,
and to all other lovers of dragons.

Other Books by D.J. Conway

Celtic Magic
Norse Magic
Maiden, Mother, Crone
By Oak, Ash & Thorn
Animal Magick
Flying Without a Broom
Moon Magick
Falcon Feather & Valkyrie Sword
The Dream Warrior (fiction)
Magical, Mythical, Mystical Beasts
Lord of Light and Shadow
Magick of the Gods & Goddesses
Soothslayer (fiction)
Shapeshifter Tarot (with Sirona Knight)
Perfect Love
The Mysterious, Magickal Cat
Warrior of Shadows (fiction)

Dancing Dragons

The Sun is out. The day is bright.
The dragons dance upon the grass
And trees and flowers brilliant.
On the winds they pass.
In and out among the clouds
They frolic in the light,
Sliding down the sunbeams,
Dragons crystal bright.
When the Sun has passed beyond
Mountains turned purple-blue,
The dragons dance on through the night
On strands of Moon-lit dew.
They dance to strains of music
Unheard by human ears,
As they have danced through eons,
Untouched by human years.
Teach me, lovely dragons,
To dance with joy life's plan,
To lift myself to higher planes
Above the limits of common man.

Contents

What Are Dragons?

Many cultures around the entire world have stories of dragons in one shape or another. Some are depicted as huge wingless serpents, others more like the traditional picture we of the Western world have of dragons: heavy bodied with wings. Dragons are shown with four legs, two legs, or no legs at all. Some dragons were said to have arrowhead-pointed tails, while others had a spiked knob on the end of the tail. Some had twisted horns, others long antennae rather like those of moths. But the dragon, in whatever form, is there in thousands of folk stories, regardless of the description attached to it. Humankind has a subconscious knowledge of the dragon and its powers that even the assumed thin veneer of so-called civilization cannot remove.

I discovered dragons and their potential powers years ago as a child. Being open-minded and noncritical, as most children are, I enjoyed the company of dragons, faeries, elves, and similar beings on a daily basis. My activity, however, was deeply frowned upon as "imagination." I soon learned to keep quiet about my special ability in order to stay out of trouble with adults. Soon I began ignoring these other beings because I was afraid of making a slip and talking about them. Ridicule and punishment were severe when this happened; the subconscious negative programming had begun. When I finally rebelled against family control, I found the inner door not only shut, but locked. It took years of conscious retraining and experience before I could again understand how to call upon these beings, especially dragons, and use their magickal powers.

Negative programming has created havoc and unhappiness in a great many lives. This type of programming is inflicted upon others because of fear and a desire to control. The perpetrator forgets, or does not care, that they are dealing with an individual who has the right to her/his special abilities, dreams, and goals in life. This happens not only to children, but to anyone who is less than sure of themselves, dependent upon someone else, or unable for whatever reason to leave the situation and people who are causing them great mental and emotional pain. If these beleaguered souls could make contact with their own special dragons, they could build the inner power to either remove themselves from the problem or at least refuse to accept the guilt, fear, and control being placed upon them.

But what are dragons? Are they real or imaginary? In the Western world, our word dragon comes from the Greek *drakon* and the Latin *draco*. *Drakon* comes from a verb meaning to see, to look at, or possibly to flash. Certainly in most legends dragons spend their time watching, whether it be treasure, territory, or the supposedly captive maidens. The word "dragon" is used in many different fields, as diverse as astrology, astronomy, alchemy, magick, heraldry, psychology, and the study of dreams. From the time that humans began to record things, dragons have been mentioned.

In astronomy, the ancient constellation of Draco is in the northern heavens and curves in a winding pattern between the Big and Little Dippers. It ends in the Dragon's Head, a trapezium of four stars. The star Draconis is a brilliant double star. The constellation has probably shifted over the millennia and may have once been the polestar to which the pyramid of Cheops was aligned.

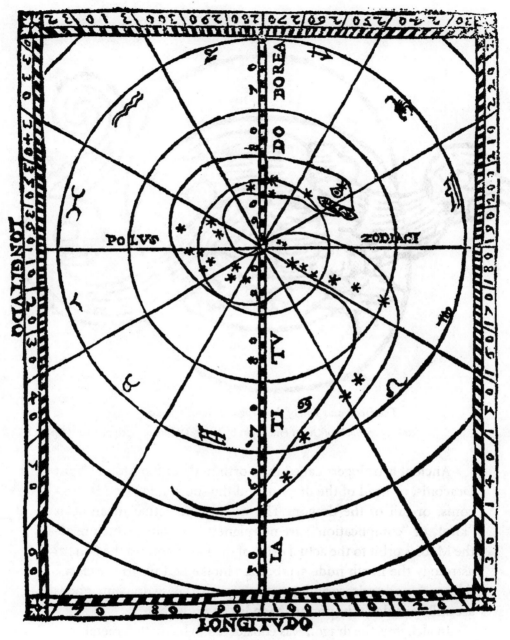

The Constellation Draco

from *Theatrum Mundi* by Giovanni Paolo Gallucci (Venice, 1588)

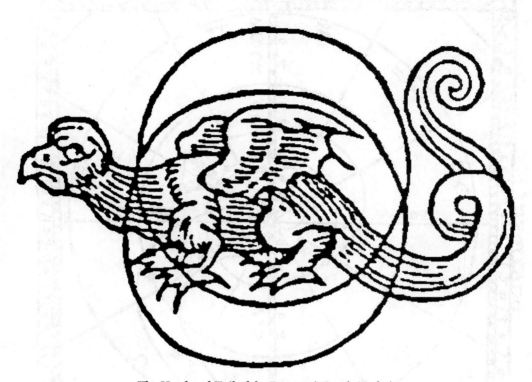

The Head and Tail of the Dragon (Moon's Nodes)
from *Three Books of Occult Philosophy* by Henry Cornelius Agrippa (Antwerp, 1531)

Ancient astrologers called the north node of the Moon Caput Draconis, or head of the dragon, and the south node Cauda Draconis, or tail of the dragon. The nodes (the actual meaning is "knot" or "complication") are not planets but points which relate the Moon's orbit to the actual orbit of the Earth around the Sun. In astrology the north node symbolizes intake and positive aspects, the south node release and negative aspects. These draconic nodes are still considered important to today's astrologers.

In alchemy, the dragon was considered to be matter, metal, and the physical body. Often mentioned in conjunction with the dragon was the dragon's sister: spirit, metallic mercury, and the soul. Ancient alchemy used the picture of a dragon or winged ser-

Alchemical Dragon
by V. Feil, from *Vögelin Praktik* by Hans Singrieners. 1534

pent as one of its many secret symbols. A common symbol of spiritual alchemical work was the dragon or serpent holding its tail in its mouth, an unending circle of eternity. Near this circled dragon was written the Greek motto *en to pan,* or "all is one." The fabled Philosopher's Stone of alchemy was also considered the One Which is All. This Stone was closely connected in ancient writings with the Great Work of alchemy; the Great Work simply means humankind becoming God, or merging with the Supreme Creative Forces within, thus completing the cycle of human growth by returning to the Source.

Jung wrote that the alchemists considered the winged dragon as female, the wingless dragon as male. Jung also considered water in dreams and analysis as unconscious spirit or the water dragon of Tao. This water dragon of Tao symbolized the yang embraced in the yin, or balanced growth in spirit. In Chinese Taoist symbolism, the dragon was seen as "the Way," the bringer of eternal changes. Often it was depicted as guardian of the Flaming Pearl, or spiritual perfection. Joseph Campbell also speaks of the winged dragon or

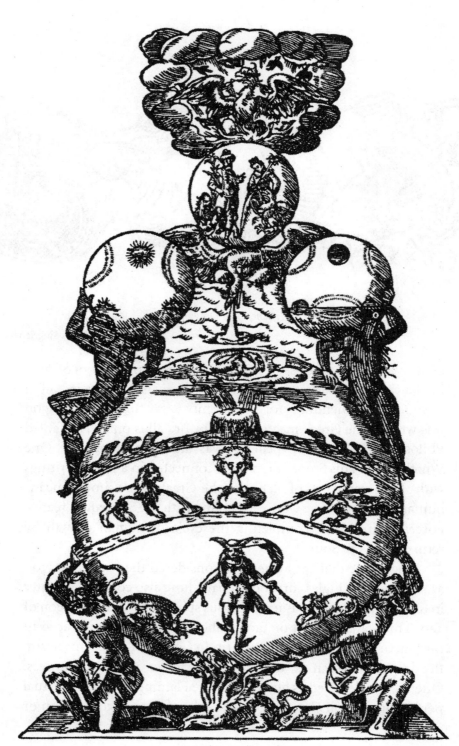

Alchemical Process

from *Alchymia* by Andreas Libavius, 1606

serpent as being the balance between Earth and Spirit. To the Chinese, the dragon was a potent symbol of luck and power. Silver dragon amulets were worn to help gain these qualities.

Everywhere the legged dragon is associated with creation or life-giving. Throughout the world the Goddess, or Great Mother, is connected with serpents, dragons, and spirals. As the great whale-dragon, Ishtar brought about the catastrophic flood which made it possible for a new order of humans to develop. Tiamat of Mesopotamia was the Mother-creator-dragon whose body was shaped into the heavens and Earth. Worldwide, dragons and serpents are symbolic of the energy source of life, healing, oracular powers, fertility, and maternal blessing.

H.P. Blavatsky states in her books that the dragon is a very old sign for Astral Light or Primordial Principle. This means that there is always wisdom in chaos, even if humans cannot see it. The dragon stood for psychical regeneration and immortality. Perhaps the stories which insist that dragons were partial to virgins simply meant that the seeking of wisdom and true innocence of the spirit were traits which attracted draconic beings.

In some cultures a full initiate was called a dragon or snake. Priests of Egypt and Babylon called themselves Sons of the Serpent-god or Sons of the Dragon. Even the Druids of the Celts spoke of themselves as snakes. In Mexico, the priests of Quetzalcoatl referred to themselves as of the race of the Dragon. The Welsh word *Draig*, or dragon, was used to denote a leader, hero, war-leader, or prince. King Arthur and his father Uther Pendragon were said to have used a dragon as their emblem. Even today the royal banner of Wales has a four-legged red and gold dragon on it.

The dragon became a symbol of evil and the Christian devil only after the church gained power. In an attempt to crush the ancient beliefs of Pagans, the Christians spread their propaganda of their devil, calling him the Dragon.* By instilling deep fears, particularly of eternal punishments, the priests and church leaders

---

*The Christians tied a great number of ancient deities and symbols to their devil in hopes that the people would desert the old beliefs. The god Pan and the horned god Cernunnos were said to be the Christian devil.

managed to grasp control of rulers and governments. By becoming the controlling force behind governments, the church could control the people themselves, either through making their own Christian religious belief the state religion or by influencing the laws that were passed. Even then, though, there were truly individualistic people who refused to give up what they knew to be, for them, true spiritual paths. These Pagans had to go underground, living in fear of persecution and death, for centuries until they were once again granted the freedom to follow their ancient ways, freely speak of contacting the powerful astral beings who aided them.

Even through these times of persecution, the dragon did not fade from sight. In European countries, and China in particular, the draconic image remained alive in stories. European families, especially, used the dragon in coats of arms. The European art of heraldry and coats of arms still employs the depiction of dragons in its art. The Prince of Wales has a red and gold dragon in his coat of arms and on his flag. The families of de Drago, von Drachenfels, de Draek, de Dragon de Ramillies, and Dragomanni, among others, all have a dragon on their coats of arms, as did the family of Sir Francis Drake.

In heraldry, a dragon with two legs is called a wyvern; a dragon without wings is a worm; a serpentine dragon with wings but no legs is an amphiptere; a dragon with wings and legs is termed a guivre. Further meaning of these draconic images was determined by how the dragon was posed: rampant (forelegs raised), passant (one foreleg raised), statant (all four feet on the ground), wings endorsed (upright over the back), displayed or depressed, tail nowed (knotted). Even further definition was determined by the color: or (gold), gules (red), sable (black), or vert (green).

Today true practical dragon magick and power are almost a forgotten art in the world of magick. Generally speaking, only those practitioners and believers in the Faerie Tradition speak of the existence and validity of dragons. Few people know of the joy

The Goddess Tiamat

from relief carving, Temple of Enurta, Nimrud, Assyria

and companionship and spiritual knowledge that come from dancing with dragons. Dancing with dragons takes cooperation, not
master-slave relationships; it takes great self-discipline to reach into
another level of existence and contact a dragon as a co-magician.

It has been my experience that, although dragons have form
and existence, they do not exist in this physical world as we do.
Dragons inhabit the astral plane which co-exists with and inter-
penetrates this physical plane. Astral beings are as real as we are;
they just have a body that vibrates at a different rate than physical
matter does.

Dragons can be everywhere and, in a matter of speaking, in all
things. Every elemental action and reaction has the possibility of
being an extension of a dragon and its power. This is not to suggest
that dragons go about controlling people and incidents. Usually
they take little note of ordinary humans, deeming them beneath
their notice. There are two reasons a dragon might become
involved with humans and their problems. First, if there appears to
be an immediate danger to the dragon's area itself. Second, if a
magician knows how to properly contact and communicate with
dragon power, and if she/he can persuade the dragon to help.

The only exception I know to this are dragons talking with children. Some dragons take a delight in communicating with small
children, particularly those who have psychic ability. Unfortunately, parents and society take a dim view of such ability, hedging
it about with so much disfavor that most children stop using it.

One of my grandsons, when quite small, saw dragons all the
time. He described them to me in great and accurate detail,
although I had never discussed them with him. When he finally
realized that this made his mother very angry, he shut off the ability. The programming may be effective enough to keep him from
re-opening and exploring his early friendship with dragons while
he lives at home, but the desire is still there. When he visits us, the
first place he goes is to the bookcase full of dragon statues. He is

very quiet and intent while he looks over every single one, although he is familiar with them all. I leave him to his silent contemplation as I realize it is a form of communication between him and his "lost" dragon friends. Someday, if and when he feels strong enough to dispense with his subconscious programming, he may decide that acknowledging the existence of dragons is not wrong.

On rare occasions an astral being, such as a dragon, will manifest itself so clearly on the physical that people see it with the physical eyes. It is my opinion that some of the so-called monsters, such as those of Loch Ness, are astral beings. Nessie is possibly a kind astral sea dragon. For this reason, I do not expect that there will ever be any hard physical evidence, the kind scientists can put under a microscope or dissect, produced to validate Nessie's existence.

Carl Sagan, in *The Dragons of Eden,* spent a lot of time and paper trying to discredit dragon stories around the world. His narrow-minded, tedious explanations tried to convince the public that the stories of dragons came from racial memories of dinosaurs. This is really stretching things, since scientists are always telling the public that humans did not exist at the time of the great dinosaurs. But then more than a few scientists, unless they can capture and dissect something, are not about to admit they do not know everything about this world and its creatures, let alone admit that there might be other planes of existence that interact with ours.

There is not only one way to see and work with dragons. There are many magickal systems in the world, and they each tend to look at dragons in their own way. Some systems think of them as elemental energies without independent existence. Others think of them only as symbolic, again having no true existence. It has been my experience that dragons are real creatures who come and go from the astral plane as they please. I have seen them, heard them, and felt their power. After working with dragons in ritual, I leave it to you to form your own opinion.

Japanese Dragon

from a painted ewer, Edo period

Dragons in Mythology and Legend

The world's mythologies are full of tales about dragons. Sometimes they are portrayed as huge serpents, sometimes as the type of dragon known to the Western world, sometimes in the shape known to those in the Orient. But dragons have always played a part in the shaping of this world and its many diverse cultures. They have also had an important part in cultural perception of spiritual ideas.

Dragons have been portrayed in many forms and variations of these forms. Ancient teachings say dragons can have two or four legs or none at all, a pair of wings or be wingless, breathe fire and smoke, and have scales on their bodies. Their blood is extremely poisonous and corrosive, but also very magickal. Blood, or the life force, is a symbol of the intensity of their elemental-type energies. Depending upon the reception they received from humans in the area where they lived, dragons could be either beneficial or violent. One thing is for certain: dragons were regarded with awe by all cultures affected by their presence and interaction with humans.

Although one can speak of dragons as a separate species of being, there are numerous subspecies and families within the dragon community, as one can deduce from reading ancient histories and stories. The subspecies and families may have greater or lesser differences in appearance but still retain the basic traits that are common to all dragons wherever they are. One family of dragons, with very similar characteristics, lived in Europe, especially northern Germany, Scandinavia, and islands of the North Atlantic. A second family was recognized in France, Italy, and Spain. A third family dwelt in the British Isles, including Ireland; these dragons, commonly called Firedrakes, included the subspecies of Wyverns (dragons with two legs) and the winged but legless Worm. A fourth family was found in the Mediterranean area, especially Greece, Asia Minor, southern Russia, and northern Africa; the dragon with many heads was common in this region. A fifth dragon family, and the largest in number, was the Oriental dragon of China, Asia, and Indonesia. The sixth family, of very limited size and number, was found in the Americas and Australia.

In the Eastern world, dragons seldom breathe fire and are more benevolent, although hot-tempered and destructive when provoked. They are sometimes pictured as wingless, but can propel themselves through the air if they wish. The dragons of the Orient, Mexico, the Americas, and Australia propelled themselves through the skies by balancing between the Earth's magnetic field and the winds.

In China, for instance, dragons are portrayed with four legs, a long sinuous serpentine body and a snake-like tail; they ranged in size from a few feet long up to the Great Chien-Tang who was over a thousand feet in length. They could speak, were able to alter their forms and sizes, and had a varying number of claws.

Chinese emperors adopted the five-clawed dragon as a sacred ancestor, symbol of their power. Only Imperial dragons were said to have the special five claws on each foot. All other Oriental dragons had only three or four claws. It became a law that only the Emperor could have a five-clawed dragon embroidered on his robes or painted on anything.

Five-Clawed Imperial Dragon

from an embroidered court robe, late Ming Dynasty

*Oriental Dragon
of the Sky*

According to tradition, China's history dates back to 3000 BCE,* although modern historians only go back to 1600 BCE. A clay vessel from about 2000 BCE is decorated with a dragon picture. The dragon symbol and figure still exist in modern-day Chinese art and celebrations.

The Chinese divided their dragons into groups or classes, each with different characteristics. There were four major Lung Wang dragons, or Dragon-Kings. The names of these brothers were Ao Kuang, Ao Jun, Ao Shun, and Ao Ch'in. They also had specific duties: the *t'ien lung* supported the mansion of the gods; the *shen lung* brought rain; the *ti lung* controlled the rivers; and the *fu-ts'an lung* guarded hidden treasures and deposits of precious metals. The Lung Wang, or Dragon Kings, resembled the Indian Nagas, or sacred serpents. They were the patron deities of rivers, lakes, seas, and rain. They had valuable pearls in their throats and lived in magnificent underwater palaces.

Further divisions produced the *kiao-lung*, or scaled dragon; *ying-lung* with wings; *k'iu-lung* with horns; *ch'i-lung* which was hornless; the *p'an-lung* which was earth-bound. The *ch'i-lung* dragon was red, white, and green, the *k'iu-lung* blue. Chinese dragons were also entirely black, white, red, or yellow, with yellow considered superior.

When it came to using dragons for decoration, there were nine distinct categories: the *p'u lao* was carved on gongs; the *ch'iu niu* and *pi hsi* on fiddles and literature tablets; the *pa hsia* at the base of stone monuments; the *chao feng* on the eaves of temples; the *ch'ih* on beams of

*Oriental Dragon
of the Sea*

---

*BCE stands for "Before Common Era," a nonreligious way of dating time instead of using BC. CE, or "Common Era," takes the place of the Christianized AD dating.

Chinese Dragon
from a bronze mirror, Warring States to T'ang Dynasty

bridges; the *suan ni* only on the throne of the Buddha; the *yai tzu* on the hilts of swords; and the *pi han* on prison gates.

Chinese experts were said to be able to tell the age of Oriental dragons and their origins by their colors. Yellow dragons were believed to be born from yellow gold a thousand years old; blue dragons from blue gold eight hundred years old; red, white, and black from gold of the same color a thousand years old.

To the Chinese, dragons could be either male or female. They laid eggs, some of which did not hatch for a thousand years. When a hatching did occur, it was known because of great meteor show-ers, violent thunderstorms, and great showers of hail.

The number of scales on a dragon was also of importance. Some ancient dragon experts in China maintained that a true dragon has exactly 81 scales, while others stated that the number was 117. They were never said to be covered with anything except scales. This is a characteristic of dragons worldwide.

Chinese dragons were said to have the head of a camel, horns of a stag, eyes of a demon, neck of a snake, scales of a carp, claws of an eagle, feet of a tiger, and ears of a cow. Although, as one can see from ancient pictures, all Oriental dragons did not fit convenient-ly into this description, they all were said to have a lump on the top of the head. This lump enabled them to fly without wings. Although this flying-lump was considered an essential part of Ori-ental dragons, it is rare to see it portrayed in pictures.

Oriental dragons could change their forms by intense concen-tration or when extremely angry. All dragons are said to have the ability to take on human form. One can see reasons behind a dra-conic being passing as a human; dragons are intensely curious about all things and may wish to directly experience human life from time to time. It is a possibility that, while in such a form, a dragon could contact a human and establish a line of communication that could be continued after the dragon resumed its own form.

The Chinese even had methods of protecting themselves from annoying dragons. It was said that they could be frightened away or controlled by the leaves of the wang plant (or Pride of India), five-colored silk thread, wax, iron, or centipedes. It is difficult to imagine a dragon being deterred by wax or centipedes. Perhaps this idea grew from a single dragon who reacted in fear to these objects, just as some humans fear crawling things, heights, or mice. After all, drag-ons have very distinct and individual personalities, just as we do.

In Chinese medicine, the skin, bones, teeth, and saliva were considered very valuable. Powdered dragon bone was a magickal cure-all. Old medical textbooks are quick to point out that dragons periodically shed their skin and bones, like snakes do. Since the skins glowed in the dark, presumably they were easy to locate. Some of the bones were listed as slightly poisonous and could only be prepared in non-iron utensils. How "bones" could be shed is a mystery unless it is not really bone, but something that looks like it. The shedding and regrowth of teeth is known to occur among certain animals, reptiles, and amphibians.

Dragon saliva was said to be found as a frothy foam on the ground or floating on the water. It was usually deposited during mating or fighting. One Chinese story tells of a great battle just off the coast near a fishing village. The people watched the great dragons rolling in the black clouds and leaping waves for a day and a night. Their echoing roars were clearly heard by all the villagers. The next morning these people set out in all their fishing boats to the place of the battle. They scooped up whole boatloads of dragon saliva that they found floating in huge piles on the ocean.

The blood of Oriental dragons was sometimes red, other times black. Dragon experts said it changed into amber when it soaked into the ground. Wherever dragon blood fell, the ground became incapable of supporting any vegetation. Although the blood was considered dangerous, sometimes deadly, in Oriental myths, European heroes bathed in it to create invulnerability or drank it to become wise. This transformation of the blood into amber could well be an alchemical expression of the manifestation of magickal power and elemental energies into a desired physical result.

Oriental dragons did not figure in Chinese creation myths. Only rarely, and then only by accident, did they come in conflict with the gods or heroes. They tended to mind their own business and keep a beneficial attitude toward humans. Oriental dragons had specific duties such as controlling the weather and keeping the land and animals fertile, as well as assignments to help humans learn certain civilized arts. Although dragon parts were widely esteemed in Oriental medicine, these magickal creatures were not hunted down as were Western dragons.

In the Mideast, there seems to have been a meeting ground for dragons, some being like Chinese dragons, others more like Western dragons. Phrygian history tells of dragons that reached ten paces in length, lived in caverns near the River Rhyndacus, and moved with part of their bodies on the ground, the rest erect. Islam gives hints of Muhammad's magick horse rising to heaven with the aid of dragon's breath. An illustration from a Turkish manuscript now in the Bibliotheque Nationale in Paris shows this scene.

The Egyptian Apep was described as a huge serpent-dragon that lived in the Underworld. The Canaanite god Ba'al is said to have killed the dragon Lotan and made the world from its body; the Hittites had a similar legend about the dragon Illuyankas. The Mesopotamian god Marduk killed the she-dragon Tiamat and created the world from her body. Ancient heroes of Persia battled with dragons.

In the Classics, the Greeks told of their hero Herakles slaying the seven-headed hydra, a form of dragon. While still in his cradle, he slew two giant serpents sent by Hera. Later the hero saved Hesione who was chained as a sacrifice to a sea dragon. Perseus did the same for Andromeda. As a baby, Apollo also killed a serpent (dragon) sent against his mother by Hera. Jason killed a hydra (many-headed dragon) to get the Golden Fleece; scenes of this story can still be seen on Greek dishes from about 480-490 BCE, showing a definite dragon creature. Both the Greek Medea and the Roman Ceres were said to ride in chariots pulled by dragons. Ancient Greece and Rome considered the dragon both beneficent and evil, depending upon the activities of the creature. The Purple Dragon became the emblem of the Byzantine emperors. There is a wall painting of a dragon still existing in the ruined Roman city of Pompeii.

In legends from India there was ordinarily no conflict between the gods and the Nagas, or serpent-dragons, as shown by the sto-

Hydra
from *The History of Four-footed Beasts and Serpents* by Edward Topsell (London, 1658)

ries of Krishna and Vishnu. Both of these gods had a fine working relationship with Ananta, king of the serpent-dragons, and the Nagas. The greatly revered Indian god Vishnu was on good terms with Ananta, the Endless One, a giant serpent with eleven heads. Vishnu slept on Ananta while the serpent guarded him. Ananta is considered by the Hindus to be the symbol of cosmic energy which is vital for creation.

The one exception to this friendship between the Nagas and the gods was the slaying of Vritra, a great serpent who coiled around the navel of the Earth, holding back the waters. Indra killed him to create the world-mountains.

The Nagas were known for their great magickal powers and the pearls of great price that they carried in their foreheads. The Nagas, also patrons of lakes, rivers, rain, and clouds, lived in wonderful palaces, often visited by the gods. But as with all dragons in whatever form, the Nagas were capable of killing people and causing problems when annoyed. There are stories of their creating drought, pestilence, and great suffering when humans broke their rules.

Sometimes the Nagas were pictured with serpent heads and human bodies. They were said to live at the top of Mount Meru, where they had a golden palace full of music, gems that fulfilled wishes, wonderful flowers, and beautiful companions. In the center of this garden, which once belonged to Varuna, stood a dragon-guarded tree of life and reincarnation.

In Africa, the country of Ethiopia was said to be heavily populated with dragons at one time. The Roman poet Lucan and other Classical authors wrote that African dragons could fly, that their brilliantly colored scales shone brightly, and that some of them were so huge that they could be mistaken for hills when they lay asleep.

Generally speaking, Western dragons were different in physical structure from Eastern dragons. Most of them had two strong hind legs, two shorter forelegs, a thick body and a long tail. Their wings were membranes, like those of bats, and had long ribs or bones. Their wedge-shaped heads were carried on long sinuous necks. Western dragons were fully armed with long claws and sharp teeth, besides their fiery breath. They talked with humans by means of telepathy and were extremely cunning and wily.

The ancient Celts had traditions of dragons, considering them wily but wise. Unfortunately, so much of Celtic lore was lost to deliberate destruction that we have only remnants of tales and fragments of dragon lore left today from that culture. The Celtic ram-snake, or dragon, is connected with Cernunnos, the antlered Earth god. This Celtic ram-dragon is also connected with the number

Naga Design for Ballustrade-End

drawing by Linda Norton, from a photograph (in *Asiatic Mythology* by J. Hackin et al.,
New York: Thomas Y. Crowell Company, n.d.) of an artifact in the Musée Delaporte

eight, this being the number of spokes on the solar wheel; the solar wheel is set in motion by the ram-headed dragon. What few carvings we have of the god Cernunnos picture him with a bag of gold at his feet and a double-headed ram-snake belt about his waist. This belt with its two ram-dragon heads symbolizes the spiritual bridge between various planes of existence. The Celtic shaman-magician-priest knew that in order to travel this bridge, she/he must go inward to meet the dragon guarding that bridge. A lack of self-discipline and self-knowledge would prevent any seeker from being able to pass the dragon and enter the realms of the Otherworlds.

Conchobar of Ireland was said to have had both a divine and a human father. He was born at the Winter Solstice with what the story calls a water-worm in each hand. From the description these water-worms were probably baby dragons.

The Irish hero Finn MacCumhaill also killed dragons. Some magickal systems would look at Finn's activities as not physical, but as battling his own destructive inner thoughts.

The dragon has been depicted on the Welsh banner since at least the departure of the Roman legions. And in England, Scotland, and Ireland the dragon has been drawn with four legs and the wyvern with two since the 16th century. On the European continent, however, the two-legged wyvern is still called a dragon, the same name given to the four-legged variety. Even today, the dragon, alone or with other designs, is part of the heraldic heritage of some two hundred English families and some three hundred from Europe.

In Scandinavian legend, the hero Sigurd (called Siegfried in Germany) killed the dragon Fafnir. This story clearly details the benefits from a dragon's blood. Sigurd accidentally swallowed a drop of it and immediately could understand the language of birds. This saved his life from the dragon's treacherous brother who was plotting to kill him for the treasure. Sigurd also was bathed with the blood when he struck Fafnir from a pit. This made him invulnerable to weapons, except where a leaf covered a tiny spot.

Sigurd Slays Fafnir
from *Myths of the Norsemen* by H.A. Guerber (London, 1909)

The god Thorr once caught the World-Serpent while fishing. Considering the power and negativity of the great serpent-dragon, Thorr was fortunate that his companion cut the line. The god did not feel that way about it, though, and clouted his friend alongside the head for letting his big "fish" get away.

If one reads the very best of translations of the story of Beowulf, it is quickly seen that he fought three dragons. Although the first he killed was described as a young two-legged male monster who was raiding for food among the houses at night, it could have been a wyvern (who has two legs) or a four-legged dragon who walked upon its hind legs or a dragon in human disguise. The second creature was a mature female, finally killed in her spawning ground, who definitely took on human form. The third dragon came later in his life, and was specifically listed as a dragon. This one was a mature flying male with a poisonous bite. Well into middle age at the time, Beowulf used himself as bait to draw the last dragon out of its lair so it could be killed.

Probably the greatest of Northern dragons was Nidhogg (Dread Biter) who lived in Niflheim and was constantly gnawing at the World Tree. Nidhogg would be classified as a chaos dragon, one who destroys in order to re-create. This idea of destruction-resurrection extended to the Norse belief that Nidhogg stripped all corpses of their flesh.

In the Northern regions, dragons were said to live in cold seas or misty lakes, storms, and fogs. When these were not available, dragons lurked in deep underground caverns, coming out when hungry or when there was a thunderstorm. Even after conversion to Christianity, the Scandinavians, especially the Norwegians, placed carved dragon heads on the gables of their churches to guard against the elements, as for years they had guarded their ships with dragon-headed prows.

In the original legends of Scotland, Scandinavia, and northern Germany, dragons were not winged, nor were they totally evil. Up

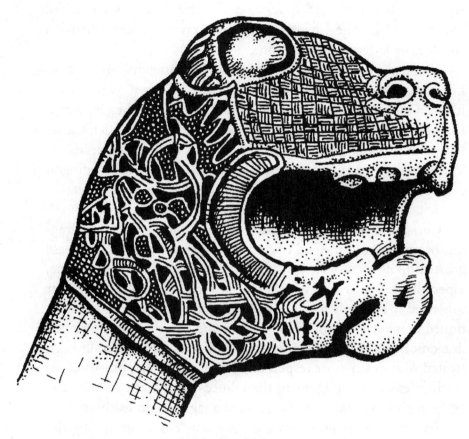

Viking Ship's Prow

from Oseberg ship burial

until the early Middle Ages, it was reported that flights of dragons were as common as migrating birds. By the Middle Ages when the Christians had grabbed control of nearly everything and were fanatically persecuting Pagans, they changed the ideas of dragons into winged monsters, always menacing and evil, some with multiple heads. They described some of them as having the throat and legs of an eagle, the body of a huge serpent, the wings of a bat, and a tail with an arrow tip; we now call these two-legged dragons wyverns. Christianity was quick to equate dragons with their Devil and their Hell. The Christians also portrayed all non-Christian rulers as evil, destructive dragons.

There are many Christian references to dragons, all of them negative, which generally speaking meant "down with Pagan ideas." One such tale is told in the book of Bel and the Dragon in the Apocrypha; another is described in the book of Daniel. Christian tales of saints and dragons always picture the dragon losing. The Christians want you to believe that they have killed dragon power, but this is not so. They have not, and never will destroy magick or the wily, elusive dragon.

Christianity and its admonition to hunt down and destroy dragons brought about the end of common dragon sightings, for these great and knowledgeable beasts withdrew from the physical plane, especially in Britain and Europe. In the Orient dragons were never subjected to the malicious hunting practices of Europe and so continued to involve themselves in human and cosmic affairs. Oriental dragons, being as a whole gregarious extroverts, have generally been treated with much more respect and honor than other dragons.

In Mexico the dragons of the Olmecs were pictured with the body of a rattlesnake, the eyebrows of a jaguar, and feathers. This combination of serpent-jaguar-dragon was common among the civilizations of Mexico, Central America, and certain portions of South America. This combined sinuous and hungry form symbolized the ambiguities of the universe, the process of destruction and re-creation, subconsciously understood by even the most primitive peoples. Although these cultures were primitive by our standards, they were certainly not without knowledge, cultural advancements, and scientific studies. After their own fashion, they were very spiritual people, who would have been perfectly capable of discovering dragon power; their strange half-dragon, half-jaguar carvings represent their understanding and acknowledgement of the dragons of their continent. Quetzalcoatl, the Feathered Serpent, a dragon-

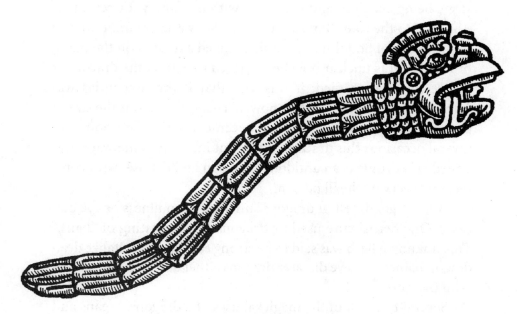

Mayan Feathered Serpent

from Chichén Itzá

serpent figure known and revered over much of the area, bore many of the same characteristics as Oriental dragons.

All legends do agree on certain characteristics concerning dragons. Legends say that you should never look a dragon in the eyes; he has hypnotic powers. A dragon is not likely to give you his real name; that would give you power over him. Several legends from different cultures speak of the draconic ability to appear in human form. When a dragon does appear in human form, it is very difficult to see through his disguise unless he wants you to.

Dragons have a precious stone, called the dracontias, in the forehead. This stone is credited with amazing powers of many kinds. For the stone to hold its powers, however, it had to be removed before the dragon was dead. There is a story of such a stone being acquired and then kept within a family for centuries. About 1345 the Chevalier do Gozano, who was later Grand Master of the Order of St. John of Jerusalem, killed a dragon on the island of Rhodes. It is unclear how he managed to extract the dracontias before the dragon died; it was said that if the dracontias was extracted after death it lost its power. This stone, about the size of an olive and beautifully colored, became a family heirloom. On several occasions this dracontias was put into water; the water was boiled and drunk as an antidote to poison and disease, with complete recovery by the ill person.

A few legends tell of dragons suffering from illness or eye diseases. One herbal cure used by dragons was the eating of "balis." This unknown herb was said to be strong enough to revitalize dead dragon babies. For eye diseases dragons either ate fennel or rubbed it on their eyes.

Several tales tell of the magickal uses of a dragon's organs and blood. In European lore, the blood was said to make a person invulnerable to stab wounds if they bathed in it, able to understand the speech of birds and animals if they drank it. One of Bothvar's companions, in the Danish *Hrolf's Saga*, ate a dragon's heart and became extremely brave and strong. Eating the tongue gave eloquence and the ability to win any argument. The liver cured certain diseases, as did various other parts.

Medieval medicine and magick mention the use of dragon's blood many times. Since dragons are not going to willingly give up their blood, magicians had to turn to other sources. There were said to be several sources of this material, other than from an actual dragon. The "bloodstone" hematite, an ore rich in iron, and the mineral cinnabar, a compound of mercury, were both called forms of dragon's blood. However, the most widely used "dragon's blood" was a gum resin. It was said that trees which originally grew from actual spilled dragon's blood produced a reddish-brown sap of great magickal value. This species of tree is still called *Dracaena draco* by botanists. Incisions were made in the bark and the sap collected as it congealed into resin. Most of these trees are found in the East Indies, southern Arabia, and the Canary Islands. Dragon's blood resin is still known and used in magickal procedures today.

Dragons are long-lived, hoard treasure, and are very wise. The older a dragon, the wiser he is. Conversing with an old dragon is a double-edged sword. He may be wiser, able to give you greater knowledge, but he is also touchy and extremely untrustworthy, unless you handle him correctly. After all, he has been around long enough to have experienced human unreliability and deceit.

Dragons have control of deeper currents of elemental energies than is usually felt by humans. They are always connected in some manner with various forms of the four elements. Sightings of dragons have also been reported in areas where other psychic phenomena have occurred, such as ghosts and other astral creatures.

Depending upon the behavior of the dragons under observation, their appearance can be considered an omen of good fortune. Oriental dragon-watchers said that it was possible to predict the weather and fortune of any community by studying the part of the sky in which a dragon appeared and the way it behaved, such as breathing fire, fighting with another dragon, screaming, or frolicking in and out of the clouds.

Dragons tend to speak in riddles and symbols, avoiding straight answers whenever possible. The only weapon dragons respect is a sword, but only if it is wielded by a confident magician who is prepared to stand his ground. Please notice I say respect, not fear. I believe this is because dragons like strong humans with a healthy, balanced opinion of themselves. They do not care for vacillating humans, who are afraid to make a decision or take responsibility. Do not make the mistake of trying to physically attack with the sword. In the first place a dragon could melt the blade like ice in a flame. In the second place, the dragon is an astral

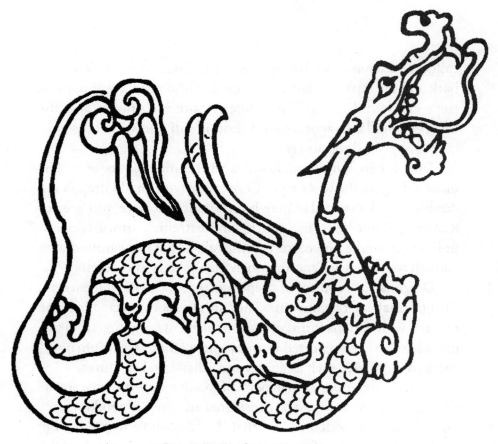

Dragon Design from a Garment

Hopeh, Han Dynasty

creature, incapable of being actually harmed by a physical weapon. The sword is only for magickal gestures.

As one can see by the legends, there was a time when dragons materialized from the astral into the physical plane on a fairly regular basis. Considering a dragon's intelligence, it is no wonder that they now choose to stay away from humans. Most humans want to control, dissect, or vanquish everything they do not understand, and even a lot of what they do understand.

But that wonderful, vast storehouse of dragon magick and power is still available if a magician will take the time to learn how to approach dragons and their deep magickal energies.

Seeking and Working with Dragons

It should be obvious by now that I have a deep respect and love for dragons, a belief in their powers as co-magicians that is backed by years of personal experience. And I hope I have piqued your interest enough to want to work with them.

So how does one go about finding dragons? And how do you use their power? Should you do co-magick with dragons, or should you avoid the partnership?

I assume, since you have read this far, that you either already practice some form of magick or are seriously contemplating doing so. If you are experiencing any doubt about your worthiness (Goddess forbid!) to work in the area of magick, any area of magick, you have some serious work to do on your self-image and the programming you have undergone that created your poor self-image.

Every magician, indeed every person who even uses prayer, constantly walks the fine line between an overinflated ego and an appreciation of her/his self-worth. She/he understands, without any cover-ups, exactly why they are choosing to work magick at any given time. This understanding is vitally necessary in order to assess the end-result of the spellworking, the type of magick used, and the consequences that may be forthcoming for certain actions. What others think of a magician's reasons is not important; they do not pay the penalties, gain the advantages of the rituals, or know exactly what that magician may think and feel. However, the magician must know what is deep within her/his own mind and heart, know it and deal with it if there is negative programming or intentions that are selfish and unjustified.

A good magician is neither white nor black. A good effective magician is what I call gray, one who understands completely the consequences of actions and is willing to do what is necessary, particularly in the areas of protection and the removal of evil. An effective magician knows her/himself like no one else does; she/he has to be brutally honest about real intents and purposes for using any type of magick in the first place, but especially so when practicing dragon magick.

In dragon magick, the magician cannot afford any lingering doubts as to her/his right to ask help from these powerful entities. Like many other beings, physical and nonphysical, dragons will take advantage of anyone who vacillates in her/his commitment or who is unclear about their intent of a ritual.

I have yet to meet an "evil" dragon, although I have encountered a few who distrust humans so much that one must take special care when working with them. Dragons become "evil" only when there is an imbalance of energies, a disruption of the powers flowing from the Earth and humans to dragons and back again. To re-establish a positive flow of this power, the magician does not join every fanatical group out picketing and rioting. She/he knows that all changes begin within the self. Like ripples in a pond, when the self becomes balanced, the immediate atmosphere and community are affected. When the community becomes balanced, this spreads further, taking in countries, and eventually the entire world. But, as with all things, a majority of individuals must desire and seek the balance and improvement, or it will not occur.

An Evil Dragon?

from *St. George and the Dragon* by Albrecht Dürer, 1508

Does this mean that unless you are perfect in all levels of your being that you cannot attract, contact, and learn from dragons? Of course not! But if you desire a continued companionship with them, you must strive to better yourself, balance the ebbs and tides of energies within you, and make this effort an on-going project. Every magician and spiritual seeker should be aware that there is no such thing as complete perfection within the human body and mind 100 per cent of the time. If you could become that perfect, you would no longer inhabit a physical body. The laws of the universe do not allow anything to remain static, non-moving, or non-growing. Perfection is static in whatever form it currently has; therefore, in order to confirm to the laws of the universe, that perfect form must evolve into something else, some form of being that can continue to evolve to the next higher stage of life. Change is one of the few constants of universal law.

So how does one go about finding dragons? You begin by learning as much about dragons and their magickal habits as possible. Then you look at your reasons for wishing to practice dragon magick with an objective and critical eye. When you feel comfortable with these steps, and only then, you begin building an atmosphere that will attract dragons. You perform certain actions that arouse their curiosity and will draw them to your vicinity. You beam a mental welcome, setting aside time and place to communicate with them on the astral level through mental visualization and speech. And you have to believe they exist, even if you cannot see them with your physical eyes or prove their existence to someone else.

You have to cast aside social taboos on "seeing" things and know with your heart that dragons do exist, if you wish to attract dragons. Mentally invite the dragons to make their presence known by thought or deed. Be sensitive and extra aware of what is occurring around you. Most dragons tend to be subtle in their first contacts with humans. They may choose to make an appearance in dreams or as flashes of movement seen in the peripheral vision. They may even forego these types of appearance to simply touch your psychic "feelings."

Guardian dragons, the easiest to contact, often appear as little voices or faces and forms in the mind. Dragons may show up unannounced at any time, but especially during meditation or magickal rituals, either singly or several at a time. They love the power flow of ritual and will make an appearance just to bathe in the energy. They may well have been there all the time; you just did not notice them. Since dragons are masters at concealment this is not surprising.

These smaller dragons delight in sharing the vibrations of tarot and rune readings and other psychic practices. One of our guardian dragons likes to play with my crystal pendulum. He either pats it with a claw or mentally sends it spinning in nonsense directions. The only solution to using the pendulum is to let him tire of his game before attempting to get a reliable answer. He and his companions like to peer over my shoulder during tarot readings, muttering their own interpretations all the while. One just has to be patient with them, as one would with a small, curious child.

You have to be willing to practice a great deal of patience, self-control, and self-discipline, learning to work within a specific set of magickal laws in order to consistently attract and elicit the help of dragons. As with all magickal procedures, nothing is cast in concrete, but there are certain aspects of these procedures which can-

A Small Dragon

from *St. George and the Dragon* by Carlo Crivelli

not be eliminated or changed to any great extent without disturbing the flow of magickal power.

Not all dragons are of positive magick. I dislike using the words "good" or "evil," because negative power is just as important to the existence of life as is positive power. Negative energies have nothing to do with evil, unless you have evil thoughts and intentions within yourself. And the Goddess knows that evil thoughts and intentions exist within those who are totally against magick! It is easy for people to understand what positive energy is and does. But negative energy has received a lot of bad press. Both positive and negative aspects of many things besides energy are needed to create, indeed for the universe to stay in existence.

What most people mean by using negative energy is the deliberate use of this type of power against another human. The magician realizes that sometimes, and after great deliberation of possible consequences and the true reasons behind her/his decision to use this type of energy, calling upon and sending forth negative energy can be justified. The best examples I can give of this are in the areas of rapists, child abusers, spouse beaters, drug dealers, dangerous fanatics, and serial killers. Allowing such evil to continue to exist unrestrained is potentially harmful to everyone. Working magick to get these offenders caught and punished is helpful to society as a whole in the final analysis. Even for these reasons, the magician must end the ritual with detached, unemotional involvement, an extremely difficult state of mind to reach.

Casting aside the magickal laws for working with dragon power is certain to get you into trouble. Even the most positive dragon is a wily beast who, like many humans, tends to look out for him/herself first. Dragons likely developed this attitude after trying to work with humans thousands of years ago and finding that puny mortals were unreliable, often treacherous, allies.

Tuning yourself in to dragon power for magick is discussed in greater depth in later chapters. But your attitude toward the existence of dragons must be the first big step in preparation for meeting them. The power of dragons is a tremendous force, amplifying a magician's ability to new heights.

Why bother cultivating the cooperation and companionship of dragons? Because their wisdom and elemental-type energies are unequaled, boundless. They have access, by means of their extremely long lives and unique thought-processes, to forgotten information and knowledge, especially in the field of magick. Dragon power also helps the magician to make personal, inner changes that may be necessary. Helping to remove past negative programming or self-destructive habits is well within the abilities of dragons; of course, the human involved must desire those changes. Dragon magick, like all magick, does not produce miraculous results without work. Dragons can create opportunities, provide encouragement and guidance, even back the magician into a

Emperor Ki Harnassing Dragon Power
from *Myths & Legends of China* by E.T.C. Werner (New York: Brentano's, n.d.)

figurative corner so that she/he must face problems and make decisions. But they will never, never, do for you what you can and should do for yourself. Once befriended, dragons make excellent protectors, powerful fellow-magicians.

A true, knowledge-seeking magician weighs all possibilities for use in her/his magick, keeping what feels right to her/him and discarding the rest. Dragon magick is not for all. Dragon magick is only for the self-disciplined seeker who realizes the potential dangers, yet dares to communicate with and befriend this vast astral power of the ages. It is for the magician who is serious about changing her/his life and the living space around her/him. It is an asset for those who can give trust (not blindly, but with common sense), love, and a desire for true friendship.

If you use dragon magick for unjustified purposes, or try to manipulate and control dragons, you can expect a terrific negative backlash. In the matters of self-protection or bringing justice down upon dangerous members of society, I have absolutely no second thoughts about employing dragons. As to manipulation and control, one simply does not do that with friends and co-magicians. Common sense tells you that such behavior will terminate the friendship and cause other magicians to cease their cooperation, perhaps even to work against you. If you prove a danger to dragons, they are likely to enspell you to such a point that your magick does not work.

What if you have attracted a dragon or dragons who make you feel uncomfortable? I have known this to occur with other spiritual guides, so I suppose it can also happen with dragons, although I have not personally experienced this. If a dragon makes you uncomfortable, it is very likely that you are not ready yet to work with its energies. First, become clear in your own mind why you feel this discomfort. Perhaps the actual root of the discomfort is a bit of programming struggling to make itself felt and keep control over your activities. Perhaps the dragon's coloring has triggered old conditionings. A black dragon produces this feeling in people who have been taught that dragons, and particularly black dragons, are evil. The further into the subconscious you dig, the more you are amazed at what is in there, controlling your thoughts and actions when you least expect it.

If you still feel uncomfortable, set aside a time for a brief meditation and mental conversation with the dragon. Explain carefully and politely that you are attempting to remedy the situation, but at this time you just do not feel that the two of you can work positively together. Project as much good will as you can. The dragon will understand. I have never known a dragon to stay where it is not welcome.

The first dragons I saw were the huge elemental ones who appeared one night about a week before we discovered that some

A Black Dragon

by Johann Melchior Dinginger, 1701–8

bikers up the road were operating a meth lab. By the time the ATF forces, FBI, and local law enforcement descended upon the area, the dragons had put up very strong defenses around our property. At no time did we have any problems with the bikers. And, although some of their members shot it out with officials in another location, the arrests near us were quiet. After that, all colors and sizes of dragons made appearances, joining in rituals and generally hanging about the house. They are still with us.

Ancient mapmakers drew dragons at the edges of their maps to denote unknown territory that explorers entered at their own risk. Some explorers took this quite literally, venturing no further. Others looked upon this as opportunity, fully accepting the responsibility of their actions, and willing to take the risk for the sake of discovering something new.

Like the old mapmakers who wrote "Here be dragons" on the unknown edges of their maps, I wish you a safe journey into dragon country. Go prepared for a fantastic voyage on which you can make new friends and magick-working partners, and you will be pleasantly surprised at the knowledge you will learn. Dance with the dragons in their endless round of energy, and feel all areas of your life lifted into new, powerful realms. Go prepared to wrest what you want from the astral plane, and you may well (and very likely *will)* have an unprofitable journey filled with unpleasant experiences. Would-be conquering invaders have never been met with friendship, whatever plane of existence they were on. Exploring traders who were willing to listen and bargain a bit always had the most successful, profitable voyages of discovery. Travel into dragon country with caution, an open mind, and friendship in your heart. The journey will be well worth it.

Dragon Power in Magick

Working with dragons in magick is different in many ways from other magickal procedures, but not so different that you can disregard certain rules. You need to know how to practice visualization and self-discipline, ethics, absolute truthfulness with yourself, consistency of practice, and meditation. And there must be an exchange of energies while working, an absolute when working with dragons. All of these are important components of any magickal system.

Visualization begins with unlearning many so-called value systems shoved on us by other people, the most common of which is that use of the imagination and daydreaming are not productive and good. The imagination and daydreaming *are* a negative practice if they occupy most of your life and time; if you daydream about what you want to happen instead of planning and taking action, then you are avoiding responsibility. However, for any type of magick to become truly effective, you must learn how to vividly picture in your mind the event or result that you wish to happen. Once you firmly have the event or result in your mind, you perform your ritual and then release the mental energy for manifestation.

Self-discipline and ethics go together. A magician should not, for his/her own good, dabble in controlling other people or indulge in questionable personal behavior. Jealousy, envy, lust, greed, and anger should not control what a magician does during his/her rituals. In fact, these undesirable emotions should not control any part of a magician's life. These intense emotions tend to cloud judgment, either bringing an emotional backlash on the magician or causing deliberate harm to others, which in itself brings an eventual backlash on the magician. Either way, it is not worth the misery.

A magician must sincerely desire what she/he is asking for in ritual. If it is a half-hearted wish with little emotional intensity behind it, the dragons, or any other entities for that matter, will simply not be interested in helping. And do not think you can put one over on spiritual or astral plane entities because they can see straight through to the truth. The truth is never hidden from these creatures.

One of the worst things a magician can do is take something away from another person by means of magick. This includes health, property, life, or freedom. Very often I find that beginning magicians want to control another's decisions and life on the subject of love. Too often I hear that "I know so-and-so is the true love of my life, but they show no interest. How can I use magick to make them love me?" Forget it! The price is very high for doing this kind of manipulative magick! If they were meant to love you, they would already show interest. Obviously, they are not the love of your life except in your own mind. Any magician considering such a dark use of magick had better take a long, truthful look at their ulterior motives. If someone you were definitely not interested in started taking away your personal freedom to choose, how would you feel?

The second part of the use of magick is that the magician must release the emotions and desire after the ritual is finished. To constantly think about what you want accomplished after the ritual is ended binds the energies to you and they cannot manifest. To con-

A Disinterested Wyvern

from a 17th-century treatise

stantly talk about your desires, or to talk about the rituals you are performing to get them, will surely keep them from manifestation. To want something so much you can taste it and yet not care if you get it is a very difficult mood to cultivate. I have never known any magician who reached perfection in this area, but getting as close to it as possible is what is important.

There must be an exchange of energies between the physical, emotional, mental, and spiritual planes for any spellworking to result in a manifestation. Playing at ritual magick, particularly dragon magick, will not get you anywhere. Without mental concentration, physical working, emotional involvement, and intensity of purpose, in other words energies, dragons will not be interested in adding their vast energies to yours. No entity or companion, whether of this plane or another, is going to do all the work for nothing and let you sit on your hands. Dragons are attracted by the energies you raise during ritual, a kind of astral pay-off since they "feed" on this energy.

Belief in powers beyond yourself is important in any kind of magick. There is an old saying: "If you believe you can, or you believe you can't, you're right." We may not understand how these powers and energies work; we may not be able to describe them to anyone else; we will not be able to prove "scientifically" what they are. But we magicians know they exist. A magician believes in them because she/he sees the results of their use.

Every magician who wishes to be effective in ritual and manifestation, who desires to grow and expand in knowledge, sooner or later comes to the conclusion that magick is a very serious practice. They learn to set aside time for study and self-improvement through meditation. They practice what are commonly called the psychic arts: tarot, runes, the pendulum, crystal reading, dream analysis, and so on. They cultivate the senses, especially observation, which includes what is in both the physical and astral realms. They learn to read their own intuitive feelings and the vibrations of others.

Tarot Card Showing Perseus, Andromeda, and the Sea-Dragon
by Sandra Tabatha Cicero, from The New Golden Dawn Ritual Tarot

Meditation is important for the magician. She/he uses meditation to relieve stress, improve the physical and mental, alleviate emotional upheavals, and above all clarify her/his needs into the proper forms. It is also a time for listening, a time when spiritual guides and entities can bring valuable information. I am not an advocate of daily meditation, although some are. I believe that meditation performed from one or three times a week is very beneficial and not so much that it begins to blur the line between the physical and spiritual realms.

Having to live in a demanding physical world, full of stress and problems, makes meditation a very enticing way to escape. The physical, mental, and spiritual can become unbalanced; oftentimes the person loses her/his sense of reality and what is important at that moment. We see this all the time with people who sit back and say "God/Goddess will provide," meaning since they are "spiritual" they need do nothing but meditation and ritual and hold out their hands.

This type of behavior brings us back to self-discipline and balance in the magician's life. Through magick and ritual the magician gains guidance, opportunities, and a better sense of timing in order to take advantage of those opportunities. However, she/he never expects to get something for nothing. She/he knows the responsibility for action to fulfill and gain the desires is theirs alone. The dragons will not provide the magician with a magick lamp full of instant wish fulfillment; neither will any other entity, and that includes God/Goddess.

Whatever advice a person receives during meditation, or even through divination or other avenues of the psychic, must be filtered through good common sense. I have known people who received messages to leave a spouse, quit a job, move completely across country, and other drastic things. Those who followed these messages without further clarification and the use of good common sense generally found themselves in a worse situation than they had been in before.

Rebecca was what I call a fence-sitter in magick. She used it to try to get what she wanted, but did not follow the ethical laws of magick. She and her brother had a long-standing dislike for each other which ended up in court when her brother had her charged with forging a check on her mother's account. Since the check was actually for her mother's benefit (Rebecca was totally responsible, without pay, for the sick woman), her actions were not without a good motive, although she should have chosen another way to get the money. To fight the charges, Rebecca hired a lawyer. In the course of events, she decided that she was in love with this man, who was happily married. She informed me that a spirit, through use of the tarot and other divination, told her that this love was meant to be. She dropped all efforts to find a job, moved into the lawyer's town, and generally made a fool of herself. She became so obsessed with this "love" that she began to use controlling love spells. The last I heard, Rebecca was struggling along as a sometime mistress, unprovided for and unhappy.

Not every entity on the spiritual or astral planes is of a high character. You would not blindly follow such advice from just any-one in the physical. In fact, you should not blindly follow such advice from anyone *ever!* The old law of "as above, so below" means just what it says. We have perpetrators of evil and malicious troublemakers here, so obviously the spiritual and astral planes do also. Creatures totally born of the astral do not think as we do; their perceptions of physical life can often be totally unusable for us. As to the departed spirits who once lived in the physical, one must take care not to make them into something they are not. Too many people erroneously assume that once a person dies, they turn into a good, caring, reliable spirit, even though they were selfish, uncaring, and cruel while in the physical body. Being physically dead does not change a person's character.

Develop your relationship with your spiritual personal guardian. There is no difference in whether you call this entity your guardian angel or your spirit guide or an astral teacher. Unless you drive these personal guardians away by evil, totally selfish behavior (and yes, this can be done), they will remain with you throughout your physical lifetime. They help you through the birth experience when you enter this world, try to guide you throughout life, and are there waiting for you when you die. Other guides and teachers come and go as you progress and have a need of their special expertise, but your personal guardian can be a lifelong friend and companion.

Dragons are much the same as other astral entities, although I have yet to meet an "evil" dragon. Their view of what is vital to your growth and advancement may exceed your present abilities to perform. To dragons, the physical is simply a hindrance that they tend to ignore. After listening to their advice, carefully consider if you can or should make the changes now or at all. Be certain that you are not holding back because of fear of the unknown or simple laziness. And always look at the end results sure to occur from taking action. You, and only you, are responsible for your life, regardless of where you received the advice you decide to follow.

The types of dragons who are attracted to you will be the ones who have the most to offer you at the present time. Before rejecting a dragon, find out what she/he has to teach you. Be brutally truthful with yourself. If you find that you need what the dragon offers, but do not feel that you can endure the teaching and results in large doses, do some negotiating. Present your case for a modified lesson plan; be plain-spoken about your emotional and mental inability to withstand the great stresses of immediate and upheaving change. When you do start working with a particular dragon on specific issues in your life, make an honest effort. As long as you are trying, even though you fall short at times, the dragons will be patient.

You can also acquire a personal dragon guardian. See chapter 13 for more in-depth information on this. The guardian dragon does not automatically come into this life with you as does your

Guardian Dragons Tend to Be Fun-Loving Creatures

from *St. George,* an engraving, n.d.

spiritual guardian. It is a personal choice by that dragon (or dragons), just as one would choose a close friend. Although you can attract guardian dragons by cultivating certain attitudes and atmospheres, they can show up without any encouragement at all. They are gregarious little creatures, full of curiosity and mischief, who enjoy their own brand of practical jokes and the company of humans and animals.

Although guardian dragons tend to be fun-loving creatures who enjoy a good laugh, they are very serious about protecting you and your property. You might think of them as a spiritual watch-dog with boundless energy, influence, and power. Cultivating their friendship helps when dealing during ritual with the other dragons.

If you do not develop the friendship of your guardian dragon, the other dragon powers are not likely to be so cooperative.

Not all dragons are the same, no more so than are humans. They each have their own personalities. Their appearances vary according to the subspecies to which they belong, as do their special talents. Even individual dragons within a subspecies have identifying characteristics, markings, and bodily appearances. Dragons can be even more individualistic than we are.

Different species of dragons have different abilities and interests. Dragons connected with the element of Fire, or those of fire and volcanoes, for example, are primarily effective in getting things moving or tearing down impossible barriers. Wind and Air dragons are creatures of creative and mental aspects. Water dragons help stabilize emotions, heal emotional pain, and point you in the right direction to discover love and friendship. Earth dragons are interested in the acquiring of material possessions and the accomplishment of goals. These are very general descriptions of dragon interests and abilities, as draconic abilities overlap in many areas. It is best to work with a balance of types of dragons, with one particular dragon-aspect predominating, according to the intent of the ritual.

Above all, a magician must know her/himself, all the good and bad habits, and face them squarely. There cannot be any self-delusion if ritual is to be effective and positive in nature. And why would anyone want their rituals to be negative when there will eventually be such a price to pay?

The magician may choose to begin working dragon magick as an effort to better the physical life, and this is not a bad or wrong procedure. Working on physical needs and desires, and seeing them manifest, gives a budding magician greater trust in her/his inner powers. When the physical body and the surrounding area in which the magician must live and work are well and cared for, when there is less struggle and strife in life, then the next logical step for the balanced person is to seek spiritual enlightenment.

After all, when the very foundation of magick and ritual is finally uncovered, the magician finds that *all* ritual and spellworking is meant to be a means for spiritual growth and development. Whether or not we choose to follow that upward path is an individual responsibility. We are each responsible for our choices in life, how we react to the choices of others around us, even to our being here in the first place. We have no right to place any blame on others for what is going wrong in our lives. If you make a wrong decision, change it and learn from the experience. Dancing with the dragons can make this life-path a little easier and a lot more interesting.

Set Slaying Apep

Dragon's Breath in the Earth

Many of the old legends speak of killing the dragon. Sometimes, the real meaning of this term is clarified when one is told that the dragon continued to live. Of course, if you are reading Christianized stories of dragons, the dragon is always killed by a faithful saint or hero; this is a less than subtle reference to Christianity "killing" Paganism. But a great many of the legends were in existence long before the Christians came along; therefore the term "killing" must mean something far different than destroying your religious rivals.

If you look at ancient Egyptian paintings of Horus and his Sun Boat sailing over Apep, sometimes called Apophis, serpent of the Underworld and the dead or winter season, and read the ancient stories of these daily and seasonal voyages, you become aware that the word "killing" has another meaning. The pictures show the god Set "staking" or guiding Apep by a series of rods driven into the ground. A similar practice is still used to control or change the Earth's energy in certain areas of the world in the belief that out-of-control dragon energy adversely affects humans, crops, animals, and the land in general.

The Chinese emphasized the importance of controlling the "dragon's breath" in architecture and landscape. This is still a respected belief in Hong Kong and other places having Chinese communities. There are professionals adept at finding imbalances of the dragon's breath, and they are in demand, not only by home owners, but by businessmen. If a series of unexplained illnesses or misfortunes strikes a business, for instance, the owner will go through the ordinary procedures to discover the cause. If there is nothing found, or nothing appears to alleviate the problems, he will send for a person skilled in detecting a disruption of dragon's breath; this person is called a Feng-shui diviner.

A visit to the premises is made. This Feng-shui diviner sometimes uses a special magnetic compass that has as many as 38 concentric rings around the needle. Each ring is divided into special traditional measurements of space and time. The diviner takes sightings along what are called the veins of the dragon. These veins are raised features of the landscape, such as trees, rocks, watercourses, valleys, etc. Within buildings, the diviner considers such things as doorways, halls, the directions of corners, and so on. Any recommendations made by the diviner are implemented with great seriousness. If possible, a small garden, aligned in certain ways, is made outside for the dragon of the region. Inside, a shrine is placed in a particular corner or area to accommodate the reigning draconic being. Dragon images are placed in both the garden and the shrine to honor the dragon, and also to remind it of its good fortune to be recognized and given respect by the human residents.

Although cultures in the rest of the world may scoff at this, the Chinese businessman will tell you that the problems have ceased and business has improved.

The Chinese word for dragon's breath is *sha,* a term which may correspond to what European dowsers call "black radiations." For the past 50–60 years European dowsers have traced lines of black radiation which seem to follow underground water-bearing fissures or "black streams." These black streams produce an energy imbalance in the Earth, affecting the landscape, its vegetation and crops, and any humans or animals that live there or frequent the area. Dowsers say that this imbalance of energy can be caused by quarrying, cutting through hills for roads or building, landslides, etc. Like an acupuncturist "staking" a node on an acupuncture

Feng-shui Diviner at His Compass

meridian to restore balance in the human body, these dowsers stake the black streams with iron rods. In Chinese terms, they are restoring the Yin and Yang of the land where the dragon's breath has turned sour or noxious.

This staking or guiding the dragon's Earth energies may have been an ancient art which both balanced and collected these energies within a specific place. Dragons are connected in legends with mazes, spirals, labyrinths, and hills, coiling around or within them. It is possible that the terraced and spiraled hills, the circles of stones, indeed the single monoliths, were a method of controlling and directing this dragon energy. With the spiraled mounds and labyrinths the energy would have been guided into the center of the structure where it would have been of use to initiates who understood its great potential and power. In legends this guided dragon energy would be symbolized by the dragon coiling around a hill and squeezing the hill into its spiral form, such as in the legends of the Wormington Hill and Bignor Hill dragons in Britain. The Vurm of Shervage Wood was said to lie in and out among the trees of its area, its winding coils marking the boundaries of an ancient so-called campsite. Archaeologists have long called these spiral-marked areas ancient campsites, although common sense tells you that they could not be defended from invaders.

This dragon energy may be a form of static electrical energy flowing naturally through the Earth. It would explain the strange sensations one gets within specific areas, especially in what are called sacred spots. The sensations range from tingling in the fingers, spine, or back of the neck to a great sense of peace to an unidentifiable strange feeling. Whatever this energy is, it is extremely strong wherever it is concentrated into a contained area, such as the center of a stone circle or a spiral. There are other places, commonly called power spots or power-sinks, where this energy appears to rise from the ground without any human-made structures. These power spots cover a specific area of ground and have definite edges where the energy phenomena cease to exist.

Barrow mounds have long been associated with strange happenings. It may be that the priests of the original builders knew now-forgotten techniques of situating these sites over power flows so that they collected and stored the energy as would batteries. Among the Celts, it was a common practice for trained seers to spend the night on such a mound or grave and communicate with the dead, either to gain information from the past or predict the future. It has been documented several times within the last few centuries, that when a barrow mound was opened, strange and violent thunderstorms occurred soon afterwards. It would appear that there was a release of some kind of contained energy, and that the release was done in such a way as was not safe for such a build-up.

Many old stories tell of the dragon using a regular path, whether by air or land, whenever it journeyed from one place to another. These paths were not necessarily in straight lines. It is possible that these dragon paths followed underground streams of energy that moved from one sinkhole of energy to another. In his book *Folklore of Prehistoric Sites in Britain,* L.V. Grinsell tells of a mysterious light commonly seen moving from a cairn at

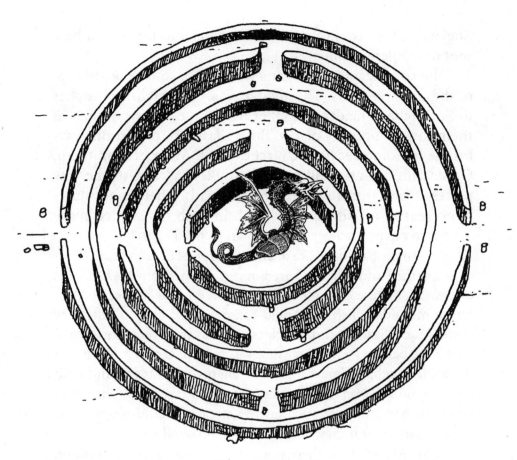

Dragon in Labyrinth

Torhousetie to a water conduit and back; the conduit had been covered with a stone slab taken from the cairn. In this instance it would seem that the cairn slab had become so magnetized that the energy set up a new line of flow from the sinkhole (cairn). Legend says that when the dragon's blood is spilled, no vegetation will grow there. Dowsers say that if something goes wrong with the Earth energy, the same thing happens. One story about spilled dragon blood is connected to the bare spot called Dragon Hill, which lies just below the White Horse at Uffington in Berkshire,

England. There is another such legend connected with a bare spot near Aller in Somerset.

The conquering Christians were quick to take advantage of these power spots. They had a policy of building churches to St. Michael the dragon-killer over these old sites, some of them in very unlikely places. Both Glastonbury and Burrowbridge in Somerset have churches to St. Michael atop them. Other churches are built in the most illogical, out-of-the-way places, areas far from towns or even roads. There is absolutely no reason for siting the church in such an isolated place except to cover a power spot known to the Pagans.

The Anglo-Saxons spoke of another type of dragon Earth energy when they said dragons laired in certain sites to protect hoards of treasure. These sites most often seemed to be connected with burial mounds which the Anglo-Saxons called dragon hills. The Celts, Anglo-Saxons, and the Norse all said that were-fire burned above the barrows where treasure was buried. It may well be that the ancient peoples knew where the energy streams ran and built burial mounds over them for some specific reason. The grave goods in barrows over such energy streams would absorb that energy, particular if they were made of gold or silver.

In the *Mabinogion*, there is a story of Peredur, son of Efrawg, who refers to a Welsh barrow that is guarded by a Worm. The *Mabinogion* is filled with symbolic stories that can be interpreted on a spiritual level. On the physical plane, the burial treasure was considered to be magickally charged. Perhaps the treasure in the dragon lairs really meant spiritual treasure which could be discovered through the use of the streams of "dragon" energy. Physical treasure which has been removed from such mounds often carries with it strange vibrations which precipitate very weird events.

The ley lines, which have been mapped in Britain proper, may well be streams of positive dragon energy, while the black streams would be imbalanced energy flows of the same type of force. I sus-

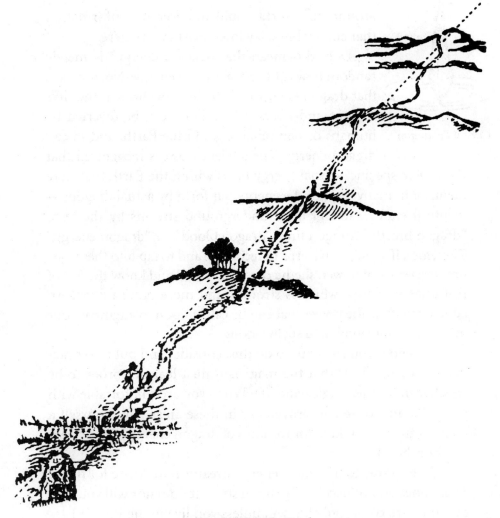

The Old Straight Track

from *The Ley Hunter's Manual* by Alfred Watkins (1927)

pect that these underground Earth energy streams crisscross the planet and can be found in every country, if a magician is willing to put forth a little effort to discover them. We have always assumed that such lines of energy existed only in Britain with only the occasional power spot to be found elsewhere. I feel certain that magicians

Crystal Pendulum

around the world could uncover the information that energy lines, ley lines, exist everywhere.

Does this mean that "dragon energy" is merely random flows of Earth electrical energy? No, it means that dragon energy has specific flow lines, rather like streams and rivers. Water flows can be diverted by humans or natural changes in the Earth, and so can dragon energy. The ancient peoples recognized that there were specific, special energy flows within the Earth that were identical in many ways to the energy put forth by actual dragons— identical enough to call these underground streams by the term "dragon breath," "dragon fire," "dragon blood," or "dragon energy." Therefore, if a magician learns to recognize and to tap into these natural reservoirs of power, she/he can understand and know the feel of real dragon energy, which is stronger and more powerful yet. An added benefit is the power that can be called upon to augment your own energy for rituals and spellworking.

But before you rush out to do this, consider and put into practice all the methods that the magician must learn in order to be effective in her/his magick and life. When you are comfortable with your schedule of self-improvement in these areas, give yourself a relaxing treat by looking for the lines of dragon energy in your own neighborhood.

The best way to find these energy streams is to dowse for them. These lines do not necessarily run in straight lines nor will you find that they are commonly known, unless you live in the British Isles proper where they have been extensively studied and mapped.

For dowsing* you can use a pendulum or dowsing rods, neither of which have to be professionally made. A pendulum can be a small weight or crystal suspended on a thread or chain. The pendu-

---

*There are three books on pendulums and dowsing rods that I consider good. There are very likely others which I have not read that are just as good. *Everybody's Dowser Book* by Ona C. Evers (San Rafael, CA: Onaway Publications, 1977); *Divination by Magic* by Noud van den Eerenbeemt (York Beach, ME: Samuel Weiser, 1985); *The Complete Book of Dowsing & Divining* by Peter Underwood (London: Rider & Co., 1980).

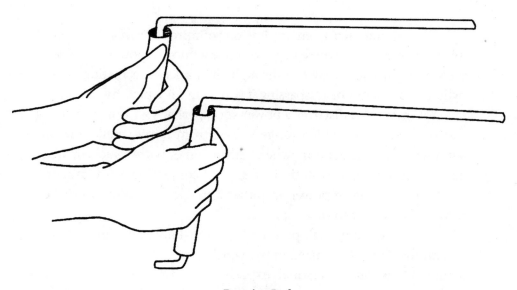

Dowsing Rods

lum is held suspended by the chain in your power hand while you walk over an area. For some people, the pendulum will swing in a clockwise circle, for others back and forth, when an underground flow of power is crossed. By marking the ground wherever this occurs, you can trace a power line's underground flow for long distances. Don't try to walk along over the top of the flow, but rather cross it from the side. Back and forth working will allow you to be aware of any twists and turns the line might take.

Dowsing rods can be made from two coat hangers. Using a pair of wire cutters, cut off the hook and then straighten the remaining wire. Bend this long piece of wire in such a way as to provide short hand-grips and longer right-angle bars. Holding a bent rod loosely in each hand, the dowser walks slowly over an area until the long bars cross. The problem with dowsing in an inhabited area is that you will find every water line there. But it can be productive if you combine dowsing with watching for unusual anomalies in the vegetation growth or lack of plant life altogether. Energy flows have been known to shift position, following underground water or electrical lines.

Discovering such an energy line on your property makes it possible for you to know where to go to access a burst of power when you need it. Other lines may run through city parks or recreation areas, where you will not be trespassing if you go in for a pick-me-up.

You may even discover a power spot, perhaps within your own yard. These areas, which range in size from fairly small to large enough to lie in, can be anywhere. Sitting on or within such an area is a great aid for meditation or simply contacting your dragon allies. The radiating power amplifies a magician's ability to make contact with the astral.

There are many such power spots, well-known in Europe and beginning to be recognized in the U.S.A. One such large spot with which I have had personal experience is the Oregon Vortex. Although you first must go through the area with a guided tour, you are allowed to freely look about afterwards. Some people find they cannot tolerate the energy fields within the Vortex; they get headaches or nausea. I experimented with a crystal pendulum there and had strange but wonderful results. At first the pendulum refused to move at all. It merely hung straight down and quivered; this quivering was visible as well as being strongly felt all through my arm. When I stuck my arm in through the open window of the old assay shack, the pendulum came back in a straight line nearly touching my arm. It stayed in that position until I withdrew my hand from the window. At no time could I get the pendulum to move normally within the Vortex area. However, as soon as we left, it worked as it always does.

At one time, power spots in the U.S.A. were probably well-known by the Native Americans. Since these peoples rarely built permanent structures on these sites, there is no way to readily recognize them, as we can in Britain where stone circles and monoliths, not to mention ancient Christian churches, cover the landscape. Machu Picchu in South America is such a power spot, as are Mount Shasta and Mount Tamalpais in California.

I plan to study further on the connection between dragons and these power spots and energy lines. I know that dragons can be seen either within the spots themselves or moving along the lines. They tend to be particularly visible at night. It is not uncommon for people to see "ghosts" in connection with these places. I assume they are seeing both disembodied and astral entities, with the dragons being mistaken for ghosts. Few people take the time or effort to discriminate. Most people are programmed with too much fear of the subject.

Dragons use the projected power of these energy lines and spots, probably in much the same way they do energy given off by rituals. Having an energy line in your back yard is not a prerequisite for dragon magick, but you may discover that you find a disruption of flow. If you do find what you think is a black stream, consider whether you have trouble growing plants within or near that area. Do animals and people avoid that spot in favor of other places in the yard? Have you had difficulties with Earth slippage or unusually swampy ground? Do you just feel uncomfortable in that area? Be very careful about designating such a place as a disrupted power line until you are more familiar with the idea, because first contacts with dragon's breath can give you some very strange sensations.

If you decide that there definitely is a disrupted line of energy, you can take active steps to help correct it. A few carefully placed stakes, whether wood or iron, can change the atmosphere in such conditions. If you have underground water or other utility lines, be very careful about driving stacks anywhere near them. If you decide to use iron rods, do not go anywhere near them during a thunderstorm; they are capable of acting like lightning rods! Take your time deciding about staking, though, because you do not want to worsen any possible existing problem. And use a lot of forethought before you do any major excavation or dirt moving, even though you do not detect an existing break in the power flow.

If you locate dragon energy lines on your property, you can

guide the energy into a central place much as the ancients did by laying out a simple spiral pattern with rocks. Even if you think you do not have such energy streams, a rock-patterned spiral may very well collect energy and concentrate that power into its center.

A rock spiral can be as simple as a widely spaced line of small stones that curves inward until a center is reached, rather like the design of a snail's shell. The best way to provide for a working center is to first establish a circular space big enough to stand and move around in; center this over a power spot if you are fortunate enough to find one. Surround this center with a border of rocks, leaving an opening on one side. Then curve your spiral path out from this at least three times around the center area. Be sure that the path is wide enough to comfortably walk in. Make the path turn clockwise.

In the very center of the spiral, you can place a flat stone. It does not have to be very large. Whenever you find such a stone, before placing it within your power area, cleanse it with a bath of salt and water. This flat stone can do double duty as an altar and also to stand or sit upon when you are working within your sacred place.* There are some human-constructed flat stones used for facing buildings that work quite well. Stay away from plastics. Several bricks set up in a square or oblong pattern can be substituted; however, they are not very good at conducting energy into your body. The real stones can become power-sinks in their own right, drawing in and storing Earth dragon power or even the power produced by repeated rituals.

Much more elaborate labyrinths can be formed if you first plan them out on paper, but I cannot say they are any more effective than the simpler design. One side effect of such a spiral is an improvement of the atmospheric vibrations throughout the immediate neighborhood, as well as on your own property.

---

*A flat stone can also be used inside in your ritual room as an altar or standing place. Marble, however, is an excellent substitute for an indoor altar. Slabs of marble made into kitchen cutting boards are easily available. Marble is an excellent material for holding power that is raised around it. It becomes a power-sink, or holder of power, and that energy can be drawn upon when needed.

Rock Spiral

Circles of stones will work in the same manner, especially if they are built over lines of dragon power. In *Circles, Groves & Sanctuaries* (Llewellyn, 1993), Dan and Pauline Campanelli wrote of a man who built a wooden henge, as in Stonehenge, in his yard. This circular structure would work on the same principle as a stone circle or labyrinth.

Although the mere laying out of the spiral or circular rock pattern will activate and center the dragon's breath energy, you might want to specifically tie it to your own energy vibrations. This can be done with a simple welcoming ritual. Using your staff, walk along the spiral path into the center. Take with you a small gift of herbs. If you have laid out a circle, choose one particular direction to use as a consistent entrance place. Stand in the center facing north and tap the ground three times with the staff, saying:

> *Arise, O breath of dragon.*
> *Fill this land with goodness.*
> *Bless me and mine with your positive energies,*
> *And repel all those who wish us harm in any form.*
> *I welcome all dragons who come to this place of*
> *   power.*
> *May we work in harmony and in love.*
> *May this sacred spot become a haven of centeredness,*
> *A refuge that revitalizes,*
> *A door that leads to Otherworld knowledge.*
> *May your powers become one with mine* (kneel and
>   touch the ground with the palm of your hand)
> *That I, my family, my community, my country, the*
> *   world,*
> *May become whole and healthy again.*

Tap the staff three times on the ground. Sprinkle the gift of herbs about your center space. Exit the circle or spiral with dignity and thanksgiving, knowing you have begun a neighborhood change in vibrations for the better.

Sometimes you will find a house or building that sits on a line of dragon's breath energy. Some of the older houses that exude an atmosphere of either welcome or repulsion are often situated on such lines. Disembodied spirits, or ghosts, are frequently seen in these buildings, and not just by psychics. If the energy stream is a positive one, the ghosts will not be troublesome. However, if the house sits over a black stream, one finds poltergeist activity, malicious ghosts, and a general set of negative vibrations that harass the family living there. It may be that these ghosts are trapped by the negative energy flow or that they use it to boost their own power.

I rented such a negatively situated house once and never was able to stake the energy line right or get rid of the hateful ghost who stayed there. One of the two stairways in that house was always as cold as the inside of a freezer, even on the hottest days of the year. The evil that was felt on that stairway made everyone, even nonbelieving visitors, avoid going that way. I found out that forty years before, a teen-aged boy had died in the room at the top of the stairs. What his reasons were for staying on after death, I do not know, but the noises, evil feelings, and trouble he caused were unwelcome. No renters stayed for any length of time.

Tracing flows of "dragon energy" is an excellent exercise for strengthening your psychic abilities. The vibration of such power is quite similar to that felt when dragons are in the vicinity, so it helps the magician become familiar with the feeling of arriving dragons. Best of all, it is just plain, inexpensive fun!

Ritual Candle

Ritual Tools

very sincere, dedicated magician is always searching for new ways to amplify her/his magickal power so that her/his manifestations will be more accurate and consistent. Using the elemental-type power of dragons to help in your rituals is an excellent method for increasing the flow of energy within the cast circle.

There are certain ritual tools that you will find helpful for dragon magick. If you are already practicing magick, you will have some of them. If you are just beginning to work in magick, acquire your tools slowly and with care. Tools do not have to be elaborate or expensive to work magick. For example, I have never found that a little silver wand (these are really expensive!) could do more than a piece of dowel lovingly decorated by the magician. And the tools do not have to all be acquired at once or before you can start your magickal workings.

If your budget does not allow any purchases at the moment, do not put off beginning your practice of dragon magick. Start off with the kitchen table or the nightstand in your bedroom as an altar. One white candle in a fireproof holder is better than none; however, if you cannot have a candle, substitute an electric candle

Standing Brazier

or small light. A paring knife will work as a ritual dagger for carving script onto the candle. A pleasant cologne or aftershave can become an emergency incense. A glass can be a chalice. Use your imagination and inventiveness until you can manifest enough prosperity to purchase better tools. Ritual manifestations have been

Magickal Book

successful with some of the most outlandish equipment in a pinch. But it does work better and more efficiently when you have special ritual tools. I think this has to do with the budding magician's subconscious mind and the development of the magickal personality.

An altar can be any table, chest, or microwave cart that is large enough and of a comfortable height to stand and do magick. If you find it impossible to stand during ritual, choose an altar that is a comfortable height while you sit. Colored scarves coordinated to the elements or various dragons can be used to cover the altar. For magicians who are hampered in movement, whether by a broken leg, physical disability, or confinement to a wheelchair, do not despair. Sit at your altar and visualize yourself going through each moving step of the ritual as if you were physically doing it. I know one magician who, while flat in bed for a time, meticulously visualized her way through rituals and got excellent results, although she was unable to do so much as light a candle.

To illuminate the altar, use a black candle on the left end and a white candle on the right. A knowledgeable magician knows that using black candles is not evil magick. The color black is merely the

Incense Burner

opposite of white; it balances the energies. If you feel you cannot use black, use a very dark blue, purple, or indigo.

However, if you do have an aversion to the color black, it signals a need for you to do some intense work on the programming you have accumulated in your subconscious mind. All of us have, at one time or another, received and accepted undesirable programming from others, whether it be from parents, teachers, friends, colleagues, a religious group, or simply society in general. Unfortunately, much of this programming is given to us at a very impressionable age when we are not aware enough to reject it. What we acquire at an older age is accepted because we want to fit in with a special group, etc. Although it takes determined effort to undo this programming, it can be done.*

An incense burner is also very helpful for dragon magick, just as in all magickal rituals. A burner with chains is best because the magician can move it about without getting burned. One can use the little self-lighting charcoal tablets especially made for incense to burn the appropriate herbs and gums. A list of these herbs and gums is given later in Appendix 1. In a pinch, the magician can use incense sticks or cones, choosing the scents to match the ritual.

The prime ritual tool for dragon magick is a sword. It does not have to be an elaborate, expensive sword. Choose one that is not too long or heavy because you will often hold it out before you for long

---

*Childhood programming is discussed in greater detail in my book *Celtic Magic* (Llewellyn, 1990).

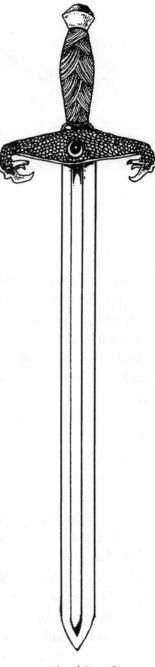

periods of time. For a woman, a sword 18 to 20 inches in length is usually the right size. I love Scottish claymores and other large reproductions, but have enough sense to know that my shoulders would be aching miserably after a few minutes of holding it out in front of me. Besides, long swords are notoriously clumsy and difficult to maneuver within a cast circle. It is quite easy, when totally involved in magick, to sweep everything off the altar with a swinging sword. Men should also chose a lighter, shorter sword for the same reasons. Swords do not need a sharpened edge.

I suppose the magician could use a painted wooden sword as a substitute for a metal one, although I would personally find it difficult to adjust my thoughts to the use of such a ritual tool. However, a dragon is not impressed by the weight or elaborateness of a sword, just the fact that you have one. The sword is of the element of Fire.*

A double-edged dagger with a blade no longer than your palm and fingers is used to carve on candles and do other small jobs within the circle. However, it does not have to be very sharp to do this. In fact, it is probably better that it is not, as you can get a nasty cut when working. The very tip of the blade is the part you will usually be using to incise

Ritual Sword

---

*My assignment of the sword and dagger to the element of Fire and the wand to the element of Air differs from that of some other magicians and writers. This is not a contrary assignment on my part. It simply seems more logical to me.

Ritual Dagger

anyway. The dagger is also of the element of Fire.

For dragon magick, both the sword and dagger should have names. Choose any name that reminds you of their power and might. However, I would suggest not using any name such as "Dragon Slayer"; such names will not help you when trying to gain the cooperation of dragons. "Dragon Claw" is appropriate, as would be "Star Fire," "Wind Cleaver," or "Foe Slayer."

It is best to have your wand no longer than the length of your forearm plus your fingers. Like a sword, a wand that is too long becomes a detriment. A wand can easily be made out of a piece of dowel. If at all possible, glue or attach a crystal or a very small crystal ball to the directing end of the wand. Dragons love gems and crystals. If you wish to paint the wand, good colors are black with silver markings if you are a woman, black with gold markings if you are a man. However, there is no reason you cannot use whatever colors appeal to you. The only problem with using other colors is that later, when you have grown beyond those shades, you will either have to repaint your wand or make another one. Sometimes this happens anyway, as when you get new ideas or come across a ready-made wand that really speaks to you. Paint your magickal name on the wand in Dragon Script, if you wish. (See the chart in Appendix 3 for Dragon Script.) In dragon magick, the wand is used to consecrate the wine, water, and salt. The wand is of the element of Air.

At some time you will want to include a staff among your tools. You can choose a piece of dowel or natural wood about shoulder-high or head-high. It has been my personal experience that shoulder-high is quite long enough; as with swords and wands, a staff that is too long can create disaster in one movement. You may wish to attach a crystal or small crystal ball to the top end.

If using a smooth dowel, you can purchase four lengths of cording the length of the staff. These should be in the colors of the elements. Traditionally, these are red, yellow, blue, and dark green or black. (For information on other magickal systems and their element colors, read the next chapter.) Tack or glue a length of cording down each side of the staff to correspond to the elemental directions (see next chapter). Attach tassels of the same color at the top end of each piece of cording; if you cannot find colors, use white instead. If you do not want to tack or glue the cording, it can be attached near the top of the staff by decorative brads or nails and allowed to swing free; if you do this, use short pieces of cording to avoid getting tangled in them. You can further decorate the staff with small bells, glass beads, or whatever seems appropriate to you. If you choose a limb or twisted wood staff, it can be decorated with dangling ribbons of the appropriate colors attached near the top in the correct order. Attach the bells, glass beads, etc. to the ribbons.

When decorated in this manner, the staff becomes the dragon bridge, or the connecting link between the magician

Staff

Chalice

and the astral planes. The staff is a symbol of magickal authority, your right to call upon and work with dragons. It is also symbolic of the center of the circle or the element of Spirit. At times it can be used like an oversized wand. Be careful when gesturing with the staff because it is very easy to knock things over.

For convenience, you might consider having some type of holder or a deep bucket of sand near one end of the altar to securely hold your staff when not in use. Or it can be laid on the floor before the altar. The problem with this method is that you may tend to stumble over the staff when deeply involved in the ritual unless you are careful. But then, a deep bucket of sand is attractive to cats and small children. Experiment until you find what works for you.

You will need two chalices, one for water and one for wine. The water chalice can be of any material, but it is advisable that the other chalice be lined with a good coating of silver if it is pewter, brass, bronze, or copper. Wine and other acidic beverages create a dangerous reaction with certain metals. Of course, if the magician chooses a wine chalice made of glass or ceramic, this is not a problem. If you cannot drink wine for whatever reason, substitute apple cider, grape juice, fruit juice, or even soda. The water chalice is of the element of Water, the wine chalice the element of Earth, sometimes of Fire when used for "blood."

A small container for salt is handy. A small jar with a lid is best because you will be keeping your ritual salt separate from the kitchen salt after consecration. Salt is the element of Earth.

Since you may want to collect very small amounts of earth from sites you visit, you will need a pottery, glass, or metal bowl with a lid. Whenever you are on an outing and feel within the area a power that draws you, take an extremely small amount of the dirt or sand back for your dragon bowl. The last information I had is that it is illegal to bring some foreign soils into the U.S.A., so check with customs before trying this. Remember that a *very* small amount of soil is all you need. This dragon bowl and its contents will be used to empower objects in magickal ritual. This bowl and its contents, naturally, will be of the element of Earth.

It is also useful to have a clear glass bowl for stones and gems that you collect or buy. Expensive, polished gems are not necessarily any better than those you find rough in Nature or the tumbled ones found in a rock shop. This gem bowl does not need a lid because stones radiate power at all times without any loss. The gem bowl is of the element of Earth.

If you plan to work with water or sea dragons, you need to purchase a number of small bottles with lids that can be securely fastened. Again, you will be collecting extremely small amounts of water from various sites where you feel the radiation of dragon power, or strong elemental energies. I am not certain as to the legalities of bringing foreign water into the U.S.A., so check with customs before doing this. Even rainwater has power. Carefully label each little bottle so you can remember where you got it. I will explain later how to add these to larger amounts of regular water for special rituals. These containers and their contents will be of the element of Water.

A pentacle disk is necessary for consecrations and other ritual work. This is usually a metal or wooden disk with a pentagram (five-pointed star, one point upwards) painted or etched on it. However, there is no reason that the pentacle cannot be made out of cardboard. The pentacle is of the elements of both Spirit and Earth and helps to control and balance all the other elements.

Pentacle Disk

When used as an element of Earth, the pentacle grounds Spirit in the ritual. (See the illustration for the design.)

The dragon pentacle can be used as either a picture or disk. It is presented during specific rituals as a means of establishing your authority to call upon the dragons, and is also of the element of Spirit. You can copy the picture from the illustration and mount it on cardboard or wood, or put it in a frame.

Another element of Earth and Spirit is the mirror. This may be of any shape. A plain wooden or plastic frame around the mirror makes it easier to write on your magickal statement. Around the

Dragon Pentacle

edges in Dragon Script should be written: "By the power of the eye of the Dragon, I capture and harmonize all airborne thoughts."

A small gong is useful for certain dragon rituals. You can, however, substitute finger cymbals or a small brass or glass bell as long as the tone is clear and attractive. The gong is of the element of Air, because sound is carried on air. Gongs, cymbals, or bells are one means of attracting the dragons' attention during certain portions of the ritual. They also signal to the magician's subconscious mind that deep personal attention is needed at that point.

Last but not least, over time you may want to collect pictures or images of dragons. Role-playing figurines are excellent for this. Some of these are quite large. Grenadier Models* has a wide variety and a considerable number of dragon model figurines that work quite nicely for this purpose. They are easy to assemble and can be painted in any colors you wish. Another source of dragon statues (indeed of anything with dragons on it!) is Dancing Dragon,** a mail order firm. The idea behind the figurines is that they help the magician to better visualize various types of dragons.

The personal apparel of the magician is just as important as the ritual tools. It is not a good idea to wear everyday clothing into a cast circle. Too many times disruptive vibrations cling to your clothes; besides, the magician wants her/his subconscious mind to get the message that the ordinary is being laid aside. Robes color-coordinated to the primary dragon power being used are very nice and help the magician assume the magickal personality and confidence necessary when dealing with dragons. However, more than one robe is not necessary; a black or white robe is quite acceptable.

The robe should be a loose, comfortable fit and can be decorated with dragons, dragon script, astrological symbols, or decorative braid and beads—in fact, anything that appeals to you. Sometimes you may be fortunate to discover a ready-made caftan or robe already decorated with dragons or other symbols that appeal to you.

---

*Grenadier Models, P.O. Box 305, Springfield, PA 19064.

**Dancing Dragon, 5670 West End Rd., Suite 4, Arcata, CA 95521. For the price of their catalog, see the ads in *Llewellyn's New Worlds of Mind & Spirit*.

A gold and silver cord can be tied around your waist. If having something tied about your waist is uncomfortable or does not appeal to you, at least have the cord among your magickal items. If you cannot find a cord with both these colors, choose silver if you are a woman, gold if a man. These colors are traditional in the magickal system within which I work. Again, the magician may choose other colors, realizing that later growth may make it necessary to change them. The cord is for more than ornamentation, as you will see in later rituals. The magician can wear sandals or slippers or go barefoot.

It is nice if any jewelry (headband, bracelets, pendants, etc.) has dragon designs. I have both a pendant with a dragon and a dragon claw clutching a crystal, both of which have proved excellent fascinations for dragons and their energies. More and more pieces of jewelry with dragons on them are appearing on the market, many of them inexpensive.

Dragon headbands are rare, so the magician may want to make one for her/himself. To do this, you can use a plain metal headband, obtain a small dragon charm, and glue it on the band. If you cannot get a metal headband, substitute a strip of cardboard covered with aluminum foil. Fasten the dragon charm to this.

All herbs and oils are useful but certain ones have excellent drawing power for enticing dragons into your ritual work. Those needed for a particular rite will be listed at the first of the various rituals; the herbs are fully discussed in the Appendix.

Keep your ritual supplies of herbs and oils separate from others you may use for medicinal or ordinary purposes. In fact, it is important to magickal power to keep all your ritual supplies separate from your everyday life, or at least as much as possible. I was taught that magick is a part of everyday life, but that all ritual supplies should be set apart. I have found this particularly effective. This also keeps other people from handling your tools and possibly leaving negative vibrations on them.

The worst offenders for leaving negative vibrations are those who do not believe in magick and either openly or privately condemn you for practicing it. If necessary, and if possible in such circumstances, put your tools under lock and key. It would be ideal if a magician did not have to contend with such people, but it is not always possible or desirable to remove yourself or the offenders from your environment. Most of these types of conflicts stem from prior religious programming, something the magician cannot and should not try to change because she/he would then be guilty of the same offense of trying to control another.

A word of warning to any magician who may have small children in her/his home. Although children rarely leave negative vibrations on objects, they can hurt themselves with some of the tools, herbs, or oils. Make certain that your equipment and supplies are off limits and safely out of the way.

The magician should take the same precautions with pets, although I have yet to find a cat who would do more than absorb ritual energy or be fascinated by a crystal. Cats and dragons seem to enjoy each other's company with few disagreements. I cannot say about dogs, since I have had no experience with them.

Stones are also used in dragon magick. In the list of gems and stones in Appendix 3, I have listed the names of various kinds according to color. However, unpolished stones you pick up in nature can be just as powerful; you do not have to spend a fortune buying precious and semiprecious gems. Whether you purchase your stones or find them, be certain that the vibration feels right to you. Keep these in your gem bowl.

All of these ritual aids and tools are important to the performance of rituals that will entice dragons to help you in your work. However, it is not an absolute necessity to have all of these things before you can begin working with dragons. As you read through the various types of dragons and their rituals given throughout this book, you will come to further understand the value and uses of these tools.

The magician must learn to practice meditation, at least on a regular basis for it to be helpful.* Meditation stimulates the psychic centers and teaches self-discipline and patience. Every magician also must learn and practice silence. Silence, in this sense, means that you do not talk about the magickal rituals you are performing. Talking about your magick dissipates the energy you have raised. The only exception to this that I know is if you are working with a like-minded individual or group. Then sharing can help to focus stronger energy toward your goal. I strongly suggest that you be absolutely certain that the people with whom you share your activities and plans are in total agreement. Otherwise you will find yourself struggling to get results. A person may say they do not oppose what you are doing, but inwardly disagree completely.

One important fact to remember whenever you do dragon magick (or any magick) is that it is definitely not a game. If you plan to only dabble in magick, I strongly suggest you forget trying any of these rituals. Stick to simple candle-burning spells. Dragon power, or elemental-type energies, are not something to play around with. You can get a terrific negative backlash from just playing at dragon magick. Dragons are not noted for being cooperative or patient with insincere practitioners of magick. Dragons, like other types of powerful spiritual and astral entities, quickly weed out the dedicated from the dabblers in magick.

Dragon magick and power are only for the serious magician. If you are sincere about advancing your skills as a magician, then I heartily wish you well. Becoming acquainted with dragon power is an extremely satisfying experience.

Celtic Magic (1990) and *Norse Magic* (1990), two of my books published by Llewellyn, give examples of how to meditate.

Two Elizabethan Magicians, Edward Kelly and Paul Waring

from a 17th-century English engraving

The Magickal Personality

Every magician begins building her/his magickal personality as soon as she/he begins to seriously work with ritual. The magickal personality is the subconscious way the magician perceives her/himself as a magician. We create these types of images all the time by the way we think of ourselves: shy, too thin, fat, not pretty enough, whatever. What we image ourselves to be, and tell ourselves mentally we are, eventually comes to pass.

Others, to whom we give power over us, can do the same thing. This programming can be quite open, with others or ourselves constantly harping on our appearance, our behavior, or our beliefs. Most people, however, are adept at the art of subliminal programming. This is a very insidious thing to do, either to ourselves or to others. It is like little drops of water constantly wearing away at a stone. The single drop seems like nothing of importance, but with time the water wears a groove in the rock so that it becomes a different shape.

A magician needs to learn to choose friends and acquaintances with great care. Life is tough enough without surrounding yourself with people who belittle what you believe and do. Oftentimes it becomes necessary not to share your practices and ideas with family and friends. If they are not in agreement with your goals, they can consciously or subconsciously undermine all your efforts.

If you find yourself being self-critical too often, it is a signal that you need some inner work. Everyone has received negative or derogatory programming at some point in their life. Success comes when one can recognize it for what it is and work at weeding it out of the subconscious mind. Unfortunately, there are no instant solutions to this problem. A conscientious magician soon learns that inner work is an on-going task. It is never really finished. However, the biggest advance is made when the magician catches those programmed thoughts as they surface, recognizes them, and rejects them.

If you desire to work in the magickal field, you need to have a long talk with your inner self, not only at the beginning of your career, but at various times throughout your life. Your inner self needs to be firmly convinced that you have the right to practice magick, that it is not wrong or evil unless you have negative intentions. Even more than this, you need to feel that you can do magick. If you believe you can't do magick, or you believe you can, you're right! Whatever you believe, you become.

One way to convince your inner self, and your subconscious mind, that you are a magician is to assume what is called the magickal personality each time you enter your ritual area. This is first accomplished by firmly believing that you can do magick and that you have the right to do magick. You reinforce your image of your magickal self by laying aside ordinary life and donning a special robe for the ceremony. Your jewelry and ritual tools, the casting of the circle, the actual working of the ritual, all strengthen the image you build of yourself as a magician. Last, but by no means least in importance, is the choosing and assuming of a magickal name.

Your magickal name is an important part of your tools and your magickal personality. The use of this name within your ritual area is a signal both to your subconscious mind and to any entities with which you work that you are prepared to switch from the everyday mode of thinking to magickal workings. The name may come to you during meditation or dreams or simply be one that appeals to you and perhaps describes your desires, attitudes, or aspirations. As with any of your magickal tools, this name can be changed at a later date if you decide you have outgrown it.

Since this special name is a key to your magickal self, share it only with those you can trust. Sharing it indiscriminately with people may place power in the wrong hands; you could find yourself under psychic attack, either to limit your magickal manifestations or to control your life. This type of attack does not necessarily have to be by another magician. Orthodox religionists are experts at using what they call prayer to control and manipulate others.

Your magickal name can be anything you want. It does not have to be the name of a deity or even belong to the history of a particular culture. The name can be made up of syllables whose sounds appeal to you and only has meaning to you alone. *The Magical Name* by Ted Andrews is a book published by Llewellyn (1991) that goes into a number of ways to choose a magickal name.

If you are already into the practice of magick, you very likely have such a name. You might continue to use it, or decide that you need a special one for working with dragons. Dragon magick names might be: Firebright, Flame Dancer, Wind Rider, Storm Walker, Golden Eyes, Cloud Shadow, or anything else that reminds you in some way of dragons and their attributes and activities.

Some people like to use the study of numerology to choose a name. They use either the number of their birth date or their common name to select a magickal name with the same numerical value. The table on the following page shows the numerical values of letters and is a common feature of any book on numerology.

1	2	3	4	5	6	7	8	9
A	B	C	D	E	F	G	H	I
J	K	L	M	N	O	P	Q	R
S	T	U	V	W	X	Y	Z	

To determine the numerical value of your birth date, add the numbers of the month, the day, and the year together. For example, February 10, 1961, would have a final value of 11. Some numerologists would break this down further, giving it a value of 2, but I was taught that the numbers 11 and 22 should be left as they are.

In determining the numerical value of your name, or a chosen magickal name, add together the values of all the letters. This gives you the final number, or numbers as in the case of 11 and 22. You must use your entire name to come up with the correct value.

1—A person with great individuality, but can become a dictator if not careful. This person seldom if ever follows the dictates of the crowd. More often they are trend-setters, for good or bad. Works best alone.

2—A cooperative, sympathetic person who delights in group projects and solving problems. The diplomat who must beware becoming static through not making decisions for fear of hurting someone.

3—Inspiration and optimism are expressions of this type of person. Also has creative and artistic abilities in some form. Beware of talking too much and doing nothing.

4—The slow but steady builder of a career, business, relationships, whatever. Works best in a capacity of serving others. Penny-pinching and nitpicking are the extremes of this number.

5—This person thrives on change and new things. This person can become such an advocate of new ideas that they become a pain in the neck to everyone else.

6—Home, family, truth, and justice are very important to number 6 people. They will do whatever is necessary to have a stable life. However, they sometimes tend to be worry-warts.

7—These people often get off to a rocky start in life with many trials and tests, especially in learning to see deception. The reward for working their way through these messes is great understanding and sympathy, tempered by high spiritual ideals.

8—This number person has the strength and talent to be an effective business and financial organizer. Although they like to acquire money and position, they should also involve themselves with charitable events.

9—If this person disregards the responsibilities of her/his life, a career of disappointments can result. Compassion, love, and service must be their keywords. Works best where human understanding and kindness are needed.

11—These people are happiest when they are pursuing a life or career which expresses their religious ideals in some way. A few of them choose to withdraw from the world and pursue their goals inwardly, but most of them work in areas where they can directly help others.

22—These are the innovators on an international, community, or national scale. They are efficient organizers and communicators. Watch out for too much pride in ability.

Having a so-called numerically correct name is not necessary to magick. What your choice of name means to you inwardly is more important. Your magickal name is a vital part of the magickal personality that you create, the image that you become when you enter your ritual area. This magickal personality is the one to which the dragons respond. As astral beings, this is the real you as far as dragons are concerned.

However, the very first creature you must convince that this magickal personality exists is yourself. When you have chosen your magickal name, prepare your altar with lighted black and white candles, perhaps a sweet-smelling incense, and your dragon mirror. Dress in your robes and jewelry as if you were going to do a full dragon ritual. As with regular dragon ritual, it is important that you not be interrupted or disturbed during this time. Instead of the usual ritual proceedings, sit comfortably on a chair or stool so you can look directly into the mirror. Look straight into your reflection and say: "I am (your magickal name). I am a magician and friend of dragons."

How did you feel as you faced yourself and spoke your new name? Did the name itself make you feel uncomfortable, or was the uncomfortableness just the normal reaction of speaking to your reflection? If the name itself truly does not seem to fit, seriously consider choosing another one.

In the beginning, most magicians have to do a lot of work on themselves so that they feel at ease when putting on their magickal personality. They learn that time and ritual practice makes it easier to think of themselves as actual magicians with power.

Weed out any negative past programming that arises from the subconscious mind to tell you you are unworthy, that you cannot do magick, that magick is not real, that magick is evil. Every time a negative thought such as these arises, look straight at your reflection in the mirror and answer it out loud. Take as long as necessary to squash these negatives. You may find yourself having a one-sided conversation with a person who has put you down in one way or another throughout your life. If yelling at that person while looking into your mirror works, then yell! The important thing is to get a clear picture of the negatives hiding within you, those subtle little and not so little pieces of programming that make you doubt yourself in more than just the field of magick.

The ultimate goal is to reach a point in your mirror talk where you can tell yourself that you can, and will, rise above this type of control placed upon you by others. Rise above it, and release it. You may find that your immediate most damaging enemy is yourself. Like Pogo said, "We have met the enemy, and they is us." Stop setting personal goals which are based on comparing yourself with someone else. You are a unique individual, with your special needs, desires, goals, and dreams.

When you are comfortable with your personal mirror work and speaking your magickal name, it is time to present yourself as that magickal personality to your dragons. When your ritual area is prepared, when you are dressed in your robes and stand at the center of your circle, call out your name to your dragon co-magicians as you greet them. By trusting your dragon allies with this secret name, you are strengthening the trust you hope to build with them. As you share with them, so they will share with you. Dancing with dragons is an experience of friendship built on trust and caring.

A Flying Dragon

Music and Dance

Dragons respond to music and dance, as do a great many entities in the spiritual and astral planes. The rhythms of music and the expression of free-form dancing have been considered by many experts in the fields of psychology and cultural study to be an almost universal language in themselves. Many sources over the ages have spoken of universal harmony and music, which emanate from all things. This makes sense if one accepts the idea that everything, even that which we call inanimate, has vibrations. Vibration is movement, and movement produces sound of some kind. Music is commonly thought of as harmonious sound. And what is considered to be music is determined by each individual or creature.

Dragons, like most humans, respond differently to different rhythms and types of music. One way to understand these responses and feelings brought to the surface of the mind by music is to experiment on yourself. The most obvious rhythm-maker is the drum, a vital part of music all over the world. Spend a week listening to various kinds of music. Ignore the words. Concentrate your attention on the drum rhythms or music beats and note your responses to them. In order for this to be an accurate experiment, you must also be aware of your existing emotional feelings prior to hearing the music, as these feelings will determine how you relate and respond to any given piece of music.

Write down your feelings of emotion prior to the music and how you felt afterwards. Did the drumbeat quiet you, or did it accelerate your energy level? Did the drum, in connection with the rest of the music, make you feel like tearing down the walls, or did it make you feel as if you could regroup and take on the world? Each person is an individual and therefore will respond differently to various types of music and beats; each person will also at different times in their life respond in different ways to the same music.

Next, experiment with various types of music, from hard rock to easy-listening to classical to New Age, and everything in between. Do your listening when you are totally concentrating on the music, not sharing your attention with another person or project. Try to set aside any preconceived notions or programming you have concerning certain kinds of music. You may find that certain artists in various categories appeal to you while others in that field do not. If there are vocals, try to tune them out, listening instead to each separate instrument until your hearing becomes sensitive to your will and demands.

Now, strive to identify the memories that may arise from certain music. Are those memories from this life, or do they possibly stem from past lives or racial memory? Sometimes we are drawn to music that has a specific and definite cultural flavor. If this music corresponds to your inherited background, it may indicate that you are tapping into your racial memories, or the unconscious.* If it does not correspond to inherited background, it may well be past-life memories.

What has all this to do with dragons? A lot, actually, since dragons were and are cultural creatures also, with emotions of their own. If you really want to stir up a dragon with protective urges,

---

*My book *Maiden, Mother, Crone* (Llewellyn, 1994) goes into the areas of the mind and all the consciousness patterns in detail.

Gypsy Musical Instruments
from *The History of Man* by J.W. Buel (Richmond, 1889)

just play music with a heavy, march-like drumbeat, a rendition that stirs the blood and emotions. This does not necessarily have to be military music; in fact, strangely enough, most military music does not appeal to dragons. One must take care in stirring up such emotional feelings in dragons, though, since they often take things quite literally. Wind and water dragons, when incensed by such music, can create great destructive storms. They see nothing wrong with their activities in such circumstances; after all, they are only being themselves, even if it is at their most active and violent.

Many New Age and classical pieces of music run the gamut from calming to invigorating. Some of this type of music is now being classified as anything from New Age to rock; some of it has become quite popular with the general public. I find these types of music very useful during rituals, along with non-vocal classical music. The magician should not limit her/himself to one type of music, but experiment with many kinds. A wide variety of styles and categories can be used to interest the dragons and raise their involvement and energy levels.

Music can also include the vocalizing of sounds. All sound is vibration, the creating of a temporary, short-term source of energy. I have found that chanting prolonged versions of the vowels (A, E, I, O, U) can produce a form of energy that is sustained within the magician's aura for some time, particularly if the chanting is done within a cast ritual circle. No particular note is necessary; choose a level of sound that is comfortable for your voice. Take a deep breath and, as you begin to exhale, chant the vowel as one long, sustained sound until your breath is gone. This can be repeated as many times as you like. Be aware, however, that until you become accustomed to this practice, it is very possible to get dizzy from this kind of chanting and breathing. So, in the beginning, do not use more than two or three sustained vowel chants at any one time.

With a little experimentation with the various vowels you will discover which ones work for what purposes. There does not appear to be any hard and fast rule as to which vowel is best for channeling what power or energy in ritual. It seems that the use to which the vowels can be put changes with each magician. This would be logical if one considers that the energy levels of the chanted vowels combine with the energy levels of the magician's aura, thus amplifying whatever power and energy already exists.

When I first began to use this type of chanting in connection with dragon rituals, I had an extremely interesting, pleasant experience. I was alone in my ritual room, deep in thought while chanting the A vowel. At that time I did not realize that one could call dragons with that procedure. As I stood, arms outstretched, eyes closed, vibrating the sound for the second time and enjoying the calmness that it brought to my mind and body, I began to be aware of subtle movements and faint sounds around my feet. Since my cats have free run of the ritual room and often join me there, at first I thought nothing of it. Then a series of small dragon forms and laughing faces played across my closed eyelids. Tiny claws scratched on the floor; there was the papery rustle of little wings. Something knee-high brushed against my legs, while a very tiny form lodged itself comfortably behind my left ear. That was my first introduction to Nip and Tuck, the knee-high guardian dragons, and Tinsel, the very small one who often nestles in my hair.

When your dragons are comfortable with your singing, and you with theirs (yes, they do sing!), you can progress to impromptu songs that express your emotions, desires, and/or goals. This singing does not have to rhyme; it does not have to be a repeated, specific melody; you do not have to have a beautiful trained voice. You are using the power of universal music-language to deeply communicate with your dragons. They are very understanding about your attempts in this area. After all, some of their singing takes getting used to; some of it is very different from what humans are used to hearing. This type of impromptu singing can be used in coordination with free-form dancing during parts of your rituals.

Each dragon has a very distinct, unique song or melody of its own. Subspecies of each family of dragons have similarities in musical tone, but each draconic being has developed its own identity-signature of musical sound. They do not sing for just anyone, so recognize the honor you are being paid if your dragons share their songs with you.

Dance has always been connected with music, whether it was the folk dancing of the common people or the more structured forms of movement used in temples. Today's magicians frequently never learn about or use dance motions in their rituals, perhaps because much of magick, except for certain Pagan forms such as Wicca, are descended from forms of ceremonial magick which do not use the dance form.

Free-form dancing can be one of the most satisfying of dance routines, since one does not have to memorize steps. This type of dancing is self-expression at its highest, melding physical movement with emotional feelings and spiritual yearnings. One does not have to make great leaps and turns, but can move gently and fluidly within a small area, letting every move be different and unique. The best results come when the magician does not even try to remember how she/he danced the last time, but moves with the music in new ways each time she/he dances. If you feel self-conscious about dancing, at least let the upper part of your body and your arms move in response to the rhythm. Break through your inhibitions, that previous programming, and enjoy yourself. After all, you are dancing for yourself. Why care what some narrow-minded person thinks?

When dragons feel emotional about something, they move with the rhythms of the vibrations given off by that person or event.

Everything in the universe, not just humans, gives off vibrations, which are a type of movement of energy. Even what we erroneously call inanimate matter has vibrations or movement, although we may see no movement whatsoever. Since every happening and event is created by the actions of both animate and inanimate matter, events and happenings become imbued with vibrations of their own. Granted these vibrations only last until the event has completed its cycle, but they do exist for a limited period of time.

And dragons are experts at communing with and using all types of vibration. Dragons of wind and storm will roll and leap with the air currents, following the storm system for thousands of miles until it dissolves. Water dragons will take advantage of the storm vibrations to ride the waves of ocean, lake, or river. Even a gentle breeze becomes a celebration of movement and dance.

The vibrations of various happenings have musical rhythms of their own, if one listens. So do the vibrations of various areas of land and water. When powerful surges of these vibrations break

Sea Dragon

from an 18th-century engraving

through the Earth's crust instead of the usual steady radiation, we find uniquely energized areas, such as the ley lines, the Oregon Vortex, triangles all over the world, and so on. Magicians realize that there are also myriads of smaller power spots on the surface of the Earth, some quite probably in your neighborhood.*

Dancing during ritual draws to the magician the type of vibrational energy she/he is expressing by movement. If you are near a power place or energy line, or the pressure centers of weather are crossing over, you can tap into that energy pattern. Dancing also attracts dragons who are interested in that specific type of vibration. As with any entity, physical or otherwise, one first must get their attention and interest, then persuade them to aid you. There is little you can offer a dragon that will enlist her/his aid except an exchange of vibrations or the chance to frolic in the vibrations you have raised about you. Dancing, coupled with emotional intent and purpose, is the most satisfying and accurate method of raising the desired vibrations and attracting dragons.

---

*See the chapter entitled "Dragon Power in Magick" for information on dragon energy within the Earth.

The little guardian dragons dearly love music and dance. In fact, the easiest way to communicate with these creatures is to invite them to join you in such activities. Since young children are uninhibited experts at free-form dancing, these little dragons can be found wherever children are having fun without the frowning supervision of adults. The guardian dragons can be found frolicking around even very young babies. They are expressing the joy of life, the vibrations of self-power and hope, the ecstasy of possibility. Their movements are totally uninhibited, free-form dancing at its most unique, expressive of every little shade of their emotions. It is quite easy, even for an adult, to get one of these little dragons to dance with you.

The larger dragons appear to be more stately in their movements. Even when seen in storms, earthquakes, volcanic eruptions, floods, or fires, these dragons move with grace and balance of motion. The more forceful or violent the event, the more likely you are to see two or more dragons twining about each other in a complicated expression of dance. These adult dragons are less likely to actually dance with the magician, at least at first. It may take many dances by yourself before you attract a large dragon as a dancing partner. But when it does happen, the experience is indescribable. It is as if one is lifted out of oneself into an area of pure spiritual vibration and magickal energy.

For magicians who cannot physically participate, dancing can be accomplished by visualization within the mind. No disability of the body or restriction of living conditions can restrict the use of the mind, the imagination, and visualization. The magician, even when physically dancing, knows she/he does not enter the spiritual and astral realms of power with the physical body. The transition is accomplished through certain areas of the mind and spirit.

Dancing with dragons has a side-benefit that may take some time to make itself known, but it will happen. Besides the unique relationship the magician gains through this activity with the dragons, the

Small Guardian Dragon
from *The Chariot of Minerva*, c. 1500, France

magician's mind becomes more open and creative, her/his body more flexible, emotional states more balanced, spiritual goals more concentrated. What you, as a magician, give to your attending dragons in freely-given vibrational energy is returned to you in a number of subtle yet beneficial forms.

When you discover which music, vowels, and movements help you to become one with the music, sound, and motion, you are well on your way to opening the door to communication and partnership with dragons. When you reach this state of oneness, you will discover that the separateness built up between you and all other creations and levels begins to blur and finally to dissolve. Meditation, ritual, indeed life itself, will be richer and more rewarding. And dragons will crowd into your daily and ritual life, peering over your shoulder as you work. It is an exhilarating experience.

Basic Rituals

By using the following rituals, the magician can begin seriously attracting dragons as co-magicians and fellow companions for aid in magickal work. Before beginning even these, however, I suggest that you set aside time for work with chanting, music, and dance, as well as meditation. Consider these activities the training exercises an athlete goes through before actually participating in the main event.

While practicing these procedures, the magician can begin to collect the ritual tools she/he needs to begin performing dragon magick. Do not feel that you must rush out and buy everything at once. And do not fall into the trap of equating expensive with better. Once you have established communication with the dragons, they will lead you to many of the tools; dragons seem to be very conscious of a good buy; at least mine are. Take your time collecting what you need.

Although ritual magick is a serious practice, the magician must also make room for fun. Music and free-form dance can be very important in keeping dragons interested. These activities are also of importance to the magician, since most humans live lives full of stress and over-seriousness. Know yourself, know your real intentions for doing ritual, and enjoy your time with the dragons. Take time to be a child again, non-judgmental, full of wonder and delight at the antics of dragons. Learn from them when to be serious about life and when to lose yourself in play and pure enjoyment. My dragons have taken part in rituals with total concentration and involvement, only to spook one of the cats when we are finished.

Enjoy yourself with your dragons. Ask them for help in whatever you are striving to accomplish. Provide them with friendship and the chance to frolic in the energy vibrations you create. Learn from them. But never, never, treat them as commanded slaves or take their friendship lightly. Dragon magick is serious business. Be an honest friend, and you will receive honest friendship in return. Try to deceive and use them, and you will find yourself in trouble. Dragons are not like humans. They feel no compunction to continue a friendship or be helpful or even nice if you mistreat them.

It is helpful to the magician with dragons as co-magicians to keep a notebook detailing inner experiences while working this type of magick. Some dragons will appear only during certain phases of the Moon, while others arrive during specific weather patterns, such as storms, long hot spells, etc. Other dragons hang around for days, especially if the magician is going through a period of turmoil in her/his life. Some dragons make brief appearances during a ritual and are not seen again for quite some time.

Each dragon has a definite feel to her/his personality just as humans do. The magician must learn to recognize them individually even if she/he never learns their names. Dragon names are usually never what they seem, since dragons are extremely cautious about giving their true names to humans. I never argue or press them on this point since I feel they have a right to their privacy if they desire it.

It is quite an ordinary occurrence for a magician to work the dragon rituals several times before becoming aware that she/he has

Dragon from Bayeux Tapestry

attracted dragon-helpers. Do not become discouraged if you are not immediately aware of their presence. Be patient. Dragons have good reason to be wary of humans. Prove your trustworthiness and friendship to them. A friendship developed slowly and on a firm foundation lasts the longest.

Dragon Blessing

This is a ritual for blessing and consecrating all your ritual tools. Whether your ritual tools are chosen specifically for dragon magick or whether you plan to use them in several kinds of magick, it is wise, as well as a nice gesture, to ask your dragons to add their powerful blessings to the equipment. The stronger the power in a magickal ritual tool, the better the rituals are worked.

This ritual is best done on a Full Moon or at bright noon. All of the tools may be consecrated at once if you have gathered them, or you may consecrate those that you have at this point. Others may be blessed as you acquire them. Any jewelry can be blessed at the initiation ceremony. Have pure frankincense gum to burn in the incense burner; a little goes a long way with gums, which tend to smoke.

Tools that you will find useful at this point are the dragon pentacle, the pentacle disk, incense burner, chalices, salt dish, sword, and wand. If you cannot drink wine, substitute apple cider, grape juice, fruit juice, or soda.

Arrange your ritual area with care. It is best to set the altar in the center of your working area so that you can face the east. Light the two altar candles (black on the left, white on the right). Remember, if you are timid about using black, substitute extremely dark blue, purple, or indigo.

Play soft instrumental music if you wish. It helps to create the proper atmosphere and mask minor noises. Once the circle is cast, *do not* cross the boundary until the ritual is finished! You are dealing with mischievous creatures in this type of magick. Dragon power is a totally different and more unpredictable kind of magick; it can even be dangerous if you are frivolous and half-hearted about your work.

Begin the ritual by going to the east. With the forefinger of your power hand (this is generally considered the one with which you write), "draw" your magickal circle on floor around your ritual area. Do this by pointing your finger at the floor and seeing great flames shooting from it. Move clockwise around the circle with this flame; end by overlapping it in the east. While drawing the circle, say:

BY DRAGON POWER, THIS CIRCLE IS SEALED.

Return to the altar. Put a small amount of frankincense on the burning charcoal in the incense burner. Point your forefinger at the burner; say:

BY DRAGON POWER, I CALL YOU PURIFIED.

Lift the incense burner and carry it clockwise around the edge of the cast circle, beginning and ending in the east. Return the burner to the altar.

Slowly pass the pentacle disk through the incense smoke. Say:

> ELEMENT OF SPIRIT, BY DRAGON POWER I CALL YOU
>   PURIFIED.

Set the dish of salt on the pentacle disk. Circle the dish three times clockwise with your forefinger. Say:

> OUT OF THE DARKNESS OF EARTH AND SEA COMES THIS
>   BLESSED SALT.
> BY DRAGON POWER, I CALL YOU PURIFIED.

Sprinkle a few grains of salt on all four corners of the altar. This sprinkling purifies the altar and may be done at any time, whether during ritual or as a cleansing if someone has messed about with your altar.

Pass the dragon pentacle through the incense smoke and say:

> ELEMENT OF SPIRIT, BY DRAGON POWER I CALL YOU
>   PURIFIED.

With the dragon pentacle in your power hand, go to the eastern quarter. Hold up the pentacle, facing the east. Say:

> DRAGONS OF AIR, BEHOLD YOUR SYMBOL AND ALLY.

Moving clockwise, go to the south. Hold up the pentacle; say:

> DRAGONS OF FIRE, BEHOLD YOUR SYMBOL AND ALLY.

Go to the west. Hold up the pentacle; say:

DRAGONS OF WATER, BEHOLD YOUR SYMBOL AND ALLY.

Finish by going to the north. Hold up the pentacle; say:

DRAGONS OF EARTH, BEHOLD YOUR SYMBOL AND ALLY.

Return to the altar. Lay aside the dragon pentacle and take up the sword. Touch it briefly to the pentacle disk and pass it through the incense smoke. (You will have to keep adding small amounts of incense throughout the ritual, but not enough to make breathing uncomfortable.) Say:

SWORD OF FIRE, O (name of sword),
BY DRAGON POWER I CALL YOU PURIFIED.

Hold the sword for a few moments before the dragon pentacle. Put down the sword and take up the dagger. Touch it to the pentacle disk, pass through the incense smoke, and say:

DAGGER OF FIRE, O (name of dagger),
BY DRAGON POWER I CALL YOU PURIFIED.

Hold the dagger for a few moments before the dragon pentacle.
For each tool, set it briefly on the pentacle disk, then pass it through the incense smoke. When finished with the Call, hold the tool up before the dragon pentacle.
Water chalice:

CHALICE OF WATER, BY DRAGON POWER I CALL YOU
PURIFIED.

Wine chalice:

> CHALICE OF EARTH, BY DRAGON POWER I CALL YOU
> PURIFIED.

Dragon bowl:

> BOWL OF EARTH, YOU HOLDER OF LANDS FAR DISTANT
> AND NEAR, BY DRAGON POWER I CALL YOU PURIFIED.

Gem bowl:

> BOWL OF EARTH, YOU HOLDER OF GEMS BRIGHT AND
> POWERFUL, BY DRAGON POWER I CALL YOU PURIFIED.

Wand:

> WAND OF AIR, WIELDER OF MIGHT AND MAGICK, BY
> DRAGON POWER I CALL YOU PURIFIED.

Staff:

> STAFF OF SPIRIT, AUTHORITY AND POWER ARE YOURS. BY
> DRAGON POWER I CALL YOU PURIFIED.

Water bottles:

> CONTAINERS OF WATER, HOLDER OF GREAT SEAS AND
> RIVERS, BY DRAGON POWER I CALL YOU PURIFIED.

Gong, finger cymbals, or bell:

> You Element of Air, whose musical notes reach to the dragon worlds, by dragon power I call you purified.

Mirror:

> Eye of the dragon, you Element of Earth, by dragon power I call you purified.

Whenever you get new supplies of herbs and oils, they can be consecrated by circling them three times with your wand and saying:

> Herbs (oils) of Earth, given by dragons of light and darkness, by dragon power I call you purified.

Now is an excellent time to chant and use free-form dancing. Invite the dragons to share in the raised energy and your joy of being a magician. Talk to them about your hopes and dreams. And listen to see if they have suggestions or words of encouragement for you. This is an opportunity for close friendships to be forged.

To close the ritual, take your sword in your power hand, your wand or staff in the other. Hold the sword up in salute. Go to the east and say:

> Dragons of Air, behold the tools of magick, consecrated by dragon power.
> Let us be one in magick.
> Farewell, O dragons great and wise.

Continue clockwise to the south. Say:

> DRAGONS OF FIRE, BEHOLD THE TOOLS OF MAGICK,
> CONSECRATED BY DRAGON POWER.
> LET US BE ONE IN MAGICK.
> FAREWELL, O DRAGONS GREAT AND WISE.

Go to the west; say:

> DRAGONS OF WATER, BEHOLD THE TOOLS OF MAGICK,
> CONSECRATED BY DRAGON POWER.
> LET US BE ONE IN MAGICK.
> FAREWELL, O DRAGONS GREAT AND WISE.

Go to the north; say:

> DRAGONS OF EARTH, BEHOLD THE TOOLS OF MAGICK,
> CONSECRATED BY DRAGON POWER.
> LET US BE ONE IN MAGICK.
> FAREWELL, O DRAGONS GREAT AND WISE.

Return to the altar. Point the sword at the dragon pentacle and say:

> DRAGONS OF SPIRIT, HIGHEST OF DRAGONS AND MOST
> POWERFUL, BLESS THIS ALTAR WITH YOUR FIRE.
> LET US BE ONE IN MAGICK.
> FAREWELL, O DRAGONS GREAT AND WISE.

Cut the circle with a backward sweep of the sword across the circle boundary. Extinguish the altar candles. Leave the ritual tools on or around the altar overnight to be further empowered. The dragons may inspect them closer during this time and add special blessings.

It is important to realize that you work with dragons as partners and co-magicians. You have to be firm in your intentions but willing to listen to their point of view. A magician tries to gain control over dragons at her/his own peril.

Basic Dragon Ritual

This is the basis of all dragon rituals in this form of magick. The magician can insert her/his own creations, such as music, dance, meditation, or small pieces of self-written ritual, in appropriate places without disrupting the flow of energy. Every practicing magician I know sooner or later rearranges a ritual to suit their personal style and needs. As you can see by reading through this ceremony, certain things need to be done at a certain time of the ritual. Beyond that, the magician can do what feels right to her/him.

Read all notes on appropriate times and needed supplies for a particular ritual before starting. Have everything you will need inside your ritual area and make what preparations you can to not be disturbed.

If you are performing decreasing magick, any place in this ritual that says "circle clockwise," you should circle counterclockwise. Another method of decreasing circle magic is to cast a clockwise outer circle with a counterclockwise inner one.

Set the altar in the center facing east. Make certain that you will not be disturbed once you have cast the circle. This may mean silencing the telephone and hanging a "do not disturb" sign on the door. Instrumental music also helps to set the mood and mask background noises.

Begin the ritual by going to the east. With your sword in your power hand (the one with which you write), "draw" your magickal circle on floor around your ritual area. Do this by pointing the sword at the floor and seeing great flames shooting from it. Move clockwise around the circle with this flame; end by overlapping it in the east. While drawing the circle, say:

By dragon power, this circle is sealed.

Return to the altar. Point the sword at the dragon pentacle and say:

Dragons of Spirit, highest of dragons and most
    powerful, bless this altar with your fire.
Let us be one in magick, O dragons great and wise.

Set the water chalice on the pentacle. (The water used in the chalice is not to be confused with the water you collect from various watery power spots.) With the wand in your power hand, circle the chalice three times clockwise with the wand and say:

Air, Fire, Earth, bring power forth.
Water of land and sea, purified be.

Hold the chalice high, say:

Draconis! Draconis! Draconis!

Sprinkle the water lightly around the circled area, beginning and ending in the east.

Set the dish of salt on the pentacle. Circle it three times clockwise with the wand and say:

Water, Air, Fire, hear my desire.
Salt of Earth and sea, purified be.

Sprinkle a few grains of salt to each corner of the altar.

Circle the incense burner three times clockwise with the wand. Say:

> FIRE OF DRAGONS, FIRE OF EARTH,
> YOU ARE PURIFIED. BRING POWER FORTH.

Circle the incense and herbs three times clockwise with the wand. Say:

> INCENSE MAGICKAL, INCENSE BOLD,
> AWAKE THE DRAGONS, AS OF OLD.
> I CALL YOU PURIFIED.

Put a small amount of incense onto the burning coals. Lift the burner by the chains and touch it lightly to the pentacle. Lift it high over the altar, say:

> DRACONIS! DRACONIS! DRACONIS!

Then carry it clockwise around the circle, beginning and ending in the east. Return it to the altar.

Kneel before the altar with the sword in both hands. Mentally, dedicate yourself to the study of dragon magick. Project your interest and love of dragons as strongly as you can. Continue this for several minutes. Then rise and point the sword at the dragon pentacle and say:

> BEHOLD, ALL DRAGONS AND RULERS OF DRAGONS,
> I AM (magickal name), A MAGICIAN WHO SEEKS
>   DRAGON MAGICK.
> WITH (name of sword) IN MY HAND, I ENTER THE
>   REALMS OF THE DRAGONS,

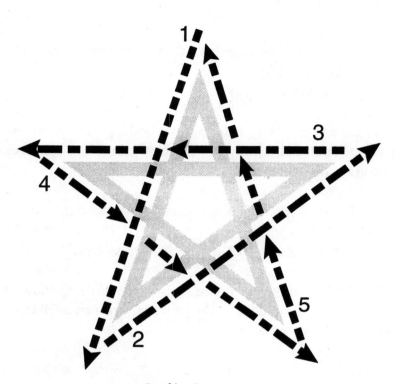

Invoking Pentagram

NOT FOR PHYSICAL BATTLE, BUT FOR KNOWLEDGE AND
    POWER.
I GREET YOU, O DRAGONS ANCIENT AND WISE,
AND AWAIT YOUR BLESSING AND GUIDANCE.

Continue holding the sword outstretched until you feel the blessings of the dragons. (Now you know why you do not want to use a heavy sword.)

When the flowing power of the blessing has lessened, lower the sword. Still holding the sword in your power hand, take the dragon pentacle in your other hand and go to the east. Point the sword at the eastern position and hold up the dragon pentacle facing outward. Draw an invoking pentagram with the sword (see illustration). Say:

From Sairys (sair'-iss), ruler of the eastern drag-
    ons fair,
Comes now the wondrous power of Air.

Feel the power of Air entering your body. When the flow stops, go to the south. Hold up the pentacle again. Draw an invoking pentagram with the sword; say:

From Fafnir (faf'-near), ruler of dragons of the
    South,
Comes cleansing Fire from dragon mouth.

Feel the power of Fire entering your body. When the flow stops, go to the west. Again hold up the pentacle. Draw an invoking pentagram with the sword; say:

From Naelyan (nail'-yon), ruler of dragons of
    the West,
Comes the power of Water, three times blest.

Draw into yourself the power of Water. Go to the north. Hold up the pentacle. Draw an invoking pentagram with the sword; say:

From Grael (grail), ruler of dragons of the
    North,
The power of Earth does now come forth.

Draw into yourself the power of Earth. Return to the altar. Lay aside the sword and dragon pentacle. Add the appropriate herbal incense to the incense burner.

(At this point in your ritual, insert the proper chants and workings for the particular spellworking or meditation you have chosen.)

If you have a problem that you have not been able to solve by physical means or by magick, ask the dragons now for advice. They will be able to give you new insight into ways of solving it. Continue to feel their power and direction as you write down the instructions.

When finished with the spellworking, tap the staff three times and chant:

> I THANK YOU, DRAGONS OLD AND WISE,
> OF EARTH AND FIRE, WATER, SKIES,
> FOR SHARING WISDOM HERE WITH ME.
> AS WE WILL, SO SHALL IT BE.

Always approach dragons as equals, not as a force to be ordered or conquered.

Set the wine chalice on the pentacle. Circle it three times clockwise with the wand and say:

> CUP OF POWER, CUP OF MIGHT,
> DRAGON MAGICK, BE HERE THIS NIGHT.

Drink the wine,* saving back some to be poured outside on the ground later as an offering to the dragons. (If it is not possible to pour the offering outside, leave it on the altar for about an hour.)

Now is an excellent time to chant and use free-form dancing. Invite the dragons to share in the raised energy and your joy of being a magician. Talk to them about your hopes and dreams. And listen to see if they have suggestions or words of encouragement for you. This is an opportunity for close friendships to be forged.

To close the ritual, take the sword and go to the east. Draw a banishing pentagram with the sword (see illustration on next page); say:

---

*Apple cider or grape juice may be substituted.

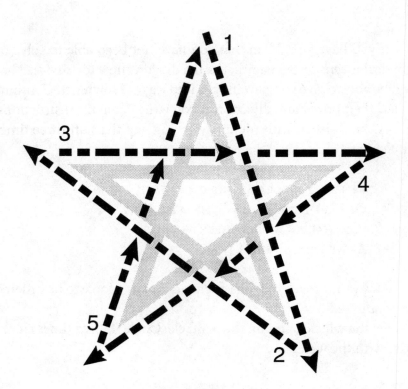

Banishing Pentagram

GO IN PEACE, DRAGONS OF THE EAST.
AND RETURN AGAIN IN THE RITUAL HOUR.

Go to the south. Draw a banishing pentagram with the sword; say:

GO IN PEACE, DRAGONS OF THE SOUTH.
AND RETURN AGAIN IN THE RITUAL HOUR.

Go to the west. Draw a banishing pentagram with the sword; say:

> GO IN PEACE, DRAGONS OF THE WEST.
> AND RETURN AGAIN IN THE RITUAL HOUR.

Finish by going to the north. Draw a banishing pentagram with the sword; say:

> GO IN PEACE, DRAGONS OF THE NORTH.
> AND RETURN AGAIN IN THE RITUAL HOUR.

Return to the altar. Raise both arms; say:

> FAREWELL TO YOU, O DRAGONS FAIR,
> FIRE, WATER, EARTH, AND AIR.
> TOGETHER WE MAKE MAGICK WELL
> BY POWER DEEP AND DRAGON SPELL.
> IN PEACE GO NOW. RETURN ONCE MORE
> TO TEACH ME MAGICK AND ANCIENT LORE.
> DRACONIS! DRACONIS! DRACONIS!

Cut the circle with a backward sweep of the sword across the boundary line. Extinguish the altar candles. Clear the altar of all tools.

Dragon Fire

Almost all dragons breathe out a type of energy we humans call fire. This fire-breathing from the nose and mouth was and is usually employed as a warning or a protective measure. However, there are a number of stories of dragons who, after being hunted and/or provoked to extremes, burned up all the houses and crops of a town as punishment and a warning to leave them alone.

A great many dragons are attracted by physical fire, which produces a form of energy. Burning candles in a ritual way is certain to attract dragons. If the magician does not have the time, opportunity, or energy to perform a complete dragon ritual, candle burning is a quick, effective form of magick. It is the quickest ritual to learn and to do.

Do not become lazy, however, and substitute candle burning for every magickal occasion. If you are new to the field of magick, begin with candle burning and work up to the other, more involved rituals. A good magician constantly seeks to expand her/his field of knowledge and expertise.

This is a candle burning ritual using dragon magick. To increase the potency of the candle, time the burning to the correct lunar and/or solar phases. For increasing and obtaining desires, burn during daylight or the waxing Moon (from after the New Moon until the Full Moon), with the Full Moon being strongest. For banishing or cursing, burn during evening hours or the waning Moon (from after the Full Moon until the New Moon), with the New Moon being strongest.

A cast circle is not imperative with this ritual. Choose appropriately colored stones to draw the attention of the dragons with which you desire to work; arrange them about the altar. With your ritual dagger, carve your exact wishes on the candle. Dragon script is very good for this, but if it proves too difficult to carve into the wax, use your ordinary language. Then anoint the candle with an appropriate oil. For moving something away from you, anoint from the end up to the wick. For obtaining something, anoint from the wick down to the end. To further strengthen the spell, roll the candle in crushed herbs chosen to further correspond to the spell-working. Either tapers or votive candles can be used.

To further concentrate the appropriate power into a candle burning, make a wide circle of your robe-cord around the candle on the altar. For safety, choose a metal or non-flammable holder and set it in a safe place.

Cast Iron Candle Holder (European, c. 1900)

With your wand, circle the candle three times clockwise for increasing magick (three times counterclockwise for decreasing magick). Hold the dragon pentacle facing the candle and say:

> DRACONIS! DRACONIS! DRACONIS! HEAR MY CALL.
> THREE TIMES I HAIL YOU. LISTEN, ALL!
> THIS CANDLE'S FLAME IS LIKE YOUR FIRE.
> DRAGONS, BRING MY HEART'S DESIRE.
> DRAGON POWER, COME TO ME!
> HEAR MY WORDS. SO MOTE IT BE.
> DRACONIS! DRACONIS! DRACONIS!

If you have been given a dragon's name and particularly want to call upon him/her, use this name instead of the word "Draconis" at the end of the Call in the above ritual.

Visualize dragon power and fire streaming from the dragon pentacle and entering the candle. After several moments, light the candle. For the fullest benefit, the candle should be allowed to burn completely out after the ritual is ended.

Entering the Mouth of the Dragon

This ritual, Entering the Mouth of the Dragon, will likely be one of the most interesting, enlightening experiences of your magickal career if you approach it with the right attitude. It is a ritual that can be repeated whenever you want, as many times as you wish. Since a magician on the ultimate spiritual path is constantly seeking and being initiated, a single initiation ceremony is not considered either adequate or a sign that nothing further is needed in the way of knowledge. Initiation must be a periodic, ongoing experience, a striving for greater contact with higher powers that has no end.

Many of the ancient pictures and carvings of humans being devoured by dragons may in fact be a symbol of initiation. It is difficult to know whether someone is entering or leaving the dragon's mouth. To a dedicated magician, this path into other planes is well-worn; she/he never feels they have learned all there is to know. The magician follows the Otherworld path confident that she/he is not the first to do so, nor will she/he be the last. The magician is driven by an inner yearning for growth on all levels of her/his being.

The experiences gained during this meditation-type ritual can help you make changes in your life, pick up your spirits when you are down, provide you with new insight and goals. It will be rare that a magician comes out of the experience with nothing. Of course, if you put nothing of your energy into the experience, you

The Entrance to Hell Seen as a Dragon's Mouth

from *Livre de la Deablerie* (Paris, 1568)

are likely to get little in return. Remember, dragons work as co-magicians only when there is an exchange of energy.

During this initiation ritual, you will be going in meditation into a huge cave shaped like the mouth of a dragon. This is best done on a Full Moon or bright noon. For 24 hours before the ceremony, try to remain aware and conscious of dragon power. You will find it flowing through all kinds of people, objects, and happenings. Just before entering the ritual area for initiation, take a cleansing bath with at least some salt and perhaps a little dragon's blood powder in the water. Be certain that you have your magickal name chosen. Dress in your ritual apparel. Carry any selected magickal jewelry to the altar; do not wear it until it has been consecrated.

Supplies: pentacle disk; dragon pentacle; water chalice with a little fresh water in it; dish of salt; wine chalice; black (left) and white (right) altar candles; sword; wand; incense burner; initiation or blessing incense; dragon's blood and thyme; dragon mirror; gong or bell.

Set altar in the center facing east. Make certain that you will not be disturbed once you have cast the circle. This may mean silencing the telephone and hanging a "do not disturb" sign on the door. Instrumental music also helps to set the mood and mask background noises.

Begin the ritual by going to the east. With your sword in your power hand (the one with which you write), "draw" your magickal circle on floor around your ritual area. Do this by pointing the sword at the floor and seeing great flames shooting from it. Move clockwise around the circle with this flame; end by overlapping it in the east. While drawing the circle, say:

BY DRAGON POWER, THIS CIRCLE IS SEALED.

Return to the altar. Point the sword at the dragon pentacle and say:

DRAGONS OF SPIRIT, HIGHEST OF DRAGONS AND MOST
POWERFUL, BLESS THIS ALTAR WITH YOUR FIRE.
LET US BE ONE IN MAGICK, O DRAGONS GREAT AND WISE.

Set the water chalice on the pentacle. (The water used in the chalice is not to be confused with the water you collect from various watery power spots.) With the wand in your power hand, circle the chalice three times clockwise with the wand and say:

AIR, FIRE, EARTH, BRING POWER FORTH.
WATER OF LAND AND SEA, PURIFIED BE.

Hold the chalice high; say:

DRACONIS! DRACONIS! DRACONIS!

Sprinkle the water lightly around the circled area, beginning and ending in the east.

Set the dish of salt on the pentacle. Circle it three times clockwise with the wand and say:

WATER, AIR, FIRE, HEAR MY DESIRE.
SALT OF EARTH AND SEA, PURIFIED BE.

Sprinkle a few grains of salt to each corner of the altar.

Circle the incense burner three times clockwise with the wand. Say:

FIRE OF DRAGONS, FIRE OF EARTH,
YOU ARE PURIFIED. BRING POWER FORTH.

Circle the incense and herbs three times clockwise with the wand. Say:

> INCENSE MAGICKAL, INCENSE BOLD,
> AWAKE THE DRAGONS, AS OF OLD.
> I CALL YOU PURIFIED.

Put a small amount of incense onto the burning coals. Lift the burner by the chains and touch it lightly to the pentacle. Lift it high over the altar, say:

> DRACONIS! DRACONIS! DRACONIS!

Then carry it clockwise around the circle, beginning and ending in the east. Return it to the altar.

Kneel before the altar with the sword in both hands. Mentally, dedicate yourself to the study of dragon magick. Project your interest and love of dragons as strongly as you can. Continue this for several minutes. Then rise and point the sword at the dragon pentacle and say:

> BEHOLD, ALL DRAGONS AND RULERS OF DRAGONS,
> I AM (magickal name), A MAGICIAN WHO SEEKS
>   DRAGON MAGICK.
> WITH (name of sword) IN MY HAND, I ENTER THE
>   REALMS OF THE DRAGONS,
> NOT FOR PHYSICAL BATTLE, BUT FOR KNOWLEDGE AND
>   POWER.
> I GREET YOU, O DRAGONS ANCIENT AND WISE,
> AND AWAIT YOUR BLESSING AND GUIDANCE.

Continue holding the sword outstretched until you feel the blessings of the dragons.

When the flowing power of the blessing has lessened, lower the sword. Still holding the sword in your power hand, take the dragon pentacle in your other hand and go to the east. Point the sword at the eastern position and hold up the dragon pentacle facing outward. Draw an invoking pentagram with the sword. Say:

> From Sairys (sair'-iss), ruler of the eastern drag-
> ons fair,
> Comes now the wondrous power of Air.

Feel the power of Air entering your body. When the flow stops, go to the south. Hold up the pentacle again. Draw an invoking pentagram with the sword; say:

> From Fafnir (faf'-near), ruler of dragons of the
> South,
> Comes cleansing Fire from dragon mouth.

Feel the power of Fire entering your body. When the flow stops, go to the west. Again hold up the pentacle. Draw an invoking pentagram with the sword; say:

> From Naelyan (nail'-yon), ruler of dragons of
> the West,
> Comes the power of Water, three times blest.

Draw into yourself the power of Water. Go to the north. Hold up the pentacle. Draw an invoking pentagram with the sword; say:

> From Grael (grail), ruler of dragons of the
> North,
> The power of Earth does now come forth.

Draw into yourself the power of Earth. Return to the altar. Lay aside the sword and dragon pentacle. Add more dragon's blood powder and thyme (or other appropriate incense) to the incense burner.

Lay any magickal jewelry on the pentacle disk and touch it with the point of your sword. Say:

> BY DRAGON POWER, I CALL YOU PURIFIED.
> BY DRAGON FIRE, I CALL YOU BLESSED.
> BY DRAGON MAGICK, I CALL YOU POWERFUL.
> THROUGH DRAGON WISDOM, I WELCOME YOU.

Slowly pass the jewelry through the incense smoke. Then put it on.

Take up the mirror, the Eye of the Dragon. Hold it before you and gaze deeply into it. Picture yourself as a confident magician of dragon magick. Say:

> I AM A SEEKER OF DRAGON KNOWLEDGE.
> I COME WILLINGLY FOR INITIATION.
> INTO THE MOUTH OF THE DRAGON I GO OF MY OWN
>   FREE WILL.
> WELCOME ME, DRAGONS OLD AND WISE.
> DRACONIS! DRACONIS! DRACONIS!

Lay aside the mirror and sit before the altar. Either lay the sword across your knees or at your feet during this meditation.

Close your eyes and mentally see before you the mouth of a huge cave. It is shaped like the mouth of a dragon. Inside, from some deep terrestrial fire, comes a red glow. Long drops of stone hang around the opening like teeth. Enter the cave and follow the dim passageway deep into the Earth. After many twists and turns, you will enter a circular subterranean chamber with crystals embedded in the walls. A gem-encrusted altar stands in the center of the floor. On the altar is a jeweled chalice.

At the four cardinal points of the circular chamber you see deep pits or cracks in the floor. From these pits comes the red glow of fire from deep under the Earth. The chamber is lit by their light alone. Sometimes you see the shadowy forms of dragons around the dim edges of the chamber.

Stand before the altar and announce to the dragons that you have come for initiation. Be sure to call yourself by your magickal name. You will feel power sent to you from all sides by the half-seen dragons. Listen for any messages that they may give you.

Finally, you will hear the deep voice of a dragon saying, "Drink of the cup." Visualize yourself lifting the heavy jeweled cup and drinking the contents. You will feel dragon magick coursing through your body, seeping into your bones. Thank the dragons, and follow the dim corridor upward until you reach the cave opening. Open your eyes and return to the here and now.

Rise and set the wine chalice on the pentacle. Circle it three times clockwise with the wand and say:

> CUP OF POWER, CUP OF MIGHT,
> DRAGON MAGICK, BE HERE THIS NIGHT.

Drink the wine, saving back some to be poured outside on the ground later as an offering to the dragons. (If it is not possible to pour the offering outside, leave it on the altar for about an hour.)

Now is an excellent time to chant and use free-form dancing. Invite the dragons to share in the raised energy and your joy of being a magician. Talk to them about your hopes and dreams. And listen to see if they have suggestions or words of encouragement for you. This is an opportunity for close friendships to be forged.

To close the ritual, take the sword and go to the east. Draw a banishing pentagram with the sword; say:

GO IN PEACE, DRAGONS OF THE EAST.
AND RETURN AGAIN IN THE RITUAL HOUR.

Go to the south. Draw a banishing pentagram with the sword; say:

GO IN PEACE, DRAGONS OF THE SOUTH.
AND RETURN AGAIN IN THE RITUAL HOUR.

Go to the west. Draw a banishing pentagram with the sword; say:

GO IN PEACE, DRAGONS OF THE WEST.
AND RETURN AGAIN IN THE RITUAL HOUR.

Finish by going to the north. Draw a banishing pentagram with the sword; say:

GO IN PEACE, DRAGONS OF THE NORTH.
AND RETURN AGAIN IN THE RITUAL HOUR.

Return to the altar. Raise both arms; say:

FAREWELL TO YOU, O DRAGONS FAIR,
FIRE, WATER, EARTH, AND AIR.
TOGETHER WE MAKE MAGICK WELL
BY POWER DEEP AND DRAGON SPELL.
IN PEACE GO NOW. RETURN ONCE MORE
TO TEACH ME MAGICK AND ANCIENT LORE.
DRACONIS! DRACONIS! DRACONIS!

Cut the circle with a backward sweep of the sword across the boundary line. Extinguish the altar candles. Clear the altar of all tools. You have now entered the mouth of the dragon and become an initiate into dragon magick. Being an initiate does not mean mastery of magick. An initiate is a beginner on the path.

Calling the Dragon

I do not know a magician who is not interested in calling a spiritual or astral entity who will project their presence with such clarity that there is no question of knowing the being is there. Dragons are such fascinating entities, how could a true magician not want to feel the unquestioning presence of such a creature?

There is also a greater reason for calling a dragon into stronger presence. The stronger the auric vibrations of such a creature within your ritual circle, the stronger the ritual and power sent into your motivation for the ritual. Magicians perform rituals for praise and enjoyment; they perform them for special intentions. I know of no true magician who does rituals for no purpose whatsoever. To perform a ritual properly, a great amount of time and energy are expended, a complete waste if one has no specific goal in mind.

When you use the dragon call and feel the presence of one or more dragons about you, treat them with respect. Take time to make their acquaintance before asking their help. Most dragons are beneficial and helpful, but all draconic temperaments are extremely sensitive; treat them with the greatest respect.

Notes: Perform during bright noon or the waxing Moon for increasing magick, with the Full Moon being strongest; during evening hours or the waning Moon for decreasing magick, with the New Moon being strongest. Use in conjunction with any ritual. This ceremony is primarily to summon the dragon for a manifestation. The manifestation may be the rare physical type or, more likely, it will be the sharpening of your inner sight.

Supplies: Pentacle disk; dragon pentacle; water chalice with a little fresh water in it; dish of salt; wine chalice; black (left) and white (right) altar candles; sword; wand; incense burner; appropriate incense; dragon's blood and mugwort; dragon mirror; gong or bell; staff. Paper and pen to write down any messages.

Use the Basic Dragon Ritual up to the point where you insert the necessary chants for specific spellworkings.

Hold the sword in your power hand, the staff in the other. Stand facing the altar and tap the staff three times on the floor while holding the sword pointed at the dragon pentacle. Chant in tones that vibrate through your body:

> COME, DRACONIS!
> BY YOUR ALL-CONSUMING BREATH, I SUMMON YOU.
> (tap staff three times)
> BY YOUR PIERCING GAZE, I SUMMON YOU.
> (tap staff three times)
> BY YOUR MIGHTY STRENGTH, I SUMMON YOU.
> (tap staff three times)
> BY YOUR WISDOM ANCIENT AND CUNNING, I SUMMON
>   YOU.
> (tap staff three times)
> BY YOUR MAGICK DEEP AND OLD, I SUMMON YOU.
> (tap staff three times)
> COME, DRACONIS, TO MY CALL!

You will feel power sent to you from all sides by the half-seen dragons. Listen for any messages that they may give you. You may feel their presence by a sudden temperature change, a prickly feeling between the shoulder blades, unusual currents of air, and other phenomena. If dragons are pleased with you, they often sound a deep vibrating rumble, almost like an enormous cat's purr.

The Charm of Making

The Charm of Making could just as well be called the Charm of Manifestation into the Physical. It is rather like the finishing touches to spellworking. The concentration used solidifies your intentions into embryonic form in the spiritual realms where all creation begins. Without this solidification and seed-planting in the spiritual, nothing can manifest in the physical.

Notes: Perform during bright noon or the waxing Moon for increasing magick, with the Full Moon being strongest; during evening hours or the waning Moon for decreasing magick, with the New Moon being strongest. Use in conjunction with any ritual. This ceremony is primarily to use dragon power and magick for bringing your desires into being.

Supplies: It is better to have a pentacle disk; dragon pentacle; water chalice with a little fresh water in it; dish of salt; wine chalice; black (left) and white (right) altar candles; sword; wand; incense burner; appropriate incense (such as prosperity or binding); dragon's blood powder and mastic; dragon mirror; gong or bell; staff; any candles for spells, talisman bags, etc. It is useful for concentration to plan what exactly you want to use before beginning this ritual.

Use the Basic Dragon Ritual up to the point where you insert the necessary chants for specific spellworkings.

Hold the sword in your power hand, the staff in the other. Stand facing the altar and hold the sword pointed at the dragon pentacle. Chant five, seven, or nine times in tones that vibrate through your body:

> BY GLOW OF SUN THE POWER'S BEGUN.
> BY MOONBEAM'S LIGHT THE SPELL IS RIGHT,
> TO CREATE DESIRE BY EARTH AND FIRE.
> WATER, AIR, MAKE MAGICK FAIR.

POWERFUL CHARM OF MAKING, CREATIVE MAGICK
UNDERTAKING.
BE FORMED!

While chanting this, concentrate deeply upon drawing on the dragon power. You will feel power sent to you from all sides. Listen for any messages that the dragons may give you.

Place the candle, talisman bag and contents, or whatever you are spelling, between the mirror and the dragon pentacle. Make certain that the dragon pentacle is reflected in the mirror along with the objects. If using a candle, light it and let it burn out completely in that position. If using a talisman bag or poppet,* leave it on the altar overnight.

Continue with the rest of the ritual.

Protection of House

Sometimes it becomes necessary to cleanse and seal your house, apartment, or even your own special room within a house where you are living with others. Vibrations can become negative and disruptive through the emotions of those within the house or left over from negative people who visit; these bad vibes will eventually disturb both your personal and magickal life. You may even find yourself host to an unwanted astral entity who has decided that it likes to feed off the energy raised in your surroundings.

Some entities are benign, spreading auras of love and helpfulness; these beings are nondisruptive and are no problem to have around. When we moved into our present home, we found we had a little elderly lady, gray hair drawn up in a bun, who was at first apprehensive about what we would do. We discovered that she had come to the house as a young bride a very long time ago; the house was built around 1895. She has been seen or felt by nearly everyone

---

*A poppet is a small cloth doll, usually stuffed with herbs or cotton soaked with the appropriate oil.

who comes here. Since the previous renters had trashed the house, it was understandable that this lady was worried. For three years she closely monitored what we did in the way of repairs. At last, satisfied that we loved the house, she decided constant attention was not necessary. Her visits now are infrequent, but we always welcome her when she comes.

Other entities are either border-negative or totally negative; these are troublemakers you definitely want to evict. I personally have found that the vast majority of negative entities have at one time lived in the physical as humans. Very rarely, one will encounter demons and devils, but I repeat, that is *rare!* The horror stories you see in films and on TV and read about in books should not be accepted as ordinary happenings. Chances are minuscule you will ever confront any demon or devil. These entities, whether positive or negative, are commonly called ghosts. Positive ghosts do not create problems for people, except to startle you on occasion. Negative ghosts can do everything from creating unpleasant odors to making you uncomfortable in certain areas of your dwelling to mentally influencing you in an effort to ruin your life. This latter effect is of interest to spirits who have usually known you in the physical and have remained jealous or dictatorial after they died.

The very first step in getting rid of what I call related ghosts is to have a talk with yourself. Decide if you still feel guilt or sympathy for them. Deep inside, there is a reason they can affect you, and it is always through the emotions. Apologize to them if needed. State firmly that you no longer wish any contact with them. If necessary, express your anger by yelling at them. Uncover and purge all the deeply held emotions that may bind you to that spirit. Unexpressed anger and hatred are two emotions which will tie people together through many lifetimes. If the entities are not related but still negative, or you cannot be certain, express your displeasure as you would with any unwelcome visitor. Then set about performing this ritual to clear your house and reform positive energies within it.

This is also an excellent ritual to perform before you first use a room you are designating for ritual purposes. In a room set aside totally for ritual, this cleansing will remove any vibrations that are not compatible with you and your magickal workings. The sealing part of the ritual will keep out disruptive vibrations, unless you bring them in on yourself or allow someone carrying such vibrations to enter your sacred space.

Since humans experience emotions on a daily basis, it will be necessary to re-cleanse and re-seal your house periodically. Humans are not perfect beings; living life is tough. We open all kinds of astral doorways through our expressions and experiences of emotions. It becomes a personal responsibility to clean up our own area astrally just as we clean it physically.

Notes: This ritual can be performed at any time. It is not necessary to coordinate it to Moon phases. A vibrational emergency requires immediate action. If you must work alone, set all your supplies on a tray in order to carry them through the house. If you have a partner, that person can take the dagger and incense while you carry the bell and water chalice, or vice versa.

Supplies: The pentacle disk; water chalice with plenty of fresh water in it; dish of salt; black (left) and white (right) altar candles; dagger; incense burner; any appropriate binding or exorcism incense; bell. It is useful for smooth procedure to plan what exactly you want to use before beginning this ritual.

Go to your altar and call all your dragons to help you. Light the black and white candles. Set the chalice of water on the pentacle disk with the dish of salt beside it. Light the incense, with plenty of additional incense available in case it is needed—which it will be as you go through the house.

Stand for a few moments communing with the dragons. You do not have to know precisely what entity, or entities, is causing your problems.

> O GREAT DRAGONS, WONDROUS, WISE,
> POWERS OF WATER, EARTH, FIRE, AND SKIES,
> LIGHT AND DARKNESS, JOIN ME HERE
> TO SWEEP THIS SPACE ALL CLEAN AND CLEAR.
> AWAY WITH EVIL, IN WITH RIGHT,
> DRAGONS OF DARKNESS AND OF LIGHT.
> ELEMENTALS, STRONG AND OLD,
> RESTORE THE BALANCE, DRAGONS BOLD.

Plunge your dagger into the dish of salt, then into the chalice of water.

> AS SALT DISSOLVES IN WATER, SO SHALL THE HOLD OF ALL
> NEGATIVES ON MY PERSON OR PROPERTY DISSOLVE.

Using the tip of the dagger blade, put three small piles of salt into the water. Stir it clockwise three times. (Remember to carefully cleanse the dagger blade when you are finished with the ritual, because salt is corrosive to metal.) Now place the bell, chalice of salt-water, dagger, and burning incense (along with additional incense) on your tray. If you have a partner, each of you can carry specific items. The instructions are given as if there are two people involved.

Begin the ritual within the room where you are, and begin your circling of the room at the door, moving clockwise. First one person carries the burning incense around the room. This is followed by drawing the banishing pentagram at each window, door, and mirror.* Next, the other person rings the bell before each window, door, and mirror; then each side of the opening is marked with an X by the forefinger of the power hand dipped into the saltwater.

---

*A mirror is oftentimes used as a focal point or dwelling place for astral entities.

The incense may have to be replenished from time to time during your ritual movements.

Move on to the other rooms you wish to cleanse. If possible, it is an excellent idea to cleanse the entire house. Plan your route so that you end up at an outside door; seal this door last. Magickally speaking, you are driving before you all the negative or bad energy and entities within your house. When you are finished, open the outside door, and yell *"Be gone!"* Shut the door quickly, and seal it with the saltwater and the banishing pentagram.

If you have a basement, be certain to include it in your cleansing and sealing. Because of the closeness to natural Earth energies, basements sometimes become safe havens for entities during cleansing rituals. I have never had a problem with attic spaces unless they were the kind people would use at some time.

Immediately pour the saltwater down the drain and clean your chalice. Take all your equipment back to your altar. Stoke up the incense again. Using your hands, pull the smoke over your body until you begin to feel a lightness of spirit.

Call your guardian dragons and, with great love and friendship, ask their aid in protecting you, your property, and loved ones. Be sure to include the names of any pets you have. Spend some time singing and/or dancing with them.

Your house or room should feel quite empty now. You do not want to leave it this way, or other negatives might find their way in. Project very positive, good vibrations while you say:

> LIGHT CALLS TO LIGHT.
> ONLY THOSE OF LIGHT MAY ENTER HERE.
> THE WAY IS BARRED TO ALL WHO WISH ME HARM.
> I GIVE MY GREETING ONLY TO THE LIGHT.

Soon you will feel the great adult dragons returning to your ritual area. Greet them with dignity and thanks for what they have done. Listen closely in case they offer any suggestions as to what caused the problems and what you can do to avoid it in the future.

When the dragons and you have finished your communications, thank them again. Finish by saying:

> FAREWELL TO YOU, O DRAGONS FAIR,
> FIRE, WATER, EARTH, AND AIR.
> TOGETHER WE MAKE MAGICK WELL
> BY POWER DEEP AND DRAGON SPELL.
> IN PEACE GO NOW. RETURN ONCE MORE
> TO TEACH ME MAGICK AND ANCIENT LORE.
> DRACONIS! DRACONIS! DRACONIS!

Be sure to clean your dagger blade of the saltwater in which you dipped it. Put more incense on to burn as a special thank-you offering. Extinguish the candles.

Dragons of the Four Elements

Dragons of the Elements

In all forms of magick, the universe and everything in it are said to be made up of four elements: Air, Fire, Water, Earth. The element of Spirit rules the center as a balance. In dragon magick, specific dragons rule these elements and help to create through their powers.

Fire and Air are traditionally positive (male) energies; Water and Earth are traditionally negative (female) energies. Male and female dragons may appear in the elemental directions in the traditional places, or may at times appear female in male directions and vice versa. This leads one to surmise that dragons may be androgynous creatures. These four elements correspond to the four directions, the four quarters of the universe, the four winds, and the four quarters of the magickal circle.

Each element has assigned traditional rulers and boundaries to their kingdoms. They possess form and force, and can influence our personalities as well as magickal procedures. Each element and its dragons has certain qualities, natures, moods, and magickal purposes; each has positive and negative traits. Because the magician calls upon each element and its ruler to protect a certain quarter of the circle, it is very important to understand them, what they are and what they do.

The traditional Pagan colors of the elements are: east, yellow; south, red; west, blue; north, dark green. However, there are other colors given to the elements. To the Celts this list was: east, white; south, red; west, gray; north, black. The Hindus listed east, blue; south, red; west, silver; north, yellow. In China and Japan these colors were: east, blue; south, red; west, white; north, black. To the Zunis of north America, east was white; south, red; west, blue; north, yellow. The following definitions of the elements lists the traditional Pagan colors. If you feel that one of the other color lists better suits you, adopt it.

The names of the dragons of the elements and the spelling and pronunciation of those names came through in trance several years ago. They have proved compatible with dragon magick. Knowing dragons, they may or may not be the actual names of the element dragons. They work as a focal point, and that is all that is necessary.

The element of Air governs the eastern quarter of the circle. Its dragon ruler is Sairys (sair'-iss), who oversees the dragons of breezes and winds. Its color is pure yellow; it is considered warm and moist. The positive associations of Air are: sunrise, spring, incense, the wand, the gong or bell, clouds, breezes, the breath, optimism, joy, intelligence, mental quickness, renewing, any kind of helpful air. Negative associations are: frivolity, gossip, fickleness, inattention, bragging, forgetfulness, windstorms, tornadoes, hurricanes, destructive air in any form.

Dragons of the element of Air belong to a family of draconic beings whose subspecies include those of wind, storm, and weather. At times they join forces with the dragons of fire and volcanoes, seas and other waters, mountains and forests, and chaos. Just as no one element works totally alone, whether in magickal endeavors or physical activities, elemental dragons join their great

Dragon of Air

powers to accomplish tasks. Sometimes there is conflict of elemental powers, producing great atmospheric and environmental disturbances, but mostly the elemental dragons work in harmony.

Many Vietnamese pagoda roofs are decorated at the end of the ridge poles with *ch'i wen* dragons (mouth drums), who swallow evil influences, and at the eaves with the *chao feng* (dawn winds), who catch and distribute the good vibrations. Several of the temples in the ruins of Angkor Wat have what are known as *makara*-dragons carved on the lintels above the doorway. These dragons are connected with the door of the imagination, an actual doorway carved near these sculptures, but also a metaphorical doorway, necessary for spiritual growth.

The element of Fire governs the southern quarter of the circle. Its dragon ruler is Fafnir (faf'-near) who oversees the dragons of Fire and the sunbeams. Its color is pure red; it is considered warm and dry. The positive associations of Fire are: noon, summer, the dagger and sword, candles, incense burner, any kind of helpful fire, the Sun, blood, enthusiasm, activity, change, passion, courage, daring, will power, leadership. Negative associations are: hate, jealousy, fear, anger, war, ego, conflicts, lightning, volcanoes, harmful fire of any kind.

Subspecies of the Fire-element dragon family are those of fire and volcanoes. The subspecies of desert and arid-region dragons, and those of chaos and destruction, often work closely with draconic entities of this element.

The element of Water governs the western quarter of the circle. Its dragon ruler is Naelyan (nail'-yon), who oversees the dragons of the seas, springs, lakes, ponds, and rivers. Its color is pure blue; it is cold and moist. Positive associations of Water are: sunset, autumn, the water chalice, any form of helpful water, compassion, peacefulness, forgiveness, love, intuition, calmness, peace of

Dragon of Fire

mind. Negative associations are: floods, rainstorms, whirlpools, any kind of harmful water, laziness, indifference, instability, lack of emotional control, insecurity.

The subspecies of the element of Water are those of the seas and various waters. It is not unusual to find this element working in conjunction with dragons of wind, storm, and weather, mountains and forests, or those of destruction.

In Cambodia, land of nagas and dragons, each reservoir has its temple where its divinity is worshipped in dragon form. In Chinese legend, the first emperor to take on a dragon form was Fu Hsi; this dragon-king put the Primordial Waters into order by digging dikes, canals, and irrigation ditches; he also tamed the Yellow River, making it safe for humans to live beside it.

The element of Earth rules the northern quarter of the circle. Its ruler is Grael (grail), who oversees the dragons of mountains, land, minerals, gems, and moonbeams. Its color is clear, dark green; it is cold and dry. Positive associations of Earth are: midnight, winter, the wine chalice, ritual salt, dragon bowl, gem bowl, dragon mirror, gemstones, mountains, caves, soil, respect, endurance, responsibility, stability, prosperity, thoroughness, purpose in life. Negative associations are: rigidity, unwillingness to change or see another side of a problem, stubbornness, lack of conscience, vacillation, earthquakes, slides.

Earth-element dragons are the most placid, unless they are required to stir up great disruptive energies such as earthquakes. The subspecies belonging to this element are the dragons of the mountains and forests and those of desert and arid regions. As might be easily guessed, the element of Earth often works closely with dragons of fire and volcanoes and those of chaos and destruction.

The white (light) and black (dark) dragons rule the center of the circle and balance all the other elements. Through invocation

Dragon of Water

of these dragons of light and darkness, the magician is able to mix a blend of elements that will bring forth the desired manifestation.

This family of draconic creatures works with all the other elements, but particularly with those of chaos and destruction. It may seem paradoxical for dragons of light to join forces with those of darkness and chaos, but it makes perfect sense to the knowledgeable magician. Sometimes, in order to create something better, old ideas, old forms, and old ways of living must be broken down and re-created. Most creatures, and especially humans, are comfortable with the way things are and do not anticipate with joy any upheavals. We think we would be happiest if there were never any negative occurrences in our lives, if everything always ran smoothly without hitches. But a static life would be very boring indeed. And universal law will not tolerate static conditions. Everything is required to keep growing and changing, or it is recycled into another, more productive form. I do not say this is pleasant. At times it can become overwhelming, unnerving, and downright frustrating.

I dislike using the terms "good" and "evil" when discussing light and darkness, because this does not give a true picture of the actual forces. Every element, including light or dark, has a negative side. The element of darkness has a definite place in magick, if properly used. The negative current of power is just as important to life and magick as is light, or positive power. We are not talking about Satanism; that is a totally different type of magick, and never has anything to do with the balance of elements.

I was taught that the most effective magician is one who uses a balanced blend of light and darkness. Certainly no magician worth the salt on her/his altar is going to be a doormat. She/he will protect themselves and their loved ones when necessary, but will not go out of their way to dominate or harm other beings if at all possible. A magician cannot possibly understand and work with the light without acknowledging the existence of the dark. What she/he does with either light or dark comes down to understanding her/himself and practicing self-discipline and good morals.

Dragon of Earth

Since elemental-type dragons of whatever color can be unpredictable, working either for or against the magician, the pentacle disk (a five-pointed star on a wooden disk) and the dragon pentacle are kept on the altar. These keep the elements within the control of the magician. To do this properly, the pentacle disk is used with one point upward, symbolizing that the dragons of light and darkness (or elements of Spirit) always rule over all elemental kingdoms.

The dragons of light, or light of the Spirit, rule positive power currents in magick. Their color is symbolized by white; a male energy, they are considered warm and dry. Positive associations of light are: all forms of day, the Sun, the pentacle disk, the dragon pentacle, the white altar candle, the staff, the salt dish, reaching toward the spiritual, balancing karma, seeking the truth, bettering life on all levels, positive attitude toward all things, psychic guidance, helpful light magick. Negative associations are: self-righteousness, I-have-the-only-way attitude.

Dragons of light exist within a space where light is completely separated from darkness, a place where Primordial Matter is constantly being formed into physical manifestation. Within their jaws they hold a precious gem that metaphorically grants wishes and desires. It is not unusual to find these dragons holding their tails in their mouths while sleeping or resting. This tail-in-mouth symbol is represented among humans' earliest depictions of dragons, a symbol of continuity and stability. When light dragons release their hold on the tail, they stand ready to use their vast powers for creation.

The dragons of darkness, or dark of the Spirit, rule negative power currents. Their color is sometimes black; a female energy, they are considered moist and cold. Positive associations of darkness are: all forms of night, the Moon and stars, the pentacle disk, the dragon pentacle, the black altar candle, the staff, the salt dish, rest, dreams, psychic guidance, balancing karma, seeking the truth,

Chinese Dragon of Good Fortune
from *Symbols, Signs & Signets* by Ernst Lehner (Dover, 1950)

helpful dark magick. The negative associations are: deep anger, hate, fear, unjustified revenge, working against karmic patterns, mentally distorting psychic messages so that you hear what you want to hear, harmful dark magick.

In Sanskrit, the dragons of darkness and chaos, or unformed matter, were given the title of *tad ekam* (That One). These dragons exist in a place where time has no authority, where physical light and darkness are actually not yet separated, where Primordial Matter waits to be formed into physical manifestations. As with the dragons of light, dragons of darkness hold within their jaws a precious stone of fulfillment. Dragons of darkness rest with their tails in their mouths, as do those of light. However, when they release the tail, they break down forms of energy; we would call this destroying. This dismantling of energy is necessary so that the dragons of light can re-create it in a new form.

The following calls and brief rituals are meant to be included in your other rituals, within a cast and sealed circle. They are used to add greater power to any spellworking because they specifically call the elemental dragons of Spirit. This taps into a vast reservoir of power current which can amplify any other power raised within the magickal circle.

Dragons of Air

Choose music that represents to you either storms or light, breezy conditions, depending upon the atmosphere you wish to create. Your dancing and singing should make you think of wind blowing across the land, stirring the plants, whistling over the mountain tops, pushing the clouds through the sky.

Notes: use candles or other objects of a pure yellow color. Choose herbs and oils that are listed as of the element of Air.

Repeat this chant three times.

> DRAGON RULER OF WIND AND CLOUD,
> I CALL YOUR SECRET NAME ALOUD.
> SAIRYS (sair'-iss)! (Ring gong once.)
> QUICKEN MY MIND, RENEW MY LIFE.
> GRANT ME JOY FREE FROM STRIFE.
> SAIRYS! (Ring gong once.)

Dragons of Fire

In your dance and singing, imitate the movement of flames. If you have ever closely watched a wood fire, for instance, you become aware that fire dances and sings in its own manner. Choose music that helps you to reflect this mental imagery.

Notes: use candles or other objects of a pure red color. Choose herbs and oils that are listed as of the element of Fire.

Repeat this chant three times.

> IN YOUR CAVERNOUS, FIRE-FILLED HALL,
> ECHOES THE NAME THAT I NOW CALL.
> FAFNIR (faf'-near)! (Ring gong twice.)
> STIR MY BLOOD WITH WILL POWER BOLD.
> CREATE NEW CHANGES FROM THE OLD.
> FAFNIR! (Ring gong twice.)

Dragons of Water

There are several good environment tapes that play the actual sounds of the ocean or running streams. Some harp music is also reminiscent of Water. Let yourself be Water in your dance and singing; feel yourself flowing along a streambed or riding the ocean waves.

Notes: use candles or other objects of a pure blue color. Choose herbs and oils that are listed as of the element of Water.

Repeat this chant three times.

> CALM WATER, MOVING WATER, SEAS AND LAKE,
> I CALL UPON THE WATER DRAKE.
> NAELYAN (nail'-yon)! (Ring gong three times.)
> TEACH ME THE PSYCHIC. GRANT TO ME CALM
> AND PEACE OF MIND, COMPASSION WARM.
> NAELYAN! (Ring gong three times.)

Dragons of Earth

As humans, we are so familiar with the feel of Earth energies that it is often difficult to imagine what being Earth is like. Earth energies are creative, maternal, slower than those of the other elements. Perhaps you can best identify with this element by feeling as if you are the mother of all, a parent who cares for her/his creations. Music should be slower and perhaps heavier, the dance more stately.

Notes: Use candles or other objects of a pure dark green color. Choose herbs and oils that are listed as of the element of Earth. Repeat this chant three times.

FROM YOUR MOUNTAIN CAVERNS DEEP,
RISE, NORTHERN DRAGON, FROM YOUR SLEEP.
GRAEL (grail)! (Ring gong four times.)
LEAD ME TO RICHES, PURPOSE TRUE,
ENDURANCE STRONG. I CALL ON YOU.
GRAEL! (Ring gong four times.)

Dragons of Light

The music for this element should be the astral, airy kind. It should make you think of floating through space, circling the Sun, and visiting the stars. Express yourself in dance as if you were dancing through the universe itself.

Notes: Use white candles or other objects along with your other chosen element color. Correspond the herbs and oils to the other primary element. Repeat chant three times.

LIGHT OF THE SPIRIT, SYMBOL OF SUN,
BE WITH ME NOW 'TIL THIS SPELLWORKING'S DONE.
HELP ME TO BALANCE ALL KARMA AND FORCE
'TIL I REACH TO THE TRUTH OF MY LIFE ON THIS EARTH.
GUIDE ME AND TEACH ME, O DRAGONS OF LIGHT.
SPARKLE MY MAGICK WITH POWER ON THIS NIGHT.
(The Charm of Making may be chanted here.)
(Ring gong once, pause, ring five times.)

Drooling Dragon of Darkness

from *St. George and the Dragon* (Italy, 15th century)

𝔇𝔯𝔞𝔤𝔬𝔫𝔰 𝔬𝔣 𝔇𝔞𝔯𝔨𝔫𝔢𝔰𝔰

This element "feels" heavier even than the element of Earth. It gives a sense of floating in the womb, of the time when each of us was being created. Choose deep, somber music with occasional rushes of energy. Dance as if you were awakening from a deep sleep and stretching for the first time in your life. Let your dancing reflect your desire to be reborn in a new and better image.

Notes: Use black (or very dark) candles or other objects along with your other chosen element color. Correspond the herbs and oils to the other primary element. Repeat this chant three times.

DRAGONS OF DARKNESS, YOUR POWER WILL RUN
UNTIL THE TIME OF MY MAGICK IS DONE.
TEACH ME YOUR SECRETS, THE DARK NOT TO FEAR.
FOR DARK IS RECEPTIVE, NOT TERROR OR TEAR.
DREAMS OF THE SPIRIT, SOAR WITH THE NIGHT.
WRAP ME IN GUIDANCE, YOU BALANCE OF LIGHT.
(The Charm of Making may be chanted here.)
(Ring gong five times, pause, ring once.)

Dragons of the Seas and Various Waters

Dragons who dwell in the seas, lakes, rivers, ponds, and other bodies of water, whether large or small, are basically shaped like Oriental dragons. They are long and serpent-like, usually without legs or wings.

They are a variety of shades of blue, from silver-blue to dark blue-green. In fact, their shades cover all the hues of the water in which they reside. All of them have a silvery hue to their scales with some shade of blue predominant on the belly scales. They have feathery fringes about their mouths and down their backs. They have large horny eye sockets set in a rather flat snakelike head. These dragons can be very large or very small, depending upon their dwelling place. They are of the element of Water and project that type of power.

Dragons of the seas and various waters help with emotions, either calming them or breaking through a barrier built around them; movement, both to get events moving and to keep things fluid; calmness on all levels of being and in all circumstances; creating changes, especially those brought about by breaking free of people who control us through our emotions.

Sightings of these creatures is so well documented that one can dismiss the skeptics' observations that people are only seeing dolphins, squids, or other common water creatures. Sea dragons have been seen all around the world, but especially off the coasts of Scandinavia, Denmark, the British Isles, and North America, as well as in various lochs, lakes, and rivers.

It was said by mariners that the only effective defense against sea dragons was to sprinkle asafoetida powder around the ship. This reddish-brown resin, obtained from the *Ferula foetida* plant, has an acrid taste and strong onion-like odor, enough to repel anything.

Scandinavian sailors, who spent a great amount of time on water of some sort, must have decided that the dragon-heads on their ships would announce their kinship to the sea dragons, thus reducing their risks of having to fight off a dragon attack. When these raiders and explorers returned to their home ports, they pulled down the dragon-heads before sighting land. This was to avoid frightening the *landvettir,* the local peaceful and protective countryside spirits.

Scotland is not the only place to have a consistent sighting of what are erroneously called monsters. The one in Loch Ness is far from being the only one around; the first recorded sight of Nessie was in about 565 CE. Other Scottish lochs, such as Lochy, Oich, Quoich, Arkaig, Fine, and the Gareloch all have stories of such creatures.

In Africa such dragonesque beings have been seen in the Congo, Nile, and Zambesi basins. As recently as 1981 Herman Rogustus and several others saw what is called "Mokele Mbembe," a 35-foot-long creature in Lake Tele in the Congo, 450 miles up the river in the jungle areas.

A lake in Patagonia, in South America, has its monster. Lakes Erie, Ontario, Utah, and many others in the U.S.A. have all had sightings. Such a creature was seen in Sweden's Lake Storsjo up until the end of World War II. The Skrimsl of Iceland was sighted

A Winged Water Dragon

from a 16th-century woodcut

as recently as 1860. The dragon was also found among the Mayans of South America, where he could be either an enemy of the rain god Chac or his helper.

In 1931 Huang Wen-chich, an official of the Chinese province of Kiangsi, reported many people seeing a dragon in the Han River. Even more recently, people at the Lan Xang hotel in Vientiane, Laos, repeatedly saw a dragon sharing the Mekong River with the giant catfish. With all of these sightings by so many cultures and types of people, how can one refuse to believe such beings exist?

In China they have a tale of a prince whose palace was guarded by a dragon that lived in a local pond. This dragon not only guarded the palace but supplied rain to the surrounding countryside. When the prince became ill, he decided that he needed the dragon's liver as a cure for his sickness. The dragon instantly knew of the prince's treachery and fled, causing a terrible thunderstorm. It was not long before the prince's enemies stormed the palace and took over the area. The story does not say what happened to the prince.

The Anglo-Saxon word *nicor* also means dragon. Both words, *nicor* and dragon, are used in the epic poem *Beowulf* to describe the first two dragons that the hero encountered. This tale was probably written down in the 7th or 8th century CE. The king of Denmark was plagued by a dragon that assumed human form, came into the palace every night, and killed his men. It became such a danger that the king abandoned his palace for twelve years, until Beowulf and his Swedish companions arrived. The Swedes spent the night in the palace and were attacked by Grendel, the dragon, who had assumed a semi-human form. Beowulf tore off one of its arms and then followed the bloody trail back to the shores of a lake. Thinking they were now safe, the Danes all returned to feast with Beowulf. But the next night Grendel's mother, who was more terrible than he, showed up and dragged off one of the Danes. Beowulf followed her back to the lake, dived in after her, and discovered an underwater vaulted chamber. There was the body of Grendel. After a terrible battle, Beowulf killed the female dragon.

In Greek lore, the hero Herakles encountered a dragon as he passed through the city of Troy. The king Laomedon had chained his daughter Hesione to a rock by the sea in hopes of placating a sea dragon that was terrorizing the city. In return for a promise of some extraordinary horses, Herakles rescued the girl and slew the dragon. When Laomedon refused to keep his word, Herakles sacked Troy.

The Greek Perseus was petitioned by a king, possibly of Ethiopia, to kill a dragon sent against the country by the sea god Poseidon. In an attempt to stop the terror, the king chained his daughter Andromeda to a rock by the sea. Perseus and Andromeda had fallen in love, so Perseus had an extra incentive to dispatch the sea beast.

When Cadmus, the brother of the kidnapped Europa, wanted to free his sister, he went first to the Delphic Oracle for advice. She

The Hero Ruggiero Rescues Angelica from a Sea Dragon

from an engraving by Gustave Doré for Ariosto's *Orlando Furioso* directed him and his companions to go to a spring near Thebes. The spring was guarded by a dragon who was a son of the god Ares. After a great battle and the death of several of his friends, Cadmus managed to kill the dragon.

One of the best known Norse stories is about the god Thorr and his fishing expedition with the giant Hymir. Disguised as a common man, since Thorr and any giant did not get along, the god claimed guest-rights from the giant. The two rowed far out to sea early the next morning. Using the head of an ox as bait, Thorr cast out his line and waited impatiently. He fully intended to try to catch the World Serpent Jormungand, but he had not told Hymir that. Suddenly the great Serpent swallowed the bait and set the hook. Thorr pulled with all his supernatural strength and Jormungand thrashed to the surface. Hymir was terrified. While Thorr was busy with the Serpent, the giant hacked the fishing line in two with his knife. Thorr was furious and knocked Hymir out of the boat to swim back to shore as best he could. Losing his catch was for the best, because the Norse said that when Jormungand's tail came out of his mouth, the world would no longer be held together but would disintegrate in chaos.

Some magickal systems look upon all dragons other than those of the elements as devic in nature. The Deva (pronounced DAY-vah) of a place is considered an inner presence, a Nature intelligence. They consider these dragons to be less powerful. This has not been my experience. Each magician must judge by her/his personal experiences in magick.

When working with Water dragons, select herbs and oils for the element of Water. Stones should be of a blue color, whether intense blue, a paler shade, or one of mottled coloring. Collect a small amount of water from a particular dragon habitat in a lake, river or ocean, and take it back to be used within your circle. Always ask permission before taking any of the water and leave a gift of herbs.

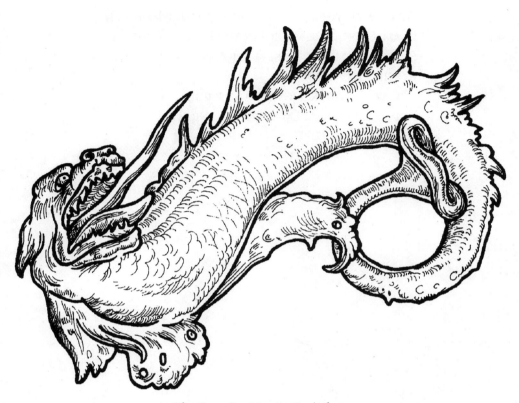

The Great Sea Monster Leviathan

from a drawing by Hans Baldung, 1515

Chant at the power source when collecting water.

I ASK YOUR BLESSING TO REMOVE THIS WATER,
O DRAGON OF THE (sea, lake, pond, river, whatever).
I LEAVE YOU THIS GIFT AND PROMISE RESPECT FOR THIS
    PIECE OF YOUR DWELLING PLACE.

Sprinkle this collected water around your magickal circle and/or over any candle or spelled object when you want to use the power felt at the collecting point. When you sprinkle this within a cast circle, say:

Dragon of the (sea, lake, river, pond, whatever),
I call upon your magick power!
Raise my spelling to new heights
In this ritual hour.
Power of Water, moving and bright,
Endless, eternal. Empower this night!

Dragons of the Mountains and Forests

Dragons of the mountains and forests are of the element of Earth. They generally have the look of Western dragons, with the heavier body, four legs, huge wings, long neck, and tail. Mountain dragons are much heavier looking in the body that those of forests.

Dragons of the mountains and forests help to build long-lasting foundations in life; long-range goals; stability; physical and mental endurance; responsibility, and oftentimes the strength to stand up under existing responsibilities; enduring prosperity and success that come through personal effort and planning.

Forest dragons inhabit stretches of deep forests, groves, sometimes solitary clusters of trees. They like the changing pattern of sunlight through the branches and leaves. They tend to get upset and sometimes belligerent if their forests are damaged or destroyed without a good explanation.

Both mountain and forest dragons have been known to inhabit areas close to human towns and farms. Sometimes this created a conflict, sometimes not, depending upon the behavior of the humans. After the belligerent Christians gained power, dragons were hunted with great determination, until they withdrew from the physical plane.

Some of these dragons are of the variety that at one time lived in or around barrows or burial mounds, especially if there was treasure inside.

One of the best known stories of this kind of dragon is told in the tale of Beowulf. The earlier two dragons in the story were obviously water dragons, but the one that appeared when Beowulf had become king of Geatasland in South Sweden late in his life was of the mountain or barrow variety. This dragon had guarded the burial mound of an ancient king for several hundred years without causing undue distress to the neighborhood, until a runaway slave crept into the mound and stole some of the treasure. Furious, the dragon ravaged the countryside, even burning the royal palace. Although Beowulf was quite old by this time, he prepared to fight the creature along with his servant Wiglaf. They tracked it to its den where, after a long fight, Beowulf killed it. However, he died soon afterwards from the poison in his wounds.

Both Teutonic and Scandinavian legend tell of the hero Sigurd (called Siegfried in Germany). Sigurd was an exceptional young man who, unfortunately, was being taught and befriended by the evil Regin. Regin talked Sigurd into going after the dread dragon Fafnir who lived in the forested mountains. Sigurd found the dragon's treasure lair but decided to dig a pit near the river in order to stab the dragon as it passed for water. The cowardly Regin did not stay to help. As Fafnir came down to drink, Sigurd stabbed him from his hiding place in the pit. The dragon's hot blood poured over the young man, and a drop of it entered his mouth. As Sigurd struggled out from under the dragon's body, the dying Fafnir warned him of Regin's treachery. Sigurd also discovered that he now understood the language of birds. Birds in the trees round about warned Sigurd that Regin planned to kill him. They also advised him to find the sleeping

Mountain Dragon

from a French engraving, 1589

warrior maiden Brunhilde who would teach him all the wisdom he lacked. When Regin returned and tried to kill Sigurd, the young man dispatched him. Following Fafnir's tracks back to the lair, he packed great bags of treasure onto his super-strong horse Grani and left the area.

One can trace past dragon activity in the Western world through such place names as Drakelow, Drakeford, Wormingford, Wormsley, Ormskirk, Ormiston, and Dragon's Hill in England; Drachenfels and Drakensberg in Germany; and Dracha, Dragashani, Draga, and Draconis in southeastern Europe.

Humans called British land dragons by various names besides the word dragon: *orme*, worm, or *vurm*. These words appear to have originated from the Norse word *ormr*, which means dragon.

Chinese maps and tradition said that the Green Dragon lies in the East, which is of the vibration of Yang. They considered mountains to be Yang, as they did large rocks and cliffs. The Yang energy was considered even more powerful if the site faced the south.

Mountain dragons usually are found in the high, rocky peaks or rugged outcroppings. Some of the older ones have staked out their domains on the very top where the wind and snow caress their great bodies.

Dragons of both the mountains and forests are shades of greens and browns and often have upright rows of sharp scales down their necks and backs.

When working with these dragons, select herbs and oils for the element of Earth. Stones should be of green or brown colors. Collect a small amount of soil or a few stones from a particular dragon habitat in a mountain or forest, and take it back to be used within your circle. Always ask permission before taking any of the soil or stones and leave a gift of herbs.

Chant for mountain dragons at the power source when collecting material:

> I ASK YOUR BLESSING TO REMOVE THIS (stone, soil),
> O DRAGON OF THE MOUNTAIN.
> I LEAVE THIS GIFT AND PROMISE RESPECT FOR THIS PIECE
>   OF YOUR DWELLING PLACE.

Put the soil in your dragon bowl, the stones in the gem bowl on your altar. The stones can be set around candles or talisman bags,

Forest Dragon
from *Moses Leading the Chilrren of Israel Through the Wilderness*, German engraving, c. 1480

etc., to further fill them with power. Objects or candles can be placed in the dragon bowl with the soil for a brief period of time before finishing the spellworking; they will soak up power. Use this chant within the cast circle when using the stones or soil:

DRAGON OF THE MOUNTAINS WHOSE ROOTS RUN DARK
  AND DEEP,
GRANT THIS SPELL PURPOSE, STRENGTH. ETERNAL KEEP
POWER DEEP AS MOUNTAINS, NEVER-ENDING SOURCE.
DRAGON OF THE MOUNTAINS, AMPLIFY THIS FORCE.

Chant for forest dragons at the collecting point when gathering material. Remember to ask permission before collecting and leave a gift.

I ASK YOUR BLESSING TO REMOVE THIS (stone, herb),
O DRAGON OF THE FOREST.
I LEAVE THIS GIFT AND PROMISE RESPECT FOR THIS PIECE
OF YOUR DWELLING PLACE.

Put the cut herbs with your other herb supplies, stones in your gem bowl on the altar. Stones are used around candles, etc. to further fill them with power. Herbs can be used in talisman bags or burned in the incense burner to release more power. This chant is for use of the collected herbs or stones within a cast circle.

FOREST DRAGON, SLITHERING, GLIDING,
SILENT AMONG THE FOREST TREES,
ANCIENT STRENGTH WILL YOU PROVIDE ME,
SELF-ASSURANCE, REST AND PEACE.

Dragons of Wind, Storm and Weather

Dragons of wind and storm and weather in general belong to a subspecies of Air dragons. They are long, slender dragons, some of them with great gauzy wings, others with the Oriental "flying-lump" on their foreheads. Down the spine of the back flutter thin fringes of membrane tissue. They tend to be pale yellows and blues, but change to angry red-orange, purple, or black when they call up storms. Long, feathery antennae rise above their eye ridges.

Dragons of wind, storm, and weather are excellent helpers to control excesses in the weather; get things moving in your life, especially in the areas of creativity and the mental processes; protection; flexibility of the mind; openness to new ideas; sweeping away obstacles, most often in a dramatic fashion.

Sometimes these dragons have feather-looking scales that surround their eyes and necks. Such a dragon was the British Henham dragon, which was well documented in 1669. It was described as being only about nine feet long with small wings and rather curious eyes surrounded by "feathers." The Henham dragon put in repeated appearances before a great number of observers for several years before it disappeared.

These dragons inhabit cloud banks or very high mountain peaks where the winds never cease. Some Oriental weather dragons live in pools and ponds. They are in almost constant motion, riding the breezy air currents or roaring along with a whistling gale. Sometimes two or more of them join forces, either in play or a temporary dispute, thereby creating tornadoes and hurricanes. When they roll together, lightning and thunder occur.

The ancient Chinese writer Wang Fu wrote that dragons scream like struck copper basins when rain is near. Their breath became clouds. After the fourth month of Summer, the dragons were said to divide the land into territorial sections, thus accounting for the wide diversity of weather in any given region. The Chinese believed that careful observation of dragon activity in the skies could predict the future and the weather. For instance, dragons fighting each other was an omen of a rough journey or approaching storms.

Chinese tradition says that the cry of a male dragon makes the wind rise, while the cry of the female makes it calm again. Their mid-air mating, which is more frequent than with Western dragons, causes great storms and downpours of rain.

The Chinese celestial dragon with the name of Fei Lin was said to appear as a dragon with a bird's head, deer's horns, and a snake's tail. The Chinese still hold dragon processions to mark their New Year and to ask for rain and fertility. These festivals are accompanied by lots of noise and dancing to give the dragon and spring a good welcome.

The greatest and Lord of all Dragons was the Celestial Lung. He was different from others of his species as he had five claws on each foot instead of the usual four and had a pair of wings, something missing from most Oriental dragons. He appears to have been a dual-element dragon, since he lived in the sky during the spring and summer and in the ocean during the autumn and winter. Celestial Lung had power over the fertility of all creatures and the

Persian Dragon

from a miniature in a *Book of Kings*

land itself. He appointed other Oriental dragons to control areas of human activities, such as music, literature, the military, bridge building, law, and architecture.

Many of the Celtic intertwined serpent-dragons were of the Air Element. Above the gate of Kilmainham jail in Dublin can still be seen a large carving of entwined Celtic serpent-dragons. The Danish Ringerike style of carving shows the same kind of dragon. These carved, twisting shapes are full of energy, giving the illusion of constant movement. A buckle from the Sutton Hoo burial site also portrays these aerial serpent-dragons.

Janet Hoult, in her book *Dragons: Their History & Symbolism* (Gothic Image, 1990), tells of seeing such an aerial display of these dragons above the houses in London. She describes it as a fiery ball of golden "serpents" which looped and writhed around each other in a strange dance in the morning skies.

When the Ringerike style went out of fashion in the Middle Ages and dragons began to be more realistically portrayed, this looping movement was retained in at least the tail if no other part of the body. Since even the vilified Christian dragons had at least one loop in their tails, this may have been a symbol for the great and limitless energy of dragons.

Although one does not usually think of the Australian Rainbow Serpent as being a dragon, it falls into the category of both weather and water dragons. The Rainbow Serpent is known as a rainmaker in Australia, North America, and West Africa. The Australians say that when the rainbows arch across the land, the Rainbow Serpent is traveling from one water hole or water course to another.

From the deserts of Arizona to the peaks of the Andes, the great Feathered or Plumed Serpent Quetzalcoatl was known as a kindly benefactor and rainmaker. When he arched himself across the heavens, he was an awesome sight, with multicolored scales and bright feathers about his neck and head. When he appeared among his human followers, he chose the form of a handsome young man attired in a cloak of feathers from the quetzal bird. Quetzalcoatl was the god of wind, creator of all life forms, the loving father who produced fertility and ample rain. He taught humans the arts and crafts of civilization and gave them the gift of fire. When Tezcatlipoca, god of war, turned the people to sacrificing living human hearts, Quetzalcoatl left the land.

Even in the British Isles, there are still a few remnants of ancient dragon processions for good spring weather. At one time there were a great many such festivals. Most of the significance has been lost because of the extreme propaganda by the church. In Britain many of the dragon figures carried in the processions have been destroyed. One of the very few remaining is carried each May as part of the Helston Furry Dance. Two very old dragon effigies now hang in the Castle Museum at Norwich. The Civic Snap,

Winged Serpent

from *America* by Crispijn de Passe, 17th century

which is the older of the two, dates from about 1795; the Pock-thorpe Snap was made by the people of a neighboring village.

Throughout the Middle Ages, these dragon effigies for the spring festivals were very elaborate. They had wings that flapped, horseshoes for gums that made a clacking noise as their mouths opened and closed, and gunpowder that made them belch smoke and fire. They were painted in bright colors and quickly became the centerpiece and most popular part of the processions.

In Central and South America and the Caribbean there was a dragon called Huracan; hurricanes were named after him. He was also responsible for earthquakes. In Olmec and Mayan carvings of Huracan, he is shown with two forelegs, one crooked up, the other down, to suggest his spinning movement. He has only one hind leg, the destructive leg that sweeps across the Earth. Other carvings show a man sitting inside what was called Dragon-mouth Cave, and identify this person as Huracan's brother; it is more likely an initiate. Dragon-mouth Cave has the dragon's eye on its top with the dragon's flaming eyebrows; the pupil of the eye is an X. Out of the cave mouth issues clouds of mist-laden breath, a symbol of both rain and the fertility of spirit. Carved near this cave mouth are four sets of concentric circles, the South American sign of precious jade-water (spiritual moisture or blessings).

In ancient Greek culture Typhon was one of the children of the goddess Gaea and Tartarus. He created powerful, destructive whirlwinds called typhoons. He was pictured with a human body, legs of coiling serpents, a hundred dragons' heads, and many wings. Fire glittered from his many eyes.

This subspecies of dragons is petitioned for weather changes, such as bringing rain, abating a storm, or calming wind. Obviously, the magician cannot collect any substance from their dwelling places, but he can entice them by using a small drum and the gong or bell to draw their attention. Wind chimes and wind socks also attract them. The magician can easily work outside with this dragon force. However, *do not* go outside, particularly under trees or with any metal objects, during a thunderstorm! Such action can be potentially dangerous, because lightning could strike you.

Chant while beating the drum or striking the gong with a slow, steady beat:

THE WINDS ARE HOWLING THROUGH THE TREES.
THE CLOUDS ARE RACING 'CROSS THE SKY.
THE WEATHER IS CHANGING ONCE AGAIN.
GREAT DRAGONS ARE PASSING BY.
BY THOUGHT I FOLLOW YOUR AIRY DANCE
THROUGH MOUNTAINS OF CLOUDS ABOVE SO HIGH.
BRING US GOOD WEATHER FOR THIS LAND.
GREAT DRAGONS, PASS ON BY.

Dragons of Desert and Arid Regions

D ragons of the desert and arid regions can be of either the element of Fire or Earth, or both. These dragons help with prosperity, manifestations into the physical realm, and the removal of obstacles, especially in conjunction with Air dragons.

Dragons whose territories are dry and rather on the cold side tend to be Earthy types, while those who reside in hot, dry climates are Fire. There are a few of these dragons who are blends of the two elements. Basically, these dragons are shades of browns, tans, whites, and other colors that match their dry-land surroundings. Generally these colors are mottled in such a way that these dragons are nearly invisible if they lie still, more so than any other kind of dragon. However, they also have chameleon-like abilities to change colors, a perfect camouflage to avoid detection by humans. They hide under the sand or in wadis and gullies when hunting or trying to avoid detection.

These dry-land dragons are serpentine in shape, with long slender tails rather like those of lizards. The larger desert dragons often have huge, membranous wings, but there are subspecies of small desert dragons who have extremely small wings that are

A Small Desert Dragon
from a painting by Hubert van Eyck or Roger van der Weyden, 15th century

actually no good for flying purposes. They use these stubs of wings to create whirlwinds of sand and dust that confuse their enemies and prey.

They have either two or four legs which are very powerful, enabling them to move rapidly. They run quite fast over the sand or desert and can easily outdistance a horse. The short flights of the smaller dragons are more like long hops or jumps than flying. If you are very cautious and remain still for a long period of time, it is possible to watch these smaller varieties frolicking in and out of the sand as if it were water. The larger ones are more reserved; rolling in the sand to clean their backs and sides of debris is as close as they get to frolicking. Heavy ridges of bony eye socket overshadow the deep-set eyes, giving shade from the hot sun. They have a powerful hypnotic gaze that can immobilize their prey or cause their hunters and enemies to forget that they saw the dragon. Tightly overlapping scales keep out the sand and fine dust.

Wingless Desert Dragon
from St. George, late medieval German engraving

Desert dragons can exist off the moisture in their prey and dew on vegetation if they have no access to oases. If they do frequent oases or water holes, they are cautious about meeting humans there. These types of dragons are the most difficult for humans to approach and communicate with, since they have been the target of hunting for centuries, probably more than others of their species. Unless the weather turns cold and stormy or their desert region has cold seasons, these dragons move around as well at night as during the day.

Desert dragons will built their lairs in rocky outcroppings or deep in areas of sand dunes, far away from human interference. The ones who lair in the dunes themselves build a cave deep within the sand by mixing the sand with their corrosive saliva; this mixture hardens to produce super-tough walls that will only weaken under heavy incursions of water. They have a magpie-like desire to acquire treasure or anything shiny. The treasure in their lairs is a combination of ancient armor, swords, gems, and modern exploration equipment, anything that glitters and catches their attention. They are skilled thieves, rather like pack rats, who like nothing better than the challenge of entering a camp and swiping some shiny object they covet while the humans sleep.

These dragons are very territorial, spending their lives in one area. Since, like all of their species, they have very long lives and exceptional mental abilities, desert dragons know the locations of all ancient, long-lost cities and civilizations that are now covered with sand or simply were deserted. They have been observers of the expeditions and activities of humans for thousands of years and know exactly what happened within their territories, what humans died there, what was built or discovered, where ancient records can still be found. However, their distrust of humans makes it very difficult to get them to cooperate with anyone except a sympathetic, well-trained magician.

In the parched deserts of the East this variety of dragon was considered just as menacing to early-day travelers as the sea dragons were to sailors. During the 13th century, while journeying through Caragian, which is now the Chinese province of Yunnan, Marco Polo saw these "serpents," which he wrote were ten paces long and as thick as a water cask. He described them as having two short forelegs near the head, claws like a lion, enormous heads, great eyes, and a mouth capable of swallowing a man whole.

It has long been acknowledged by dragon-watchers that those of Ethiopia were more poisonous than those of other regions. Presumably the intense heat of Ethiopia produced this effect, but it is more likely that this subspecies simply evolved that way. All dragons were said to consume poisonous herbs in order to make their bite more deadly. It is quite possible that the herbs in question, never mentioned by name, had something that the dragon craved and needed for its system.

Tradition says that the magicians of Ethiopia killed and ate their dragons to such an extent that they began to lure European dragons to their country. Friar Roger Bacon, in the 13th century, was complaining about this practice; however, he also said that the Ethiopian magicians saddled these stolen dragons and rode them home. No dragon is so stupid that she/he would not know what was in a magician's mind. If European dragons did allow themselves to be lured away, it would have been because they were promised safety and a better life. During the 5th century BCE, Herodotus reported a similar traffic in dragons.

In 1554, when Pierre Belon traveled through Egypt, he saw dragons that were preserved as specimens. He described them as winged snakes with feet. He was told that it was common for these desert dragons to fly out of Arabia into Egypt.

Depending upon the element-type, desert dragons can be unpredictable and difficult to work with. It is safer to take the precaution of dealing with them only within a cast and sealed circle. Particularly if they are of the Fire element, these dragons tend to do as they please with a spellworking. Since heat in some form is needed to create life, the magickal heat produced by these creatures is excellent for manifestating desires into the physical realm. However, if you are not careful, they can be quite literal, searing away anything they consider an obstacle, whether good or bad.

Desert sand, soil, stones, even herbs may be collected in the territories of this type of dragon. You will find that certain areas of a given arid region will exude more power than others, so choose carefully.

Chant for desert and arid-region dragons at the collecting point when gathering material. Remember to ask permission before collecting and leave a gift of water. These dragons, perhaps because of their hot, dry dwelling places, are not interested in alcohol in any form.

> I ASK YOUR BLESSING TO REMOVE THIS (stone, soil, sand),
> O DRAGON OF THE DESERT.
> I LEAVE THIS GIFT AND PROMISE RESPECT FOR THIS PIECE OF YOUR DWELLING PLACE.

At home, perform your chant within a cast circle. Use a candle that reminds you of the colors of the dragon's area and anoint it with frankincense or myrrh oil. Amplify your connection by burning a pinch of frankincense gum with your incense. As with Fire dragons, greet the desert dragons with your sword in your power hand, dragon pentacle in the other.

DESERT HEAT AND WIND SO COLD,
AID ME, I ASK, O DRAGON BOLD.
NOURISH THIS SEED OF MAGICK SPELL
THAT I MIGHT GAIN MY SPOKEN DESIRE.
BRING LIFE TO THIS DREAM,
RAISE MY MAGICK POWER HIGHER.
DESERT HEAT AND WIND SO COLD,
AID ME, I ASK, O DRAGON BOLD.

Dragons of Fire
and Volcanoes

Fire and volcano dragons are of the element of Fire and are in all shades of reds, oranges, and deep yellows. They have thick, heavy bodies and long snakelike necks and tails. Some of them sleep in dormant volcanoes for long periods of time before they once again become active. These dragons are also visible in forest fires and large structure blazes. They are very unpredictable, unreliable, and difficult to work with. If not properly handled, and then *only* within a cast and sealed circle, fire dragons will do as they please with a magician's spell. They will achieve the asked-for end result, but may "burn" their way through everything to get there.

Dragons of Fire and volcanoes help with personal purification on all levels of being, energy, courage, stamina to pursue goals and finish projects, remove obstacles and barriers. Be very certain you want their help in the barrier-removal, for these dragons will go through and over anything and anyone to achieve the goal. The results can be swift and difficult to handle emotionally.

Fire and volcano dragons are capable to changing their size, appearing to grow as the fire or volcano gains in strength and power. It is possible to see very tiny Fire dragons in your own fireplace or stove if you are very observant and patient. These tiny creatures were called salamanders by early alchemists and dragon-watchers—not the salamanders that we know living in water, but more of a firedrake salamander with skin like asbestos and an appetite for eating red-hot coals and cinders.

In his autobiography, Benvenito Cellini, known as a goldsmith, sculptor, and alchemist, tells how he observed such a Fire dragon as a child. He watched the tiny creature moving about in the hearth fire, eating coals, and visible for some time. When he pointed out the firedrake to his father, the older Cellini beat the boy so he would always remember what he had seen. As if one would not remember such an amazing experience!

For several years in the late 1980s and early 1990s, the West Coast was plagued with severe droughts. Forest fires raged summer after summer. Any competent magician could see and feel the great Fire dragons that came to these blazes, romping through the vast areas of flame, often rolling with the Air dragons above the super-heated infernos. Unfortunately, what gave the Fire dragons delight, frustrated and annoyed the forest dragons, sometimes precipitating battles over territory.

Obsidian, pumice stone, and lava rock may be collected from volcanic power spots. Remember, this is one type of dragon that requires a gift of a little good wine or alcoholic spirits in return. Anything less and Fire dragons get testy, to say the least, or so the legends and folktales say. If you get a feeling of the slightest hesitation about taking any of the stones, do not take any! If volcano dragons say "no," that is exactly what they mean. Try to communicate further with them to see if they just do not want you to take any from that particular spot, or if they do not want you to take any at that time. They may say "yes" at another time and place.

Chant for Fire and volcano dragons at the collecting point when gathering material. Remember to ask permission before collecting and leave a gift of good wine or alcohol.* And do not take chances by going into a dangerous volcanic area.

*Unfortunately, I do not know of any substitutes for an offering to this type of dragon.

Salamander

from *Scrutinium Chymicum* (Frankfurt, 1687)

I ASK YOUR BLESSING TO REMOVE THIS STONE,
O DRAGON OF FIRE.
I LEAVE THIS GIFT AND PROMISE RESPECT FOR THIS PIECE
OF YOUR DWELLING PLACE.

At home, chant within the cast circle. Use a red candle
anointed with cinnamon oil. Burn a pinch of cinnamon with your
incense. Or break pieces of cinnamon bark, and add a little at a
time to the burner. Always greet Fire dragons with the sword in
your power hand, dragon pentacle in the other.

CRACKLE, BURN, DRAGON TURN
NIGHT TO DAY. SEND GOOD MY WAY.
BRING CHANGE WITHIN MY RANGE.
TRANSFORM ALL AT MY CALL.
LIFT MY THOUGHTS HIGHER, LIKE YOUR FIRE.
CRACKLE, BURN, DRAGON TURN
NIGHT TO DAY. SEND GOOD MY WAY.

Dragons of Chaos and Destruction

These dragons represent the negative power currents necessary to dissolve problems and sweep away troublesome people. They are of very dark colors: black, gray, pewter, iron, dark magenta, purple, reds and greens so dark that they appear to be black. Their bodies are heavy and huge; in fact, they are the largest of all dragons. Their wide wedge-shaped heads sit atop long necks. Their serpentine tails are either barbed or with a spiked knob on the ends. Enormous wings carry them on swift flights.

When dragons of chaos and destruction make changes and help in rituals, they do everything in a big way. They go past your limited view of happenings, straight to the heart of the problem, so be certain you can stand their help before you call on them. These dragons work with re-creation of lives, relationships, and careers; breaking of barriers; changing luck; vast changes in general; work on past lives; divination; the confining of enemies or anyone who will hinder your forward growth or movement.

One of the very first recorded descriptions of a dragon is found in Babylonian records. The goddess Tiamat was considered to be the Great Mother Creator who built order out of chaos, or her own body. She was called a dragon and was said to be a monstrous creature with a scaly serpentine body, four legs, and horns on her head. After her spurt of initial creative activity, Tiamat spent her existence in repose. One of her offspring, the god Marduk, eventually killed her and build the earth and sky out of her body. This is a symbolic description of the activities of a chaos dragon: the breaking down of a static life-form and re-creation of another.

The ancient Egyptians said that before heaven and earth appeared, a great brood of serpents was created. They called these the Oldest of the Old. These serpents were very long and had only two legs. After the creation of the world and the universe, these serpents were confined, whether deliberately or by choice is not certain, in the Underworld, which every soul had to pass through on its way to judgment. The Egyptians advised that the soul should tread carefully on its journey, treating with respect the Oldest and his wife who reigned there.

The Egyptians also had a legend about the great serpent-dragon Apep who daily threatened the Sun god Ra when the Sun boat had to pass through darkness each night. The god Set who rode in the boat with the Sun god battled Apep on each nightly journey. When there was a solar eclipse, the Egyptians believed that Apep had broken out of his Underworld realm and had come into the physical world to do battle with Ra.

In Nordic myth, Niflheim was the lair of the great destructive dragon of chaos whose name was Nidhogg or Nidhoggr. Dread Biter, as he was also called, lay coiled about the root of the World Tree, constantly gnawing at it to destroy it. Nidhogg's attempts at destruction were countered daily by the Norns who sprinkled the tree with water from their sacred well. But when Ragnarok, or the end of the world, comes, the Norse say that Nidhogg will fly over the Hills of Darkness with the bodies of the dead on his wings. Another of Dread Biter's tasks was to strip the flesh off all corpses.

Although dragons in general were looked upon as bringing disaster, depending of course upon their actions, chaos dragons are

Babylonian Dragon

from tile relief, Ishtar Gate, Babylon, 6th century BCE

often quite literally omens of catastrophe. They can be seen in the area of disaster when other dragons create such things as great storms, earthquakes, or floods, but their power lies in creating or precipitating wars, bloodshed, plagues, and desolation when humans have gotten things out of balance. Unfortunately, it seems to take such occurrences to make humans want to find a better way of doing things.

Although the dragons of chaos and destruction create upheavals and complete transformations and rebirths, they are not evil. Their magick power is vital to the magician. They require as much fore-thought and caution as when working with Fire dragons. But if your life and plans have become static, your luck stuck in a negative mode, or circumstances or people are making you feel helpless and hopeless, then these dragons will turn the tide of events. Just be very certain that you are prepared for the drastic changes that will come.

As with many kinds of dragons, the chaos dragons are connected with death and rebirth; in fact, more so than others of their species. Often, when riding the dragon in an attempt to destroy barriers and remove enemies, one finds oneself face to face with oneself—the worst enemy of all. This ride can turn into a dramatic rebirth for the magician if she/he is willing to accept what is being shown by the dragon.

This connection with death and rebirth can still be seen on coffin decoration well into the Middle Ages. A wooden coffin from Zobingen, Württembergisches Landesmuseum, Stuttgart, has a beautifully carved and coiling serpent on it.

A close magician friend of mine had a problem, not of her making, with another magician. Louise's problems began when she married and no amount of magick seemed to lessen the mental attacks. Finally, she called upon the dragons of chaos and destruction. She did not specify what they should do; she only stated the problem and the fact that she wanted a definite end to the situation. Up until the final moments of the ritual, Louise had not been sure exactly how she was being attacked and had only a suspicion by whom, but the dragons let her clearly know. As she was working with the dragon mirror, she was given a glimpse of her attacker, heard an audible crack, and "saw" a second mirror shatter. The attacking magician must have had a shock upon finding *her* ritual mirror in pieces. The attacks stopped. Louise now has a huge dragon that protects her home, as well as the little guardian dragon who plays with her cat. The positive results of this ritual came from several important factors: the cause was just; there were no specifics given as to what should be done; harm was not intended.

The dragons of chaos and destruction must be called *only* within a cast and sealed circle. All movements and gestures within the circle must be counterclockwise. Burn patchouli, basil, and dragon's blood, or a binding incense. Use black or the darkest of purple candles. Greet these dragons with the sword in your power hand, the staff in the other.

Riding the Dragon

Even to an experienced and accomplished magician, the idea of riding a chaos dragon can be formidable and frightening. It is never safe to take any dragon for granted, and especially not a chaos dragon. You may find yourself on a flight much different from what you had in mind. Your thoughts on the best solution to the problem you planned to zap may not be the best solution at all, and the dragon will instinctively know this. A chaos dragon will go for the heart of the problem, with full intentions of knocking it out of existence or disabling it in such a way that you can move forward to your goal unimpeded.

Too many magicians who end up with solutions that are vastly disturbing to them, and their lives are in that predicament simply because they did not deeply consider the true nature of their problem. They accepted the surface appearance of the problem instead of delving into the heart of it. If their request to the chaos dragon had been worded differently, they could have avoided the drastic solution by bringing back balance in a slightly different manner. The magician should be really certain that she/he is prepared to accept all the results from a dragon ride with a chaos dragon.

The main reason for riding a dragon is so that the magician can remove barriers and obstacles, inanimate or animate, that impede forward progress. The ride also can impress upon her/his subconscious mind that elimination of problems has occurred. Without this deep-felt realization, the subconscious mind will continue to believe that the problems still exist because, according to the literal conscious mind, nothing has been done. Riding a dragon should ideally be a cathartic experience. The magician should be able to release all negative feelings about the situation by the end of the journey.

Notes: Perform during evening hours or the waning Moon, with the New Moon being strongest.

Supplies: Pentacle disk; dragon pentacle; water chalice with a little fresh water in it; dish of salt; wine chalice; black or dark-purple altar candles; sword; wand; incense burner; binding incense and/or dragon's blood, basil and patchouli; gong or bell; staff.

Use the Basic Dragon Ritual, remembering to cast the circle counterclockwise and call the element dragons in reverse order. When you kneel before the altar with the sword in both hands, project your interest and plea for help from the dragons of chaos and destruction as strongly as you can. Continue this for several minutes. Then say:

> BEHOLD, ALL DRAGONS OF DARKNESS AND CHANGE,
> I, (magickal name), SEEK YOUR DRAGON MAGICK.
> WITH (name of sword) IN MY HAND, I ENTER YOUR
>   REALM,
> NOT FOR PHYSICAL BATTLE, BUT FOR KNOWLEDGE AND
>   POWER.
> I GREET YOU, O DRAGONS ANCIENT AND WISE.
> I AWAIT YOUR PRESENCE.

Continue with the ritual up to the point where you may add any spellworking.

Take the sword in your power hand, the staff in the other. Stand facing the altar and tap the staff three times on the floor while holding the sword pointed at the dragon pentacle. Chant in tones that vibrate through your body:

> COME, DRACONIS!
> COME, DRACONIS, TO MY CALL!
> DRAGONS OF CHAOS, HEAR ME!
> DRACONIS! DRACONIS! DRACONIS!

Either remain standing or, to be more comfortable, sit before the altar. Close your eyes and visualize yourself astride the back of

Riding the Chaos Dragon

a great dragon of darkness. The dragon is swiftly winging through the night, blowing great billows of smoke and fire. See him/her zooming down on your problems, scattering them, turning them into ashes. Remember, do not specifically intend harm to any person. Feel the excitement and rush of joy as you realize you are now free. Open your eyes, and feel within yourself the power of the dragon. Know that you are going to win over all obstacles.

Take the sword in your power hand and go to the east. While chanting, cut and slash at the east.

> THE DRAGONS OF DESTRUCTION AND CHAOS ARE WITH ME.
> WE DESTROY ALL PROBLEMS AND EVIL COMING FROM THE EAST!

Move to the north. Cut and slash at the north; say:

> THE DRAGONS OF DESTRUCTION AND CHAOS ARE WITH ME.
> WE DESTROY ALL PROBLEMS AND EVIL COMING FROM THE NORTH!

Go to the west. Cut and slash at the west; say:

> THE DRAGONS OF DESTRUCTION AND CHAOS ARE WITH ME.
> WE DESTROY ALL PROBLEMS AND EVIL COMING FROM THE WEST!

Finish by going to the south. Cut and slash; say:

> THE DRAGONS OF DESTRUCTION AND CHAOS ARE WITH ME.

WE DESTROY ALL PROBLEMS AND EVIL COMING FROM
    THE SOUTH!

Return to the altar. Still holding the sword in your power hand, take the staff in the other. Tap the staff three times and chant:

TRANSFORMATION IS MY WILL.
USE YOUR POWER MY DESIRE TO FILL.
I THANK YOU, DRAGONS OLD AND WISE,
OF EARTH AND FIRE, WATER, SKIES,
FOR SHARING WISDOM HERE WITH ME.
AS WE WILL, SO SHALL IT BE.

Finish with the rest of the Basic Dragon Ritual, remembering to dismiss the element dragons in reverse order.

Guardian Dragons

ersonal guardian dragons come in various shapes and sizes, and usually (but not always) are quite small, at least much smaller than other dragons. They come in all colors. Often the little guardians are colored in pastel or lighter shades with belly scales of a myriad of hues. This smallness and color variety seem to point to the possibility that these dragons are more or less serving an apprenticeship, that they are younger dragons. The older adult dragons range in dimensions from tiger-size to absolutely huge; their scales are more pronounced and harder, while the little ones have softer scales, sometimes barely discernable.

Dragons age very slowly; therefore the juvenile stage could well last a hundred or more years, a relatively short period of time for long-lived dragons.

Guardian dragons would appear to be serving a type of apprenticeship by working with humans. This is their time of "schooling," of learning about humans, and of strengthening their individual powers. And as with all schools, the little guardian dragons are supervised by one or more adult dragons; you may or may not see these teachers. This supervision is for the safety of the little ones, as well as your protection. Little guardian dragons can get quite exuberant at times.

Although the powers of guardian dragons are not as strong or focused as those of larger dragons, they can help with protection; friendship; love; divination, such as tarot, runes, or crystal reading; the development of psychic abilities; dancing; singing; and general rituals.

Having a guardian or guardians from the dragon kingdom has distinct advantages. They become quite protective if you are friends with them. These little dragons are more or less astral watchdogs of both your property and your person. In this period of history with crime rates soaring, a magician, indeed any person, is foolish not to take advantage of any offered help in protection of self, family, and property. With guardian dragons, there is no cleanup; one feeds them on love and created energy. They are invisible and quiet, at least to the senses of most people. However, they can and do make disturbing noises, uncomfortable vibrational feelings, and sometimes actual appearances to those they feel might cause their friends distress or harm in any way.

Most of these little guardian dragons are quite playful. They frolic with and often tease household pets. One of our little guardians takes delight in startling Finnigan, one of our cats, but he treats the other cat, Callisto, with respect. All of our little guardians love young children, following them about with great interest. In describing dragons, one can use the pronouns he or she interchangeably, since it is difficult to know the sex of dragons unless they tell you.

Nip and Tuck are our knee-high dragons. They are quite heavy through the body and have stubs of wings; I have never seen them fly, but they run at top speed up and down the stairs. They are colored in metallic earth hues with flashes of gold and deep forest green on their scales. I have never been able to tell which one is Nip and which is Tuck; they seem to think this is a great joke. More

A Diminutive Guardian

from a woodcut by Edward Topsell, 1607

than one time I have found myself stepping over one of them, only to have a nonbelieving visitor give me a strange look. My dragons are as real to me as my cats, who also have a bad habit of lying down right behind me.

Tinsel, the tiniest of the dragons, is only the length of my hand. She is a shade of spring green, soft as silk, with transparent wings almost as long as she is. Her belly scales are colored with electric blue, deep rose, gold, and silver, like a gem-studded vest. Nip and Tuck are likely to be anywhere in the house, while Tinsel can be found nestled in my hair, draped over one of my ears like an exotic ornament, or snoozing on top of the bookcases. After working long hours in front of a computer, I often need my neck adjusted because of tension. Fortunately, my husband does this for me. One night while doing this, he started to laugh and said, "Listen to Tinsel." Tinsel was sitting on the dresser watching, while commenting with a constant stream of talk. "I don't need my neck adjusted. Ouch! Does that hurt? Don't hurt her now."

A dragon-loving friend has a guardian named Quicksilver who is black except for silver on his wings, yellow-gold eyes, and a fiery red mouth. Like most guardian dragons, Quicksilver has a delicious sense of humor and a delightful laugh.

Guardian dragons generally love to participate in rituals. Sometimes, instead of primarily defending a house, they will attach themselves to a person. Therefore, it is entirely possible to have several guardian dragons to a family and even several to a person.

Guardian dragons are the most friendly of their species and the most fun-loving. They enjoy simple impromptu rituals that include dancing, singing, and general fun. Simple, very relaxed rituals such as these are an excellent way to introduce children into the field of ritual and getting acquainted with dragons. It is also a very good way for adults to unwind and release stress.

These dragons are attracted to ginger and sweet-smelling and spicy incenses. They are greatly interested in divination and have a tendency to hang over your shoulder while you are reading cards or practicing crystal gazing, for instance. They are interested in stories, especially if the dragon is portrayed as powerful, wily, and not defeated by puny mortals.

A friend's six-year-old daughter was having difficulty seeing her dragons and was quite upset about it. Her father finally gave her a rock crystal and told her to put it against her forehead. Immediately, she saw her dragons. Now it is common for her to keep a piece of crystal handy so she can enjoy this new way of "seeing" her dragon friends.

If you are having trouble visualizing your dragons, try using a piece of rock crystal. It does not have to be flawless, nor does it have to have points. It would appear that this type of crystal acts as a kind of magnifying glass to the psychic through the third eye in the middle of the forehead. When you have mastered the technique with rock crystal, experiment with other kinds of translucent rocks. Remember, dragons have individual tastes in things, just as humans do.

Chant:
> LITTLE DRAGONS, RAINBOW BRIGHT,
> GOOD FRIENDS OF THIS FAMILY,
> SEND GOOD WISHES TO US ALL.
> JOIN OUR RITUALS MERRILY.
> PROTECT US THROUGH EACH DAY AND NIGHT,
> WHILE AWAKE OR WHILE ASLEEP.
> THROUGH YOUR LOVE AND VIGILANCE
> DO THIS FAMILY SAFELY KEEP.

Book of Magic with Illustration of Saturn-Dragon Being Ridden by the Angel Cassiel

from *The Magus* by Francis Barrett, 1801

Dragons of the Planets

T he dragons representing the planets are used basically for performing ceremonies or rituals on certain days and in certain hours, or to acquire certain physical or personality traits. If this is to be part of your ritual methods, I suggest you carefully read the charts on the next two pages for both day and night planetary hours. Remember to adjust for daylight savings time.

Some magicians feel that planetary dragons are only elemental energies and not specific beings of any kind. That has not been my experience. That is like saying there are only gnomes and no faeries. I suppose it is all in one's perception of other levels of beings.

The idea behind using planetary days and hours is that you are connecting with a stronger energy for use in your rituals. As the elements are the substance of the universe, the planets are more concerned with action and process. Only seven astrological bodies were used by the ancients: Sun (☉), Moon (☽), Mercury (☿), Venus (♀), Mars (♂), Jupiter (♃), and Saturn (♄). These correspond to the days of the week and the hours of each day. To use this system, find the planet that corresponds to the type of ritual you plan to do. Then select the proper day and hour in which to do it.

HOURS OF THE DAY

	Mo	Tu	We	Th	Fr	Sa	Su
1	☾	♂	☿	♃	♀	♄	☉
2	♄	☉	☾	♂	☿	♃	♀
3	♃	♀	♄	☉	☾	♂	☿
4	♂	☿	♃	♀	♄	☉	☾
5	☉	☾	♂	☿	♃	♀	♄
6	♀	♄	☉	☾	♂	☿	♃
7	☿	♃	♀	♄	☉	☾	♂
8	☾	♂	☿	♃	♀	♄	☉
9	♄	☉	☾	♂	☿	♃	♀
10	♃	♀	♄	☉	☾	♂	☿
11	♂	☿	♃	♀	♄	☉	☾
12	☉	☾	♂	☿	♃	♀	♄

HOURS OF THE NIGHT

	Mo	Tu	We	Th	Fr	Sa	Su
1	♀	♄	☉	☾	♂	☿	♃
2	☿	♃	♀	♄	☉	☾	♂
3	☾	♂	☿	♃	♀	♄	☉
4	♄	☉	☾	♂	☿	♃	♀
5	♃	♀	♄	☉	☾	♂	☿
6	♂	☿	♃	♀	♄	☉	☾
7	☉	☾	♂	☿	♃	♀	♄
8	♀	♄	☉	☾	♂	☿	♃
9	☿	♃	♀	♄	☉	☾	♂
10	☾	♂	☿	♃	♀	♄	☉
11	♄	☉	☾	♂	☿	♃	♀
12	♃	♀	♄	☉	☾	♂	☿

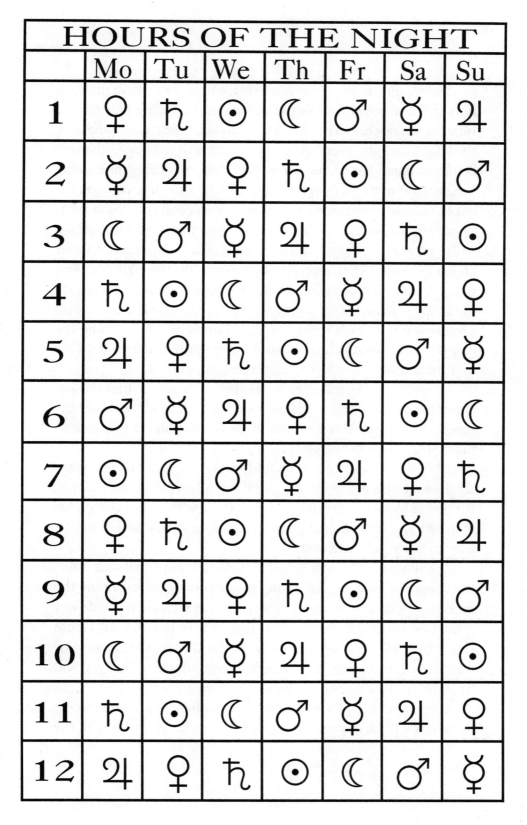

The waxing or increasing Moon is the time for spells of increase, building, and growth, while the waning or decreasing Moon is the time for decrease, destruction, removal, and binding. For the Sun, the bright daylight hours are used for increasing magick, with noon being strongest. For decreasing magick, perform during the evening hours, with midnight being strongest. Each planet has a dragon ritual chant for the physical, mental-emotional, and spiritual aspects of growth. These chants are to be used in conjunction with candles of the appropriate color. Consider carefully the reasons behind your choice of planet characteristics before you do these rituals. And never go to extremes by constantly performing the same rituals for the same characteristics. You can get overloaded and create worse problems for yourself if you do. An example would be using the planet Mars too much; this would eventually produce negative aspects, such as an explosive temper and impatience.

Carve your desires into the candle with your ritual dagger. Anoint the candle with a planetary oil, from the wick to the bottom to bring something to you, from the bottom to the wick to move something away from you.

Also part of each ritual should be the choosing of planetary herbs as an offering to the dragon of that planet. You can enhance the power more by surrounding the candle with stones chosen for their specific energies. All planetary candles should be left on the altar to burn completely out.

Use the Basic Dragon Ritual as a foundation ritual and insert the chant for your chosen planet in the proper places. Invite the dragons of that planet to join you in dance and ritual; if you do not extend an invitation, why should they bother to join you? Chose music that reflects what you feel about the chosen planet. Let your feelings be sensitive to the atmosphere around you so that you will be aware of the dragons' arrival and participation.

When you reach the part of the ritual where you insert specific spellworking, carve your desire into the candle; anoint it with the oil. Light the candle and surround it with stones. Say the planetary chant. Finish by chanting the Charm of Making:

By glow of Sun the power's begun.
By Moonbeam's light the spell is right,
To create desire by Earth and Fire.
Water, Air, make magick fair.
Powerful charm of making, creative magick undertaking.
Be formed!

When finished with the spellworking, complete the Basic Dragon Ritual.

Sun

Day: Sunday.

Color: Yellow or gold.

Metal: Gold.

Stones: Zircon, jacinth, goldstone, topaz, yellow diamond, chrysoleth.

Plants: Acacia, bay laurel, benzoin, cassia, chamomile, sweet cicely, cinnamon, clove, frankincense, ginger, juniper, mastic, myrrh, oak, patchouli, rosemary, storax.

Rules: Leo.

Oils: Bay laurel, cinnamon, clove, frankincense, ginger, patchouli, rosemary, styrax.

Rituals Involving: Health, healing, confidence, hope, prosperity, vitality, personal fulfillment, immediate family, life-energy, money, favor, honor, promotion, success, support of those in power, friendships.

Physical Chant:

> STRENGTH OF BODY, VITALITY,
> I ASK NOW THAT YOU GIVE TO ME.
> SUN DRAGON, LOOK ON ME WITH FAVOR
> THAT POWER, RICHES I MAY SAVOR.

Mental-Emotional Chant:

> I NEED A BOOST OF CONFIDENCE,
> A CIRCLE FIRM OF FRIENDSHIPS TRUE,
> NEW HOPE THAT'S BASED ON TRUTHFULNESS.
> SUN DRAGON, FOR THESE I DO THANK YOU.

Spiritual Chant:

> I SEEK YOUR GIFT OF PERSONAL FULFILLMENT.
> HARKEN, SUN DRAGON!
> GRANT ME SUCCESS ON MY SPIRITUAL PATH.
> BLESS ME, SUN DRAGON!

Moon

Notes: Perform on a Monday and/or during the waxing Moon, with the Full Moon being strongest. A silver, blue, or lavender candle.

Day: Monday.

Color: Lavender, silver, blue, pearl-white.

Metal: Silver.

Stones: Moonstone, quartz crystal, beryl, pearl.

Plants: Calamus, camphor, cascarilla, clary sage, frangipani, jasmine, henna, rosemary, sandalwood.

Rules: Cancer.

Oils: Birch, camphor, frangipani, jasmine, lotus, mint, rosemary, sandalwood, wisteria, ylang ylang.

Rituals Involving: Travel, visions, divinations, dreams, magick, love, agriculture, domestic life, medicine, luck, feminine aspects, water, birth, time, theft, emotions.

Physical Chant:

> I SEEK MAGICK DEEP AND OLD,
> ALL THE LOVE MY HEART CAN HOLD,
> GREEN MAGICK OF THE PLANTS AND EARTH,
> PSYCHIC GIFTS TO AID REBIRTH.

Mental-Emotional Chant:

> EMOTIONS AND TIME ARE SO HARD TO CONTROL
> AND TO FATHOM, O POWER OF THE MOON.
> TEACH ME YOUR MAGICKAL RITUALS AND WAYS
> THAT I MAY LEARN CONTROL VERY SOON.

Spiritual Chant:

> VIEWS OF THE FUTURE THAT COME IN THE NIGHT
> WHEN THE SILVER MOON RIDES HIGH IN THE SKY,
> I SEEK YOUR INSTRUCTION TO UNLOCK MY DREAMS
> THAT MY SPIRIT MAY GROW AND THRIVE.

Mercury

Notes: perform on a Wednesday and/or during the waxing Moon, with the Full Moon being strongest. An orange or violet candle.

Day: Wednesday.

Color: Orange, violet, multicolored, pale yellow.

Metal: Quicksilver, alloys.

Stones: Carnelian, fire opal, agate.

Plants: Anise, caraway, cassia, club moss, dittany of Crete, lavender, licorice, parsley, sandalwood, storax.

Rules: Gemini, Virgo.

Oils: Lavender, lemon, lily of valley, nutmeg, sandalwood, styrax, vervain.

Rituals Involving: Intellect, memory, science, creativity, business, magickal conjurations, divination, prediction, eloquence, gift of tongues, speed, speech, writing, poetry, inspiration, improvement of mind power, healing of nervous disorders.

Physical Chant:

> MAGICK, THE ARTS, SUCCESS IN MY TRADE,
> BUSINESS WISDOM AND DIVINATION,
> THESE GIFTS I WOULD GAIN FOR MY PHYSICAL GROWTH
> AND TO HELP IN MY CONJURATIONS.

Mental-Emotional Chant:

> THE STEADY FIRE OF INTELLECT
> THE LIGHT OF CREATIVITY,
> INSPIRATION AND ELOQUENCE,
> I ASK THAT YOU SEND NOW TO ME.

Spiritual Chant:

> THE POWER OF PREDICTION TO AID MY FELLOW MAN,
> GRANT THIS, DRAGON OF MERCURY.
> HEALING POWER FOR THE MIND AND SOUL,
> TEACH ME THE USES, O DRAGON GREAT!

Venus

Notes: Perform on a Friday and/or during the waxing Moon, with the Full Moon being strongest. A pale green, light blue, or pink candle.

Day: Friday.

Color: Green, light blue, pale green, pink.

Metal: Copper.

Stones: Amber, malachite, jade, peridot, coral, emerald, turquoise.

Plants: Ambergris, catnip, wild cherry, deer's tongue, lemon verbena, mugwort, red saunders, rose, sandalwood, savory, thyme, vetiver, violet, yarrow.

Rules: Taurus, Libra.

Oils: Ambergris, apple blossom, cherry, mint, rose, tuberose, vervain, violet, ylang ylang.

Rituals Involving: Love, marriage, friendship, pleasure, beauty, artistic creativity, imagination, fertility, partnerships, sex, spiritual harmony, compassion, children.

Physical Chant:

> MY HEART AND SOUL LONG FOR TRUE LOVE AND FRIENDSHIPS.

DRAGON OF VENUS, SHARE THESE GIFTS,
FOR THROUGH EXPERIENCING THEM, I SHALL BECOME
   STRONGER.
TEACH ME THE JOYS OF TRUE PARTNERSHIPS.

Mental-Emotional Chant:

BEAUTY COMES IN ALL DISGUISES,
EVEN IN CREATIVITY.
IMAGINATION BRIGHTENS THE LIFE.
GRANT ME MENTAL FERTILITY.

Spiritual Chant:

HARMONY OF THE SOUL IS A TREASURED GIFT.
O DRAGON OF VENUS, TEACH ME SPIRITUAL HARMONY.
COMPASSION FOR ALL BEINGS IN ALL PLACES
I SEND FORTH ON YOUR GREAT WINGS.

Mars

Notes: Perform on a Tuesday and/or during the waxing Moon, with the Full Moon being strongest. A red candle.

Day: Tuesday.

Color: Red.

Metal: Iron, steel.

Stones: Garnet, bloodstone, red agate, ruby, red topaz.

Plants: Allspice, basil, dragon's blood, ginger, patchouli, pepper, pine, squill.

Rules: Aries, Scorpio.

Oils: Allspice, coriander, patchouli, pine.

Rituals Involving: Energy, courage, battle, conflict, death, masculine aspects, surgery, physical strength, opposition, defense, endurance.

Physical Chant:

> COURAGE-FIRE, BURN MUCH HIGHER,
> ENERGY, COME. MAKE ME FREE
> OF OTHERS' WILL. TEACH ME STILL
> TO BE MYSELF, ABOVE ALL ELSE.

Mental-Emotional Chant:

> I PREPARE FOR BATTLE AGAINST MY ENEMIES.
> STAND BESIDE ME, RED DRAGON.
> OUR DEFENSE AND ENDURANCE CANNOT BE OVER-THROWN.
> TOGETHER WE SHALL BE VICTORIOUS.

Spiritual Chant:

> SOMETIMES THE CONFLICT WITHIN MY OWN SOUL
> KEEPS ME FROM REACHING MY SPIRITUAL GOAL.
> LIFT THE VEIL, AND LET ME SEE
> THAT OFTEN THE NEGATIVE IS ME.

Jupiter

Notes: Perform on a Thursday and/or during the waxing Moon, with the Full Moon being strongest. A purple or blue candle.

Day: Thursday.

Color: Blue, purple.

Metal: Tin.

Stones: Lapis lazuli, amethyst, turquoise, sapphire.

Plants: Anise, betony, cinquefoil, jasmine, lavender, oak, sage, yerba santa.

Rules: Sagittarius, Pisces.

Oils: Anise, bergamot, cedar, fir, honeysuckle, jasmine, lavender, nutmeg, orris, strawberry.

Rituals Involving: Honor, riches, health, friendships, the heart's desires, luck, accomplishment, religion, trade and employment, treasure, legal matters.

Physical Chant:

> GRANT ME HONOR AND SUCCESS.
> CHANGE MY LUCK AND MAKE ME BOLD.
> GIVE ME RICHES AND HAPPINESS.
> ALL YOU GIVE MY LIFE CAN HOLD.

Mental-Emotional Chant:

> GOALS IN LIFE ARE NEEDED
> TO BRING PEACE TO THE MIND.
> GOALS FOR HAND AND INTELLECT,
> SEND, O DRAGON KIND.

Spiritual Chant:

> ANY TASK I CAN ACCOMPLISH
> WITH YOUR AID, JUPITER DRAGON.
> SPIRITUAL PATHS OPEN BEFORE ME.
> SET MY FEET ON THE RIGHT PATH.

$\mathfrak{Saturn}$

Notes: Perform on a Saturday and/or during the waxing Moon, with the Full Moon being strongest. A black or indigo candle.

Day: Saturday.

Color: Black, indigo.

Metal: Lead.

Stones: Onyx, jet, pearl, star sapphire.

Plants: Aspen, balm of Gilead, bistort, boneset, juniper, myrrh, patchouli, storax, yerba buena, yerba mate.

Rules: Capricorn, Aquarius.

Oils: Balm of Gilead, cypress, high John the conqueror, musk, myrrh, patchouli, styrax.

Rituals Involving: Knowledge, familiars, death, reincarnation, protecting buildings, binding, overcoming curses, protection in general, retribution, duties, responsibilities, influences, doctrines.

Physical Chant:

> CLEAR OUT THE NEGATIVE. BRING IN THE GOOD.
> BIND UP MY ENEMIES, CURSES AND ALL.
> PROTECTION FOR ME AND MY LOVED ONES HERE
> SEND FROM YOUR GREAT DARK HALL.

Mental-Emotional Chant:

> RESPONSIBILITY AND DUTIES SHOULD NOT WEIGH DOWN
> THE BODY AND MIND AS MINE HAVE DONE.
> SHOW ME THE KARMA THAT I MUST SMOOTH
> SO THE BATTLE MIGHT BE WON.

Spiritual Chant:

THROUGH THE COILS OF MISTS AND TIME
I SEEK MY KARMIC PATHS TO KNOW
THAT I MIGHT REACH NEW HEIGHTS SUBLIME
AND SPIRITUALLY EXPAND AND GROW.

Dragons of the Zodiac

As there are dragons of the planets, so are there dragons of each zodiac sign. Some magickal systems look upon these dragons as devic* in nature and therefore not as powerful as element dragons. I have not found this to be so. I leave it to your own personal experience to decide the situation.

Sometimes we need to enhance the good qualities of the sign under which we were born, sometimes lessen the negative qualities. Many times we need the qualities and energies of other signs for a short period. By using the chant under each zodiac sign, the magician can add to her/his magickal energies, particularly when she/he must face a sticky situation or deal with difficult people. However, no magician should work with the powers of one sign too long or she/he may develop too much of a particular power, thereby overbalancing.

As with planetary dragons, indeed all dragons, the magician should extend a mental invitation to join the ritual. Choose music that reflects to you the zodiac sign with which you are working. Steven Halpern has recorded some very beautiful New Age music

---

*A deva is sometimes looked upon as a nature spirit or elemental spirit attached to a particular place or thing.

Dragon from a Zodiac Diagram

specifically for the zodiac signs, but these may not appeal to you. Response to music is a very personal thing. Your responses can even change from time to time, depending upon your emotions, physical health, and environmental situation. What feels right one time may not be appropriate at another.

Like the planetary rituals, these zodiac rites use candles, herbs, and oils of the appropriate sign to connect with dragon energy and draw on it. The colors in parentheses are those given by the astrologer Noel Tyl.

Use the Basic Dragon Ritual as a foundation ritual, adding the appropriate colors, herbs, etc. Insert these chants in the place where spellworking is called for. Dance with your dragons; sing with them; chant vowel sounds with them. At the end of whichever zodiac chant you decide to use, meditate on absorbing the energies and qualities for which you have asked. Listen inwardly for suggestions.

Aries

Notes: Perform during bright noon or the hour of Mars, and during the waxing Moon, with the Full Moon being strongest.

Color: Red.

Ruling Planet: Mars.

Stone: Diamond.

Flower: Geranium.

Description: Energetic, impatient, lacking in foresight, short-tempered, sarcastic, witty, lucky, demanding, sharp-minded, cutting, egocentric, adventuresome, feisty.

Chant:

> SHARPENED MIND, ENERGY,
> ARIES DRAGON, BRING TO ME.
> BOUNDLESS LUCK, ADVENTURE BOLD,
> THESE ARE THING I WANT TO HOLD.
> DRAGON RED OF LUCK AND WILL,
> HELP ME MY DESIRES TO FILL.

Taurus

Notes: Perform during bright noon or the hour of Venus, and during the waxing Moon, with the Full Moon being strongest.

Color: Pink and blue (Tyl—green and turquoise).

Ruling Planet: Venus.

Stone: Emerald.

Flower: Violet.

Description: Patient, loyal, emotionally stable, stubborn, practical, dependable, organized, materialistic, possessive, plodding, sweet, calm, determined, security-oriented.

Chant:

> I SEARCH FOR A CALM, SWEET SPIRIT.
> TAURUS DRAGON, COME!
> PATIENCE AND STABILITY MUST BE PART OF MY LIFE.
> TEACH ME, GREAT DRAGON!
> I WOULD BE PRACTICAL, ORGANIZED.
> SHOW ME THE WAY, EMERALD DRAGON!

Gemini

Notes: Perform during bright noon or the hour of Mercury, and during the waxing Moon, with the Full Moon being strongest.

Color: Multicolors.

Ruling Planet: Mercury.

Stone: Agate.

Flower: Lily of valley.

Description: Versatile, fickle, curious, high strung, a flirt, change-able, anxious, petty, superficial, communicative.

Chant:

> MENTAL QUICKNESS, VERSATILE WAYS,
> THESE I ASK TO FILL MY DAYS.
> COMMUNICATION SKILLS SO STRONG,
> DRAGON, SHOW ME RIGHT FROM WRONG.

Cancer

Notes: Perform during bright noon or the hour of the Moon, and during the waxing Moon, with the Full Moon being strongest.

Color: silver, pastels (Tyl—silver, white, dark blue).

Ruling Planet: Moon.

Stone: Pearl.

Flower: Larkspur.

Description: Caring, nurturing, moody, clinging, dependent, lazy, retentive memory, receptive, changeable, sensitive, pack rat, emotional, overprotective, messy, money-oriented.

Chant:

> MAKE ME CARING WITH NURTURING WAYS,
> RECEPTIVE WITH GOOD MEMORY.
> TEACH ME CONTROL OF EMOTIONS AND LIFE.
> THANK YOU. SO MOTE IT BE.

Leo

Notes: Perform during the day or the hour of the Sun, and during the waxing Moon, with the Full Moon being strongest.

Color: Gold and scarlet (Tyl—orange and yellow).

Ruling Planet: Sun.

Stone: Ruby.

Flower: Marigold.

Description: Positive, optimistic, warm, dogmatic, organizational, hardworking, persistent, dramatic, colorful, generous, flamboyant, arrogant, inspiring, performer.

Chant:

> POSITIVE OUTLOOK I WANT IN MY LIFE,
> WARM THOUGHTS AND FIRM PERSISTENCE.
> I WANT TO BE GENEROUS, OUTGOING TO ALL.
> FOR THESE I NEED YOUR ASSISTANCE.

Virgo

Notes: Perform during bright day or the hour of Mercury, and during the waxing Moon, with the Full Moon being strongest.

Color: Gray and navy blue (Tyl—browns, rust orange, dark blue).

Ruling Planet: Mercury.

Stone: Sapphire.

Flower: Pansy.

Description: Neat, fussy, conservative, efficient, studious, retiring, worrier, practical, logical, dependable, analytical, workaholic.

Chant:

> GOOD STUDY HABITS, LOGIC AND PRACTICAL,
> ARE ALL TRAITS OF THE SIGN OF VIRGO.
> EFFICIENCY, NEATNESS, ARE GOOD THINGS TO HAVE.
> I DESIRE THESE TRAITS, AS YOU KNOW.

Libra

Notes: Perform during bright daylight or the hour of Venus, and during the waxing Moon, with the Full Moon being strongest.

Color: Light blues, pink, soft rose (Tyl—blue-green).

Ruling Planet: Venus.

Stone: Opal.

Flower: Rose.

Description: Refined, diplomatic, vacillating, vain, social, just, artistic, gentle, tactful, gracious, peace loving.

Chant:

> SOCIAL SKILLS, ARTISTIC WAYS,
> I NEED TO BRIGHTEN UP MY DAYS.
> GENTLENESS, DIPLOMACY,
> ARE NECESSARY NOW TO ME.
> LIBRA DRAGON, GRACIOUS, GOOD,
> HELP ME AS YOU KNOW YOU SHOULD.

Scorpio

Notes: Perform during bright daylight or the hour of Mars, and during the waxing Moon, with the Full Moon being strongest.

Color: Deep reds, such as maroon (Tyl—red and black).

Ruling Planet: Pluto.

Stone: Topaz.

Flower: Chrysanthemum.

Description: Secretive, intelligent, psychic, manipulative, passionate, stubborn, well-organized, deceitful, resourceful, vindictive, tenacious, methodical.

Chant:

> METHODICAL SKILLS ARE GOOD TOOLS OF TRADE.
> SECRECY A NECESSITY FOR THE ART.
> A MAGICIAN NEEDS INTELLECT STRONG AND FIRM.
> DRAGON, WITH THESE GLADDEN MY HEART.

Sagittarius

Notes: Perform during bright daylight or the hour of Jupiter, and during the waxing Moon, with the Full Moon being strongest.

Color: Purple and deep blue (Tyl—dark blue).

Ruling Planet: Jupiter.

Stone: Turquoise.

Flower: Narcissus.

Description: Outspoken, freedom loving, independent, warm, outgoing, spiritually oriented, athletic, opportunist, inspiring.

Chant:

> FREEDOM LOVING, WARM AND FREE,
> SAGITTARIUS DRAGON, COME TO ME.

INSPIRE ME WITH DEEP SECRETS OLD,
O SPIRITUAL DRAGON, MAKE ME BOLD.

Capricorn

Notes: Perform during bright daylight or the hour of Saturn, and during the waxing Moon, with the Full Moon being strongest.

Color: Dark shades (Tyl—black).

Ruling Planet: Saturn.

Stone: Garnet.

Flower: Carnation.

Description: Rigid, practical, loner, managerial, persistent, opinionated, sarcastic sense of humor, prudent, efficient, miserly, cold, pessimistic, patient, ruthless, ambitious.

Chant:

THE SOUND OF MONEY STIRS AMBITION
TO BE PRACTICAL AND PERSIST.
I WOULD BE PRACTICAL AND EFFICIENT
THAT MY LIFE BE FULL AND BLESSED.

Aquarius

Notes: Perform during bright daylight or the hour of the Moon, and during the waxing Moon, with the Full Moon being strongest. The choice of the hour of the Moon is strictly my preference as there is never a planetary hour listed for this sign. However, I feel that, since the Moon rules water, this is a logical choice.

Color: Iridescent blues (Tyl—rust, dark orange).

Ruling Planet: Uranus.

Stone: Amethyst.

Flower: Orchid.

Description: Perceptive, temperamental, organized, erratic, cool, detached, ingenious, impersonal, goal-oriented, insightful, out-going, self-expressive, unconventional.

Chant:

> INVENTIVENESS AND INSIGHT DEEP
> BRING TO ME WHILE I'M ASLEEP.
> SELF-EXPRESSION FEEDS THE SOUL.
> HELP ME FIND A RICHER GOAL.

Pisces

Notes: Perform during bright daylight or the hour of Venus, and during the waxing Moon, with the Full Moon being strongest. Again, this zodiac sign has no corresponding usable planetary hour. However, it is considered the exaltation of Venus, so I chose this planet.

Color: Sea greens (Tyl—dark blue).

Ruling Planet: Neptune.

Stone: Aquamarine.

Flower: Water lily.

Description: Refined, shrewd, impractical, nagging, unstable, con-artist, impressionable, compassionate, escapist or drifter, paranoiac, dreamer, intuitive.

Chant:

> I SEEK TRUE INTUITION AND DREAMS,
> INSIGHT TO SHOW A CLEAR FUTURE PATH.
> LET MY ESCAPES INTO DAYDREAMS BE FRUITFUL.
> LET THE PSYCHIC TEACH ME COMPASSION.
> HELP ME TO REMAIN STABLE ON THE ILLUSIVE PATH OF
>   THE SPIRITUAL.

Dragon from a Painting by Paolo Uccello (1397–1475?)

Dancing With Dragons

When a magician dances with the dragons, she/he discovers an intensity of power untapped before. It is an exhilarating experience, a spiritual high. Dragons as co-magicians can empower magickal rituals far beyond what has been normally encountered. Their grasp of ancient knowledge is deep and profound. Their ability to see through layers of time, both backward and forward, is astounding and quite accurate, if they choose to share with you what they see. As protectors, there are no equals.

If you are a dedicated magician, your intuition, your desire to learn, will draw you, sooner or later, to call upon dragons. You may begin by asking them to better your physical life, but eventually you will find yourself more and more asking their help to improve the mental, emotional, and particularly the spiritual parts of you. That is when the real journey in the company of dragons begins.

The very foundation stones of all magick are spiritual, for all realms of existence are connected through the spiritual plane. Everything in our field of existence must first be formed and imbued with life in the spiritual realm. Whether we humans consider the event or being as positive or negative makes no difference.

If, as magicians, we wish for more positive events and surroundings to bless our lives, we must seek a better connection with spiritual forces. Every magician who continues to expand her/his personal growth and knowledge will eventually find themselves on a path more of a spiritual nature than of a physical.

In *The Evolution of the Dragon* (Manchester University Press, 1919), G. Elliott Smith writes that originally the dragon was thought of as a beneficial creature. It was identified with kings, gods, and advanced, powerful magicians. When a dragon became evil, it was considered only evil because the energy it represented was out of control or not properly balanced. As the Chinese would say, the Yin and Yang (negative and positive) were out of balance. It took greedy, cruel men and orthodox religions to brainwash humans into believing that all dragons were intrinsically evil and untrustworthy. And worse, they programmed humans to believe that dragons do not exist at all, except in their hell as their devil.

It will take hard work by Pagans and magicians to re-establish lines of communication with the ancient, powerful dragons of the astral plane. When you have been abused and maligned, trust does not return easily. The study of dragons will never be a magickal "science" available to all, nor should it be. The dragons themselves will decide the worthiness of a seeker on an individual basis. It is the responsibility of each magician to present her/his case for dragon companionship.

Under dragon tutelage, the magician has the opportunity of constantly learning and evolving her/his knowledge and magickal ability. If you have taken the time and effort to forge a friendship with dragons, they can become the best companions a human could ever want. Sometimes this friendship can seem harsh and demanding, but it is always in your best interests. Dragons will never let you slide in your responsibilities or draw back from new experiences because you are afraid. If you hesitate to go forward, dragons have no mercy. They tend to plant themselves directly behind you, gently nudging until you find yourself taking that first hesitant step into a new phase of life.

A lifelong dance with dragons is never boring. Dancing with dragons is a constant exploration of various types of energies and the uses to which they can be applied. They will start you off in "kindergarten," where you learn to manifest physical needs. Then you graduate into more complex and demanding forms of magick: healing, emotional balance, mental disciplines, spiritual seeking. And just when you think you have learned everything there is to know about a subject, the dragons will surprise you by unveiling a new view, some hidden knowledge, a different method of magick.

You may well find yourself facing an inner door, unnoticed before. The opening of this door will require you to readjust your thinking about yourself and everything and everyone around you. Sometimes this can be bitterly painful. We all like the comfortable status quo; changes bring the unknown and therefore the frightening. And none of us likes to be faced with the fact that there are still habits and traits within ourselves that need cleaning out, even though deep inside we know this to be true. It is personally painful on all levels to haul out this garbage, see it for what it is, and discard it. The wonderful thing is, although dragons will force an evolving magician to undergo this experience, they will be by your side through the whole ordeal.

The number of dragons, especially guardian dragons, around you may well grow into large numbers. What is the proper term for a lot of dragons? Herd? Flock? Swarm? Crowd? During the writing of this book, I was delighted to find that another very tiny dragon had joined my group. The first inkling I had of Rudy's existence was a warning hiss from Tinsel to not dare even think about joining her on her perch on my left ear. Rudy settled himself on top of the computer monitor, flapped his wings, and trumpeted his arrival like the cocky little male he is. I suspect from his coloring, dark gray with a silver belly, that Rudy may be a baby chaos dragon.

I have always been hesitant about dealing with chaos dragons, as I have had so much personal chaos in my life. Rudy tells me he is here to help me understand, deep within my subconscious mind, that change is not always devastating, that it can be wonderful and invigorating.

Dancing with dragons can be a joyful, daily experience, one that is eagerly sought and enjoyed by all the participants. The mutual sharing of energies helps both species in their evolution and spiritual growth. The more magicians seek out the companionship of dragons, work with them, and earn their trust, the more dragons will be encouraged to once more have a closer, positive relationship with humans in general.

At the very edges of our mental and psychic realms are signs that read "Here be dragons." The magicians who are true explorers of the unknown will be challenged, not frightened, by these signs. They will forge a friendship and partnership with these astral creatures that will lead to some of the greatest discoveries ever made. May that journey always be one of continuing interest and growth!

Appendices

1
Herbs

All magicians, sooner or later, come to realize the magickal values of the herbal kingdom. This is not a new science. The uses of herbs and their traditional values have come down to us from the earliest cultures of humankind. Herbs can be used as part of your incenses in dragon magick, in fact in most magick. Herbs and gums can be burned as the sole incense ingredient or in conjunction with other ready-made incenses.

When candles are anointed with oils, they can be then rolled in specific crushed herbs for added power. Some scents attract dragons directly; others aid in persuading them to put in an appearance and help you.

Herbs can also be added to poppets to increase their potency. Poppets are cloth dolls made roughly in human shape for the purposes of healing, prosperity, protection, love, etc. To avoid rebounding negatives, I strongly suggest that you do not make poppets to control or harm another person. There are a number of creative ways to deal with bothersome people without spelling for physical harm, financial ruin, or nervous breakdown, however much you think they deserve it.

And stay as far away as possible from the temptation of spelling someone to do something against their will! How would you feel if you discovered that the choices you made were being controlled by someone else? Besides, once you start controlling someone, you must keep at it. The effort needed to control increases because most people struggle subconsciously to get away. This is particularly true in relationships. If you did spell to make someone love you, for instance, and found it very easy to keep her/him in line, watch out! You may well have an emotional and financial leech on your hands. Getting rid of them may take more effort than it did to control them in the first place.

Herbs can be enclosed in small leather or cloth bags with a specific ritual-blessed purpose, either for yourself or someone else. These usually fall under the headings of health, prosperity, spiritual growth, protection, or good luck. These are either worn or carried by the person for whom they are made. Magickal herbal bags can also be hung in cars or houses; these are usually made for protection and good fortune.

Small amounts of herbs can also be tied up in gauze bags and soaked in bath water. Bathing in this "tea" is a relaxing way to absorb herbal energies. When magickal books speak of cleansing baths before ritual work, they are referring to this type of bathing.

Some of my element designations, planets, and powers are different from those of other herbalists. I have reached my conclusions from personal experience, which I am sure others have also. For herbs that apply to planets and zodiac signs, see the chapters on Dragons of the Planets and Dragons of the Zodiac.

ACACIA (*Acacia senegal*)
Also Called: Cape gum, gum arabic tree, Egyptian thorn.
Parts Used: Twigs, wood, gum.
Planet: Sun.
Element: Air.
Type of Ritual: Protection, clairvoyance. The wood can be burned with sandalwood to stimulate the psychic centers.
Dragons: Air, Light, Darkness, Guardian.

ALLSPICE *(Pimento officinalis)*
Also Called: Clove pepper, Jamaica pepper, pimento.
Parts Used: Immature fruit.
Planet: Mars.
Element: Fire.
Type of Ritual: Energy, money, luck, healing. The ground herb, such as is used in cooking, can be added to incense.
Dragons: Fire, Volcanoes, Earth, Mountains.

ANISE *(Pimpinella anisum)*
Also Called: Anneys, aniseed.
Parts Used: Seeds.
Planet: Jupiter, sometimes Mercury.
Element: Air.
Type of Ritual: Protection, purification, meditation. This herb has a licorice odor to it. A small pillow filled with it will ward off nightmares. Use in baths for cleansing. Place fresh in the ritual room or burn as incense to protect or help call up astral entities.
Dragons: Air, Light, Fire, Dark, Guardian.

ASPEN *(Populus tremula* in Europe; *P. tremuloides* in America)*
Also Called: White poplar, quaking aspen.
Parts Used: Bark, wood.
Planet: Saturn, sometimes Mercury.
Element: Earth, sometimes Air.
Type of Ritual: Knowledge, reincarnation, overcoming curses, protection from thieves. An aspen tree in your yard is said to repel thieves. Small shavings of this wood can be added to incense.
Dragons: Earth, Air, Chaos, Light, Dark, Guardian.

BALM OF GILEAD *(Icica carana, Populus candicans, Commiphora opobalsamum)*
Also Called: Balm of Mecca, balsam of Gilead, Mecca balsam. In the U.S.A., poplar buds of the *Populus candicans, P. nigra,* or *P. balsamifera* are used.
Parts Used: Buds.

Planet: Saturn, sometimes Venus.

Element: Earth, sometimes Water.

Type of Ritual: Protection, manifestations, intellectual stimulation, healing, love. Scott Cunningham suggests steeping the buds in red wine for a love drink. The buds tend to be very sticky. Add to magickal bags or burn as incense.

Dragons: Earth, Chaos, Guardian, Mountains, Forests, Air, Volcanoes.

BASIL *(Ocimum basilicum)*

Also Called: American dittany, alabahaca, St. Joseph's wort, sweet basil, witches' herb.

Parts Used: The herb.

Planet: Mars.

Element: Fire.

Type of Ritual: Purification, protection, wealth, exorcism, love. Added to love sachets and incenses, basil can create a bond of sympathy between two people. Carried in the pocket, it attracts money and business. Used in purification baths and sprinkled about the house, it drives out negative entities.

Dragons: Fire, Earth, Light, Dark, Seas, Mountains, Desert, Volcanoes, Chaos, Guardian.

BAY LAUREL *(Laurus nobilis)*

Also Called: Bay, bay tree, Grecian laurel, Indian bay, Roman laurel, sweet bay, baie.

Parts Used: Leaves.

Planet: The Sun.

Element: Fire.

Type of Ritual: Protection, clairvoyance, exorcism, purification, healing. Place beneath your pillow to produce psychic dreams. Burn to enhance visions; be careful, though, as burning bay leaves have an extremely strong odor. Hang wreathes or branches of bay in the house to ward off evil; these will also drive out bothersome entities, as will burning bay.

Dragons: Fire, Volcanoes, Chaos, Water, Light, Dark, Guardian, Wind.

BENZOIN *(Styrax benzoin)*
Also Called: Benjamen, gum benzoin, Siam benzoin.
Parts Used: Gum.
Planet: The Sun.
Element: Air.
Type of Ritual: Intellectual, purification, prosperity. Benzoin is usually burned as part of an incense, not by itself. Burning benzoin clears and purifies the atmosphere; purified surroundings enhance the intellect. This herb will also attract money.
Dragons: Air, Water, Light, Dark, Seas, Earth, Guardian.

BETONY, WOOD *(Stachys officinalis, Betonica officinalis, Stachys betonica)*
Also Called: Bishopwort, lousewort, wood betony, purple betony.
Parts Used: The herb.
Planet: Jupiter.
Element: Fire.
Type of Ritual: Protection, purification. Placed beneath your pillow it will produce a psychic shield that keeps others from influencing you while you are asleep. Planted around the house it makes a barrier of protection. "Washing" the smoke of burning betony over your body will purify your aura.
Dragons: Fire, Volcanoes, Dark, Light, Chaos, Water, Guardian, Wind.

BISTORT *(Polygonum bistorta)*
Also Called: Patience dock, snakeweed, dragonwort, sweet dock, English serpentary, red legs, Easter giant.
Parts Used: The herb, root.
Planet: Saturn.
Element: Earth.
Type of Ritual: Clairvoyance, fertility, money. Old traditions say to carry bistort if you wish to become pregnant. Carried in sachet bags or burned, it draws money. Burn it with frankincense to increase your powers during divination. An infusion made of betony and sprinkled around your house will drive out poltergeists.
Dragons: Earth, Mountains, Guardian, Light, Dark, Desert, Seas.

BONESET *(Eupatorium perfoliatum)*
Also Called: Thoroughwort, agueweed, teasel, feverwort, Indian sage.
Parts Used: The herb.
Planet: Saturn.
Element: Earth, sometimes Water.
Type of Ritual: Binding, exorcism. Sprinkle an infusion of this herb to drive away negatives. Burn with other incense to produce a binding effect on entities or people who are harassing you.
Dragons: Fire, Volcanoes, Dark, Wind, Desert, Chaos.

CALAMUS *(Acorus calamus)*
Also Called: Sweet flag, sweet sedge, sweet rush, aromatic rush. This is a poisonous herb. Keep away from children and pets.
Parts Used: Root, the herb.
Planet: Moon.
Element: Water.
Type of Ritual: Protection, knowledge, binding, luck. The powdered root can be added to other incenses to increase the binding power of your rituals and give protection. Small pieces can be carried to draw good luck.
Dragons: Seas, Water, Air, Earth, Guardian, Chaos, Storm.

CAMPHOR *(Cinnamomum camphora)*
Parts Used: Gum.
Planet: Moon.
Element: Water.
Type of Ritual: Anti-aphrodisiac, healing, divination. The odor of this herb lessens sexual desires and also wards off colds. Added to incenses for tarot reading, etc. True camphor is rarely available.
Dragons: Water, Seas, Air, Guardian, Light.

CARAWAY *(Carum carvi)*
Also Called: Careum, carvi.
Parts Used: Seeds.
Planet: Mercury.
Element: Air.

Type of Ritual: Protection, passion, mental clarity. Carry the seeds or hang them about in bags to drive off evil entities and thieves. When used in cooking, they increase sexual desire. Burned, they sharpen the mental faculties.

Dragons: Air, Fire, Seas, Storm.

CARDAMOM *(Elettaria cardamomum)*
Also Called: Ebil, capalaga, ilachi, ailum, grains of paradise.
Parts Used: Dried ripe seeds.
Planet: Mercury, sometimes Venus.
Element: Fire, sometimes Water.
Type of Ritual: Love, creativity, divination, prediction. Steeped in warm wine or used in baking, they set up love vibrations. Burned as incense or soaked in bath water, cardamom strengthens creativity and sharpens predictive powers.
Dragons: Fire, Air, Seas, Guardian.

CASCARILLA *(Croton eleuteria)*
Also Called: Sweetwood bark, Sweet bark, Elutheria, Aromatic quinquina, False quinquina.
Parts Used: Dried bark.
Planet: Moon.
Element: Water.
Type of Ritual: Psychic vision, divinations, magick. Use in the bath water or burn as incense.
Dragons: Light, Dark, Desert, Guardian.

CASSIA *(Cinnamomum cassia)*
Parts Used: Bark.
Planet: The Sun, sometimes Mercury.
Element: Fire.
Type of Ritual: Protection, healing, success. Can be used as a substitute for cinnamon, although cinnamon is easier to obtain. Use in incense or roll oiled candles in the powder.
Dragons: Fire, Water, Earth, Light, Dark, Mountains, Desert, Chaos, Guardian.

CATNIP *(Nepeta cataria)*
Also Called: Field balm, catmint, catnep, cat's wort, nip, catrup.
Parts Used: The herb.
Planet: Venus.
Element: Water.
Type of Ritual: Love, animal contacts. Can create a psychic bond with certain dragons. Use in love sachets or add a small amount to herbal teas. Tradition says that growing catnip near your home will attract luck and good spirits; it will also attract every cat in the neighborhood.
Dragons: Water, Earth, Light, Mountains, Guardian.

CEDAR *(Cedrus libani,* cedar of Lebanon, the Old World species; *Thuja occidentalis,* yellow cedar or arbor vitae, tree of life; *Juniperus virginiana,* red cedar)
Also Called: Tree of life, arbor vitae, cedar of Lebanon.
Parts Used: Wood, oil.
Planet: Jupiter.
Element: Fire/Water.
Type of Ritual: Purification, exorcism. Fresh cedar boughs are used as brooms for purification, exorcisms, and to clean temples. Cedar chips or shavings burned as part of your incense purifies the vibrations of your sacred area and house, driving out all negative entities.
Dragons: Fire, Volcanoes, Water, Seas, Light, Dark, Chaos, Wind, Storm, Desert.

CHAMOMILE *(Anthemis noblis, Matricaria chamomilla)*
Also Called: Roman camomile, wild chamomile, manzanilla, ground apple, whig plant.
Parts Used: Flowers.
Planet: Sun.
Element: Water.
Type of Ritual: Prosperity, meditation, sleep, purification. Chamomile tea is an excellent sleepy tea, even for small children. Use in incenses, sachet bags, or baths to draw prosperity and aid in meditation. Growing chamomile in your garden also draws good luck; get the Roman chamomile which smells like apples when cut.
Dragons: Water, Seas, Earth, Light, Dark, Mountains, Fire, Guardian.

CHERRY, WILD *(Prunus avium, P. serotina, P. virginiana)*
Also Called: Black cherry, chokecherry.
Parts Used: Wood, bark, fruit.
Planet: Venus.
Element: Earth/Air, sometimes Water.
Type of Ritual: Creativity, health. In the Orient they say to tie a strand of your hair to a blooming tree and you will be led to your true love. The bark can be burned as incense or added to sachets.
Dragons: Air, Earth, Mountains, Water.

CICELY, SWEET *(Myrrhis odorata)*
Also Called: British myrrh.
Parts Used: The herb, seeds, root.
Planet: Sun.
Element: Water.
Type of Ritual: Love. This herb is not often grown in the U.S.A. Surround a love candle with it.
Dragons: Water, Guardian.

CINNAMON *(Cinnamonum zeylanicum* or *C. lauraceae)*
Also Called: Sweet wood; see Cassia.
Parts Used: Bark, oil.
Planet: The Sun.
Element: Fire.
Type of Ritual: Protection, healing, passion. Burn to raise vibrations to a high spiritual level. Mixed with myrrh it makes a good general purpose incense. Cinnamon has long been used for ritual purposes in the Middle East.
Dragons: Fire, Water, Seas, Volcanoes, Chaos.

CINQUEFOIL *(Potentilla canadensis* or *P. reptans)*
Also Called: Five-finger grass, sunfield, five-leaf grass.
Parts Used: The herb.
Planet: Jupiter.
Element: Earth, sometimes Fire.

Type of Ritual: Protection, love, prosperity, healing, precognitive dreams. An infusion sprinkled around the house and on a person will drive out curses and bad luck. Carried, this herb will attract all good things your way. A bag of it hung over the bed helps with precognitive dreams.
Dragons: Earth, Fire, Water, Light, Dark, Mountains, Desert, Chaos.

CLARY SAGE *(Salvia sclarea)*
Parts Used: Seeds, oil.
Planet: Moon.
Element: Water.
Type of Ritual: Love, magick. Add to sachets, incenses, and baths.
Dragons: Water, Seas, Guardian.

CLOVE *(Eugenia caryophyllata, Caryophyllus aromaticus,* or *Syzygium aromaticum)*
Parts Used: Undeveloped flowers and buds.
Planet: The Sun.
Element: Fire.
Type of Ritual: Protection, memory, prosperity. Add to incenses or wear to drive away negative forces. Cloves in incense stop gossip against you and draw good luck.
Dragons: Air, Earth, Light, Dark, Mountains, Wind, Desert, Chaos, Guardian.

CLUB MOSS *(Lycopodium clavotum)*
Also Called: Foxtail, wolf claw, staghorn.
Parts Used: The herb, spores.
Planet: Mercury, sometimes the Moon.
Element: Air, sometimes Water.
Type of Ritual: Protection. Add to incenses and sachets.
Dragons: Air, Water, Chaos, Dark.

DEER'S TONGUE *(Frasera speciosa* or *Liatris odoratissima)*
Also Called: Wild vanilla.
Parts Used: Leaves.

Planet: Venus, sometimes Mars.

Element: Earth/Air, sometimes Fire.

Type of Ritual: Love, the psychic. Sprinkled on the bed or worn it will attract men. Wear it to increase psychic powers.

Dragons: Fire, Earth, Water, Light, Dark, Guardian.

DITTANY OF CRETE *(Origanum dictamnus)*

Also Called: Hop marjoram.

Parts Used: The herb.

Planet: Mercury, sometimes Venus.

Element: Earth/Air, sometimes Water.

Type of Ritual: Divination, manifestation. When burned it is a powerful cleanser of vibrations. Also produces spirit manifestations in its smoke.

Dragons: Water, Seas, Light, Dark, Desert, Chaos, Guardian.

DRAGON'S BLOOD *(Daemonorops draco, Dracaena draco)*

Also Called: Calamus draco.

Parts Used: Gum.

Planet: Mars.

Element: Fire.

Type of Ritual: Energy, purification, protection. Add a pinch of the ground gum to incenses to increase potency and effectiveness. The powder can be used to draw symbols and protective sigils during rituals; dragon's blood ink is very good for this. To make this ink, grind a small amount of dragon's blood into a powder. Dissolve this in alcohol and store in a tightly sealed bottle. This ink will be almost invisible when writing, but the legibility is not where the power lies.

Dragons: All dragons.

FRANGIPANI *(Plumeria acuminata* and *P. ruba)*

Parts Used: Flowers.

Planet: Moon.

Element: Water.

Type of Ritual: Love. Roll anointed love candles in the crushed flowers and further surround the burning candle with them.

Dragons: Fire, Water, Seas.

FRANKINCENSE *(Boswellia carterii or B. thurifera)*
Also Called: Olibanum, olibans, incense.
Parts Used: Gum.
Planet: The Sun.
Element: Fire.
Type of Ritual: Protection, purification, consecration, exorcism. A very ancient and powerful incense ingredient; can also be added to sachet bags.
Dragons: All dragons.

GINGER *(Zingiber officinale)*
Also Called: African ginger, black ginger.
Parts Used: The root.
Planet: Mars, sometimes the Sun.
Element: Fire.
Type of Ritual: Offertory, success, power. The root can be placed on the altar and around the circle as an offering to the Earth dragons. Grow ginger roots to attract success; sprinkle the powder in your purse or wallet. Burn to draw power.
Dragons: Guardian, Fire, Earth, Mountains, Desert.

HENNA *(Lawsonia alba, L. inermis)*
Also Called: Al-Khanna, al-henna, Jamaica mignonette, Egyptian privet, mehndi, mendee.
Parts Used: Leaves, flowers.
Planet: Moon.
Element: Water.
Type of Ritual: Exorcism, uncrossing, healing. Dab the powder on the center of your forehead to relieve headache. Burn in incense for exorcisms.
Dragons: Light, Dark, Chaos.

JASMINE *(Jasminum officinale, J. odoratissimun)*
Also Called: Moonlight on the grove, jessamin, jessamine.
Parts Used: Flowers.
Planet: Jupiter, sometimes the Moon.

Element: Earth, sometimes Water.

Type of Ritual: Love, prosperity. The flowers of *J. odoratissimun* are used to draw a spiritual type love. Burn or carry the flowers to attract money or prophetic dreams.

Dragons: Water, Seas, Earth, Desert, Guardian.

JUNIPER *(Juniperus communis)*

Parts Used: Berries, branches.

Planet: The Sun, sometimes Saturn.

Element: Fire.

Type of Ritual: Protection, love, exorcism. A very old European protective herb that guards against theft, it can be hung on doors, grown next to the house, or burned as incense. The berries can be added to incense by men to increase their sexual prowess. The burned berries also drive away curses and increase psychic ability.

Dragons: All dragons.

LAVENDER *(Lavendula officinale, L. vera)*

Also Called: Spike, elf leaf.

Parts Used: Flowers.

Planet: Mercury, sometimes Jupiter.

Element: Air.

Type of Ritual: Love, protection, purification. Burn as a sacrifice to the very ancient dragons. Make sachet bags of the dried flowers and store among your clothing to both attract love and give protection. Burned as incense, lavender purifies.

Dragons: Air, Water, Seas, Wind, Chaos, Guardian.

LEMON VERBENA *(Lippia citriodora)*

Also Called: Yerba louisa, cedron.

Parts Used: The herb.

Planet: Venus, sometimes Mercury.

Element: Air.

Type of Ritual: Purification, love. The scent of this herb is said to be attractive to the opposite sex of the person who has a bouquet of it in their home or grows it in their garden. Add to bath water as a purifier.

Dragons: Air, Wind, Water, Seas, Fire.

LICORICE *(Glycyrrhiza glabra)*

Also Called: Licorice root, sweet licorice, sweet wood.
Parts Used: Root.
Planet: Mercury, sometimes Venus.
Element: Earth/Air, sometimes Water.
Type of Ritual: Love, protection, prophetic dreams. Chew on a stick of the root to create passion. Use a dried stick as a wand in protection rituals. Add small amounts to incense to increase your prophetic dreaming.
Dragons: Water, Seas, Air, Earth, Chaos, Dark, Light.

MASTIC *(Pistachia lentiscus)*

Also Called: Masticke, gum mastic.
Parts Used: Gum.
Planet: The Sun.
Element: Air.
Type of Ritual: Clairvoyance, manifestations. Add to incenses where a manifestation is desired. Burn also to gain psychic vision.
Dragons: Desert, Air, Wind, Light, Dark, Chaos.

MUGWORT *(Artemisia vulgaris)*

Also Called: Naughty man, old man, artemisia, witch herb, muggons, sailor's tobacco.
Parts Used: The herb.
Planet: Venus.
Element: Air, sometimes Earth.
Type of Ritual: Protection, clairvoyance. Rub fresh leaves on crystal balls to strengthen their powers. The odor is supposed to open the third eye. If used in sleep-pillows, it will give prophetic dreaming and increase your clairvoyant ability. Bunches of mugwort hung in the house repel negative entities.
Dragons: Light, Dark, Chaos, Guardian.

MYRRH *(Commiphoria myrrha)*
Also Called: Karan, mirra balsom odendron, gum myrrh.
Parts Used: Gum.
Planet: The Sun, sometimes Saturn or the Moon.
Element: Water.
Type of Ritual: Protection, purification, exorcism. The smoke is used to consecrate, purify, and bless objects. Often used with frankincense to raise the vibrations and drive away negative entities. Increases the power of any incense to which it is added.
Dragons: All dragons.

OAK *(Quercus robur* and *Q. alba)*
Also Called: Tanner's bark, white oak.
Parts Used: Leaves, wood acorns.
Planet: Sun, sometimes Jupiter.
Element: Fire.
Type of Ritual: Prosperity, protection, fertility, power. Acorns or small pieces of wood are carried for protection of all kinds, even against illness. Carrying an acorn also increases physical fertility. Plant an acorn in the dark of the Moon to increase your prosperity.
Dragons: Fire, Earth, Mountains, Desert, Volcanoes, Chaos, Guardian.

PARSLEY *(Carum petroselinum; Petroselinum sativum)*
Also Called: Garden parsley, rock parsley, persely.
Parts Used: Root, seeds, plant.
Planet: Mercury.
Element: Earth/Air.
Type of Ritual: Fertility, reincarnation, protection. Eating parsley is said to increase fertility, while its presence on your plate is for protection against illness. The ancient Romans associated it with death; use small amounts of the dried herb as incense when meditating on past lives.
Dragons: Light, Dark, Chaos.

PATCHOULI *(Pogostemon cablin* or *P. patchouli)*
Also Called: Pucha-pot.
Parts Used: The herb.

Planet: Sun, sometimes Mars and Saturn.

Element: Earth.

Type of Ritual: Passion, love, divination, protection, death. The dried herb improves with age. Usually used in the oil form. The Hindus burn it with their dead to protect them in their journey into the spiritual; use it in incense when meditating upon past lives, especially when venturing into areas of previous deaths. Add to love sachets and baths. Use a small amount in incenses when performing divinations.

Dragons: Fire, Volcanoes, Light, Dark, Chaos.

PEPPER *(Capsicum spp.)*

Also Called: Cayenne, red pepper, capsicum

Parts Used: Berries.

Planet: Mars.

Element: Fire.

Type of Ritual: Protection, exorcism. Burn only tiny amounts mixed with other herbs, because the smoke can be stinging to the eyes of humans and pets.

Dragons: Fire, Volcanoes, Chaos, Dark.

PINE *(Pinus spp.)*

Parts Used: Cone, nuts, needles.

Planet: Mars.

Element: Earth, sometimes Air.

Type of Ritual: Purification, fertility, energy, exorcism. An excellent purifier and energizer when mixed with equal parts of juniper and cedar. Use the needles in baths and to burn as exorcism incense. Carry the cones to improve fertility.

Dragons: Mountains, Air, Light, Dark, Seas, Wind, Storm, Volcanoes, Chaos.

RED SAUNDERS *(Pterocarpus santalinum)*

Also Called: Red sandalwood, ruby wood, red santal wood, sappan, lignum rubrum.

Parts Used: Wood.

Planet: Venus.

Element: Air.
Type of Ritual: Protection, purification, healing, love. A blood-red color and an interesting scent. Use to enhance and increase the power of incense.
Dragons: Air, Wind.

ROSE *(Rosa spp.)*
Parts Used: Flowers.
Planet: Venus.
Element: Water.
Type of Ritual: Love, clairvoyance. Use in bouquets, sachet bags, baths, and incenses to draw love. These will also reduce tension within a home. Drink a tea of rosebuds to improve clairvoyance.
Dragons: Water, Earth, Light, Dark, Guardian.

ROSEMARY *(Rosemarinus officinalis)*
Also Called: Dew of the sea, incensier, sea dew, rosemarie, guardrobe.
Parts Used: The needles.
Planet: The Sun, sometimes the Moon.
Element: Fire.
Type of Ritual: Purification, love, intellect, protection. Highly valued by ancient magicians, and used in religious incenses and magickal spells. Rosemary yields its oil only to wine, not water. The scent of rosemary oil often relieves headaches.
Dragons: Fire, Air, Dark, Desert.

SAGE *(Salvia officinalis varieties)*
Also Called: Garden sage, Red sage, White sage.
Parts Used: The herb.
Planet: Jupiter.
Element: Earth, sometimes Air.
Type of Ritual: Wisdom, prosperity. Because sage is a symbol of immortality and wisdom, it became an additive to food. Add the leaves to money sachets or incenses.
Dragons: Desert, Air, Earth, Light, Dark, Mountains.

SANDALWOOD *(Santalum album)*
Also Called: Santal, sandal, white sandalwood, yellow sandalwood.
Parts Used: Wood.
Planet: The Moon (white and red); sometimes Mercury (white) and
   Venus (red).
Element: Air, sometimes Water.
Type of Ritual: Protection, purification, healing. Combine sandalwood
   and rose oils or sandalwood powder and rose petals for an excellent
   all-purpose purification and anointing oil. See Red Saunders. Burn-
   ing pure sandalwood will purify an area, producing vibrations of
   protection and healing.
Dragons: All dragons.

SAVORY, SUMMER *(Satureia hortensis)*
Also Called: Bean herb.
Parts Used: The herb.
Planet: Venus.
Element: Earth/Air.
Type of Ritual: Intellect, creativity. Slightly peppery taste and smell. Eat it,
   wear it, or burn it.
Dragons: Air, Earth.

SQUILL *(Urginea scilla)*
Also Called: White squill, red squill, maritime squill.
Parts Used: Bulb.
Planet: Mars.
Element: Fire/Water.
Type of Ritual: Prosperity, success, psychic visions. Place pieces of squill
   in a jar with money to draw prosperity and success. Burn it with dit-
   tany of Crete for psychic visions.
Dragons: Air, Earth, Water, Light, Dark, Desert.

STORAX *(Liquidamber orientalis* or *L. styraciflua,* American species,
   also called sweet gum)
Parts Used: Wood, inner bark.
Planet: The Sun, sometimes Mercury and Saturn.
Element: Fire.

Type of Ritual: Purification, success. See Styrax oil. **Note:** The storax of the ancients is not *this* tree, but *Styrax officinale,* a close relative of benzoin. If you are fortunate enough to get styrax oil, add it to your incenses.
Dragons: Fire, Earth, Light, Dark, Desert.

THYME *(Thymus vulgaris,* garden thyme; *T. serpyllum,* wild thyme)
Also Called: Common thyme, mother of thyme.
Parts Used: The herb.
Planet: Venus.
Element: Air, sometimes Water.
Type of Ritual: Clairvoyance, purification. Burn in incense to purge magickal rooms of unwanted vibrations. Wild thyme, also called mother of thyme, creates a pure atmosphere wherever it grows; it is a favorite with dragons and fairies.
Dragons: Air, Water, Seas, Wind, Light, Dark.

VETIVER *(Vetiveria zizanioides)*
Also Called: Khus-Khus, vetivert, vertivert.
Parts Used: Root.
Planet: Venus.
Element: Earth/Air.
Type of Ritual: Love, protection, prosperity. Root smells like faded violets or sandalwood. Add to incense for exorcisms. Blend with other herbs in love sachets, baths, and incenses. Carry to attract luck and money.
Dragons: Air, Earth, Desert, Guardian.

VIOLET *(Viola tricolor* or *V. odorata)*
Also Called: Blue violet, Sweet violet.
Parts Used: Flowers.
Planet: Venus.
Element: Water.
Type of Ritual: Passion, sleep, protection. Associated with sunset and twilight. Mix with lavender for sachets that create passion. The scent is said to help with sleep. Grow the flowers in your garden to bring good luck.
Dragons: Water, Fire, Seas, Guardian.

YARROW *(Achillea millefolium)*
Also Called: Seven year's love, military herb, soldier's woundwort, milfoil, arrow root, ladies' mantle, wound wort, devil's bit, snake's grass.
Parts Used: Flowers.
Planet: Venus.
Element: Water.
Type of Ritual: Love, clairvoyance, exorcism. Hang bunches over the bed for long-lasting love. Burn as part of an incense to both cast out negative entities and increase clairvoyance.
Dragons: Water, Seas, Chaos.

YERBA BUENA *(Satureja douglasii)*
Parts Used: Leaves.
Planet: Saturn.
Element: Earth.
Type of Ritual: Hexing, binding, protection. Use in sachets and incenses.
Dragons: Earth, Dark, Chaos, Volcanoes.

YERBA MATÉ *(Ilex paraguayensis)*
Also Called: Paraguay herb, maté, Jesuit's tea, Brazil tea.
Parts Used: Leaves.
Planet: Saturn.
Element: Earth.
Type of Ritual: Cursing, binding, protection. A disagreeable odor. Scatter across the outside entrance of your house to repel unwanted visitors. Burn small amounts with other ingredients to bind people or entities.
Dragons: Volcanoes, Earth, Dark, Chaos.

YERBA SANTA *(Eriodictyon glutinosum, E. californicum)*
Also Called: Mountain balm, consumptive's weed, gum bush, bear's weed, tarweed.
Parts Used: Leaves.
Planet: Jupiter.
Element: Fire/Water.
Type of Ritual: Riches, honor, health. Use in baths for health. Carry the leaves to protect you, draw honor and good health.
Dragons: Water, Fire, Earth, Mountains, Desert.

2
Oils

Magickal oils work through vibrations and scent. The rate of vibration of an oil determines its usage in magick. Scents trigger various centers in the brain and bring them into dominance, in dragons as well as in humans. In dragon magick, as in some traditions of Wicca, oil is a symbol of the element of Fire. Other traditions use oil for the element of Air.

Since the magickal power of perfumes and oils lies in the scent, I believe that good synthetic substitutes can be just as powerful as the real thing. Please do not buy oils or essences which are made from animals, such as real civet or ambergris.

Oils are used to anoint candles before burning, poppets, herbal bags, and even the physical body when a magician wishes to add an extra concentration to a ritual. Even stick incense which has been saturated with a particular odor can add desired vibrations of a specific kind to the home in a very inconspicuous manner. Do not consume or drink essential oils!

Scott Cunningham, in *The Complete Book of Incense, Oils & Brews* (Llewellyn, 1989) gives a list of substitutions for various herbs and oils that may be difficult to find or too expensive to use.

ALLSPICE: Enhances the psychic powers and gives added determination and energy. A Mars oil.

AMBERGRIS: The artificial oil works great. Resonates with the highest spiritual energy and draws the purest type of love. An oil of Venus.

ANISE: Stimulates the psychic centers, thus aiding in clairvoyance and divination. An oil of Jupiter, sometimes Mercury, it also helps in love affairs.

APPLE BLOSSOM: A Venus oil worn to promote happiness and success. Anoint candles during love rituals. Expels negativity of emotions.

BALM OF GILEAD: A Saturn oil. Use small amounts in incense for protection and manifestations. Use on candles.

BAY LAUREL: A very powerful Sun oil used for protection, meditation, visions, divination, exorcism, purification, and power in general. The ancient Greek Delphic oracle inhaled the odors of bay to stimulate the psychic for divination.

BERGAMOT: Wear on the palm of each hand during protection and prosperity rituals. Anoint the inside of a purse or wallet. An oil of Jupiter.

BIRCH: An oil of Earth and the Moon, this oil makes new beginnings. Can also be burned or used on candles to protect a lover and smooth romantic difficulties.

CAMPHOR: Wear when breaking up a relationship and either of you find it hard to let go. Also said to strengthen psychic powers. An oil of the Moon.

CARNATION: A great energy builder, especially if recovering from illness.

CEDAR LEAF *(Thuja)* or **CEDAR WOOD:** A Jupiter oil used for peace, contentment, wealth, good fortune. Also drives away all evil and negativity.

CHERRY: Especially good against loneliness. As an oil of Venus it brings peace, harmony, happiness, relaxation, wealth, and good fortune.

CINNAMON: Gives personal protection when worn. Added to any incense, it increases its powers. A Sun oil, it is good for clairvoyance, healing, wealth, problem solving, protection.

CLOVE: A Sun oil good for driving away evil influences and disease.

CORIANDER: A Mars oil used to draw purely physical love.

CYPRESS: A Saturn oil used for blessing, consecration, and protection. Vibrates on a high plane. Helps to control the self-willed. The ancient Egyptians, Greeks, Romans, and Chinese knew its uses as a high spiritual oil that brought blessings.

FIR: Peace and contentment; a Jupiter oil. Aids contact with forest dragons.

FRANGIPANI: A Moon oil that is totally erotic. Use for physical love.

FRANKINCENSE: One of the most powerful and sacred of all oils. Use to anoint yourself and magickal tools, the altar, etc. An extremely strong purifier used in exorcism, purification, blessing, meditation, and visions. A Sun oil giving great psychic protection.

GINGER: A Sun oil, sometimes Mars, that attracts Earth-type dragons. Can attract the opposite sex.

HIGH JOHN THE CONQUEROR: A Saturn oil for prosperity. Brings good luck and helps to control troublesome neighbors.

HONEYSUCKLE: A Jupiter oil used in prosperity rituals. Also for stimulating the mind and creativity.

JASMINE: A purely spiritual oil of the Moon and Jupiter. Use for psychic protection, balance, peace, sleep, meditation, prayer, astral projection. Will ease childbirth, and attract and hold a lover of a high spiritual nature.

LAVENDER: An oil of Mercury and Jupiter, it is a good vibration for the home. Use for exorcism, purification, restful sleep, peace.

LEMON: A cleansing Mercury oil that prepares the mind and body for new endeavors.

LILY OF THE VALLEY: This brings the highest blessings. A Mercury oil used to soothe the nerves, bring peace to both the spiritual and emotional levels.

LOTUS: A powerful oil with high vibrations sacred to the Moon and magick. Wear for protection and guidance if astral travelling. Use for psychic protection, happiness, good health, fertility, good fortune, peace, harmony, blessings.

MINT: A magnetic scent for attracting money and good fortune. Use to increase business. Anoint wallets and purses. An oil of Venus, sometimes the Moon.

MUSK: Universal sex scent, attraction to both sexes. An Earth oil when used for sexual attraction, a Saturn oil when used as a divinatory aid dealing with past incarnations.

MYRRH: A very sacred oil ruled by Saturn. Use for powerful protection, exorcism, purification, meditation, prayer, healing. Often mixed with frankincense and other oils.

NUTMEG: A tiny amount on your third eye aids in meditation and psychic awareness. An oil of Jupiter, sometimes Mercury.

ORRIS ROOT: A Jupiter oil that strengthens determination and will power. Also aids concentration and creativity.

PATCHOULI: A magnetic erotic oil of the Sun, sometimes Mars and Saturn, but also used for a peaceful separation. Put some on your door to keep away unwanted visitors.

PINE: An oil of Mars and the Earth, this is purifying. Also good for exorcism and defense, healing and money.

ROSE: A most sacred and powerful oil of Venus. Promotes beauty, love, artistic creativity, health, peace, balance.

ROSEMARY: Use to exorcise and protect a new home by anointing the doors and window sills with this oil of the Sun, sometimes the Moon. Also gives psychic protection, good health, dispels fear.

SANDALWOOD: A very powerful, spiritual oil of Mercury, Venus, and the Moon to raise your vibrations. Excellent for self-anointing or use on ritual objects and the altar. Use for good health, meditation, visions, protection, open the doors to past incarnations.

STRAWBERRY: Helps in the acquisition of wealth and good fortune. A Jupiter oil.

STYRAX: This oil of Mercury, the Sun and Saturn vibrates on a high plane and is good for ritual anointings. This is the same as the herb storax.

TUBEROSE: Also known as Mistress of the Night. An Earth and Venus oil that is supposed to be an excellent aphrodisiac. A very physical type of oil.

VERVAIN: A very magickal oil of Venus and Mercury for protection, material good fortune, exorcism, purification, attraction, and love. It also stimulates the mind and intellectual creativity.

VIOLET: An oil of Venus good for breaking down barriers of indifference. Also use for protection, good health, wealth, good fortune, achieving peace in marital problems.

WISTERIA: A Moon oil, it is considered a bridge to the higher planes and unlocks the door to the spirit world. Very powerful in any kind of divination, illumination, astral projection, spirit journeys, or psychic work. Wear only when in complete serenity.

YLANG YLANG: Sometimes called the flower of flowers, it is an oil of the Earth, Venus, and the Moon. Although it can soothe problems in marriage, it is mainly to attract the opposite sex. Can also make you calmer and help in finding a job.

3
Stones

The actual type of stone is not as important as the color itself and how each individual stone feels to you personally. Colors vibrate at different rates, thereby traditionally regulating their magickal uses. But each stone, regardless of its color, gives off individualized vibrations that may or may not feel comfortable when combining with your own personal vibrations. This is why a knowledgeable and aware magician will handle several stones of one type before making a decision.

Stones do not have to be polished, as they have power in their natural state. Whether you pick up the stones in nature or purchase them, make certain that the vibrations feel good to you. Stones attract dragons of similar color vibration or ritual power. Also read the chapters on Dragons of the Elements, the Planets, and the Zodiac for more specific dragon use.

Stones of the appropriate colors are set about on the altar to help attract and hold the attention of the dragons upon which you call. Since circles of stones tend to concentrate and amplify energy raised within their boundaries, using stones set about a candle or even around the edges or at the four cardinal directions of a cast circle will intensify the magickal power the magician is creating for a manifestation.

The gem bowl, which should be a regular part of your dragon magick, is an excellent place to keep your collection of stones. If your feelings tell you that particular stones should be kept apart from the others, and this does happen on occasion, keep these special stones in another bowl or a separate box.

Choose your stones carefully, whether you buy them or pick them up in nature. Like all your magickal tools, the stones with which you work should be compatible with your personal vibrations. Take your time in selecting them. If you make a choice in a hurry, you may find that you have to discard the stone when you do take the time to sit silently with it.

Sometimes you will make a choice of a stone knowing it is not for you but puzzled as to why you feel an attraction. It is quite likely that you will feel led to gift that stone to someone else in the future. You may be the recipient of such a gift yourself. Magickal tools and aids always seem to end up where they belong.

Very few stones bought in a shop, at a rock show, or from an individual will not have to be cleansed of vibrations. Most of what you discover for yourself in nature will be acceptable. But even on occasion you will have to cleanse one of these. A quick and effective method of cleansing is to put the stones in a bowl in the sink. Turn on the water in a light stream so that the bowl fills, then gently overflows for a few minutes. Remove any flecks of dirt (if you have picked up the stones in nature). Dry them with a soft cloth, then set them on your altar overnight. On the night of the next Full Moon, set the stones in a window where they will be bathed in moonlight.

Crystal quartz can be cleansed in another way. (Don't use this method if the crystal is set in a mounting of any kind.) Choose a container large and deep enough to hold the crystals, allowing plenty of space between them. Put a thick layer of salt in the bottom of the container; set in the crystals so they do not touch. Pour salt over and around the crystals until they are completely covered.

Place the salt-filled bowl on your altar for at least two days. After this "soaking" time is over, remove the crystals, rinse them under cool running water, then dry with a soft cloth. On the next Full Moon, set them in a window to bathe in moonlight. Dispose of the salt. Since all negative vibrations and impurities will have gone into the salt, you certainly do not want to use it for anything else.

Many stones, such as crystal, can be programmed with specific vibrational energies, either deliberately or by being in contact with a person. If you choose to program a crystal, for instance, be sure that you separate it from all others and label its container as to its ritual purpose. If you fail to do this, you could use a crystal for a ritual that is not compatible or even in opposition to its programming.

Many of the correspondences of stones to the planets are given in the chapter "Dragons of the Planets." However, the planets referred to are the ancient seven. The outer planets, not listed, also have stone correspondences, although not as widely known. Wally Richardson and Lenora Huett *(Spiritual Value of Gem Stones,* DeVorrs, 1983) have assigned some stones for Neptune: aquamarine, azurite, coral, crystal quartz, diamond, moonstone, opal, spinel, and tourmaline. Those of Pluto are: amethyst, jade, kunzite, spinel, and zircon. A particular shade of the stone turquoise belongs to Uranus.

WHITE
Use for spiritual guidance, Moon magick, visions, divination, dreams.
   White is ruled by the Moon. Examples: diamond, pearl, white opal, white chalcedony, white quartz, beryl. In modern America people carry white stones to attract good luck and fortune.
Quartz comes in many colors and forms. Rock crystal, a widely known form of this stone, is discussed later in this chapter. Rocks with white quartz predominant in them would be in this class.
Diamonds have been used in spellworkings to increase physical strength. The diamond is not a love stone, but rather a gem of steadfastness and purification. The diamond is connected with Fire. What are

called Herkimer diamonds are really double-terminated quartz crystals and can be substituted for diamonds in magickal workings. Diamonds promote inner searching and seeking, a balancing of the inner forces of the magician.

The **pearl** is connected with Water, Spirit, and the Moon. Real pearls are expensive, way beyond my budget, but I have found that imitation pearls work with dragon magick.

White beryl, a stone of the Moon and Water, is a gem of energy, healing, and the psychic. Beryl spheres, known as *specularii,* were used by Irish scryers in about the fifth century. The British Museum has the famous Dr. Dee's beryl sphere on display.

The **white opal** is not entirely white, but has within it flashes of other colors. Its association with misfortune was started by the writer Sir Walter Scott. Developing psychic powers, working on past lives, astral traveling.

White chalcedony is useful for banishing fears and promoting calm. It also protects against psychic attack and negative magick. It can both absorb and repel energies.

RED

Use for energy, courage, defense, physical love and sexuality, strength, power. As the color of blood, red symbolizes birth, death, and rebirth. Red is ruled by Mars. Examples: garnet, ruby, red jasper, red agate, dark carnelian, fluorite, rhodochrosite, light rhodonite, chalcedony, beryl.

Garnets, particularly the deep purplish-red ones, are wonderful sources of extra energy. They are of Mars and Fire. At one period in history, the garnet was considered a protective gem, especially against demons.

As a Fire stone, the **ruby** promotes success in business and money projects, protection from all enemies and spirits, and an increase in energy during rituals.

Red jasper, a gem of Mars and Fire, is an excellent protective stone. It can defend the magician by returning negativity to the sender.

Red agate, also known as the blood agate, is a Fire stone. It promotes atmospheres of peace and calm.

Dark carnelian, a gem of the Sun and Fire, is worn to gain courage and self-confidence. It counteracts negative thoughts and defends you against others who are trying to read your mind.

Red fluorite helps you to get your thoughts in order and free yourself from emotional decisions and attachments that may be hindering you.

Rhodocrosite, although usually a pink color, can sometimes be found in a deeper shade nearing the red tints. It draws energy without stress.

Rhodonite comes in many tints and intensities of red. It helps to get rid of doubts, but also helps to shut down the psychic centers. This is particularly helpful if you feel you are being bombarded by the vibrations of others.

Chalcedony creates energy and success in lawsuits.

Beryl can strengthen the attraction between lovers or simply attract love.

PINK

Healing, true love, friendship, relaxation, calming, smooth difficulties, build self-love,* peace, happiness. Venus rules pink. Examples: rose quartz, agate, beryl, fluorite, spinel, rhodochrosite.

Rose quartz is a stone of Venus. It can be used to balance the energy flows through the chakras. In magick, it creates peace, happiness, and fidelity in friendships and relationships.

Pink agate, often banded with other colors, is basically a Water stone that vibrates to rituals on love and friendship.

Pink fluorite helps you to be analytical about relationships, something that is often needed to override the mental blindness caused by intense emotions.

Pink spinel can be used in magickal workings to increase physical energy.

Pink rhodochrosite has the same properties as pink spinel, but also is soothing to the emotions. It draws love.

YELLOW

Power and energy of the mind, creativity of the mental type, sudden changes, communication skills, heighten visualization, travel. Mercury rules yellow. Examples: amber, topaz, citrine, yellow jasper, sunstone (sometimes called goldstone), yellow diamond, fluorite.

---

*Self-love means liking yourself, not narcissism. If you want friends or a close relationship, you must first see yourself as you really are, make changes where you can, and like yourself.

Amber, a gem of the Sun, Fire, and Spirit, is really not a stone at all, but fossilized tree resin. The ancient Chinese said that the souls of tigers inhabited amber. It was a sacred substance among the Norse, Celts, Greeks, and a great many other cultures. Sometimes one will find a piece of amber containing insects or plants; unfortunately, these are quite expensive. When rubbed, amber becomes electrically charged and will attract pieces of paper. It is very effective against negative magick.

Topaz, a Sun and Fire stone, was at one time thought to make the wearer invisible. An all-purpose protective stone, topaz wards against negative magick, mental imbalance, depression, intrigue, anger, accidents, and disease, while drawing money at the same time.

Citrine, a form of yellow quartz, is a Sun and Fire stone. By itself, or with other stones, citrine enhances psychic awareness.

Yellow jasper, an opaque form of chalcedony, is a stone of Mercury and Air. It attracts good luck, especially in connection with use of mental abilities.

Sunstone is a Sun gem. True sunstone is expensive and rare; however, there is a type called Oregon sunstone that is quite useful in magick. It draws money that can be accumulated through ideas. It also strengthens visualization of prosperity.

Yellow diamond gives off vibrations of courage and victory and draws good luck.

Fluorite with a yellow tinge to it helps to eliminate anger and straighten out thoughts.

ORANGE

Changing luck, power, protection by control of a situation, illumination, personal power, building self-worth, attract luck and success. Orange is ruled by the Sun. Examples: carnelian, zircon (jacinth), jasper, orange sunstone.

Carnelian protects, grants eloquence, and can increase sexual energy. Orange carnelian is a stone of Mercury and Air. This shade of carnelian is excellent for procrastinators as it creates a desire to get going and do something.

Jacinth, also called zircon, as a stone of spiritual insight, helps with changing luck through spiritual influences. It also helps you to get control of your own personal situation.

Orange jasper is really a lighter shade of the red variety. It can be of either Mars or Mercury, Fire or Air. It helps with defensive magick that comes through the mind and spirit.

I have a beautiful piece of **goldstone** in a ring; this is orange-brown with gold flecks all through it. This color of goldstone, also called sunstone, would attract good luck through clear use of the mind and bursts of illumination.

BLUE

Healing, harmony, understanding, journeys or moves, peace, calm emotions, stopping nightmares, restful sleep, purification of the inner being. The color blue is by Neptune, according to Cunningham, and by Jupiter, according to others. Examples: lapis lazuli, labradorite, sapphire, azurite, fluorite, blue quartz, sodalite, chalcedony.

The Venus/Water stone **lapis lazuli** has been known since very ancient times. An expensive stone, it is very powerful. The journeys or moves it helps to create are those which will benefit you on all levels of your being. It is not a stone to be used lightly. The purposes of any ritual in which it is used will be raised to a higher, more spiritual vibration.

Labradorite is an iridescent blue stone sometimes mixed with magnetite or titanic ore; this gives it beautiful points of light on its polished surface. Blue and green colors move over the stone when it is turned in the light. It is a stone of Jupiter and gives harmony and healing.

Sapphire, a gem of the Moon and Water, has long been considered a very powerful, potent enhancer to magick, especially star sapphires.

Azurite is a beautiful deep blue stone that can be used for divination and healing. It increases psychic powers and prophetic dreaming. Its vibrations are especially easy for a beginner to handle. On a spiritual level, azurite cleanses and purifies, but not so deep as to be disturbing.

Blue fluorite can strengthen the power of other stones, also adding its calmness and clearing thinking to any situation.

Sodalite is a blue stone with white veins in it. It looks much like lapis lazuli without the gold flecks. Use it to help in meditation and to gain wisdom.

Blue quartz is a receptive stone, giving off vibrations of peace and tranquility.

GREEN
Growth, fertility, money, marriage, good health, grounding and balancing. Green is ruled by Venus. Examples: jade, malachite, amazonite, emerald, aventurine, nephrite, chrysoprase, tourmaline, olivine, fluorite, green quartz.

Jade comes in many colors, which can be used under their color-category. But green jade, especially the beautiful apple-green coloring, is particularly powerful for money and any type of growth in the field of business and success. It is a Venus/Water stone.

Malachite, a tranquil green-blue stone, has bands of various green and white hues through it. As a Venus/Earth gem, it guards and protects its owner in both love and business success. The magician must be very aware and very careful of her/his emotions when using malachite, as it will absorb both negative and positive energies.

Amazonite is a bluish green feldspar, a stone of Uranus and Earth, that helps when gambling. The term gambling could be applied to any new venture, whether it is business, relationships, schooling, or whatever.

Emeralds are one of the most expensive stones there is. As a Venus and Earth gem, the emerald is valuable in magick, so you may want to purchase a low-quality one; if this is too much for your budget, use a substitute stone. The emerald's power is through making others aware of your business, your talent, or your worth in a field. The emerald attracts mental wisdom and helps to correlate it with spiritual wisdom.

The Mercury and Air stone of **aventurine** is said to attract money through increasing your perception, creativity, and intelligence.

Nephrite is closely related to jade and is a lovely soft green color. This stone has been used around the world for magickal items. It was said that Tamerlane's burial monument was built of blocks of nephrite. As an Earth stone, it both draws and preserves wealth.

Chrysoprase is an apple-green translucent chalcedony and a Venus and Earth stone. It is considered a lucky stone which attracts success in any new ventures and better monetary conditions.

Tourmaline comes in a variety of colors other than green, but the green shades, of Venus and the Earth, attract money and business success and stimulate creativity. Tourmaline should be used with great caution, since its ability to energize can create emotional and mental havoc if the user is not properly balanced on all levels of being.

Olivine is a translucent green stone of volcanic origin. It can be found throughout the world. It attracts good luck, love, and money. It also protects from thieves.

Green quartz stimulates creativity, increases money, and generally attracts an easier life through good fortune.

BROWN

Amplifies all Earth magick and psychic abilities. Brown is ruled by the Earth. Examples: smoky quartz, zircon, topaz, jasper.

Smoky quartz is sometimes mistaken for certain shades of topaz. It is an excellent grounding stone, particularly valuable in overcoming depression and negative emotions.

Brown zircon, known as malacon, is also excellent for grounding and centering your emotions and your life. It is primarily useful in money and prosperity spells.

Topaz has many uses. It protects against negative magick, injury, illness, and plots against you. Topaz also helps to remove negative emotions that may arise within yourself, such as fear, depression, and anger. It draws money and prosperity from earthly pursuits.

Jasper in a brown shading is especially good for grounding after working intensely in ritual or the psychic. It helps you keep your feet on the ground if you tend to live too much in the spiritual or daydreams.

BLACK

General defense, binding, repel dark magick, cursing, reversing thought-forms and spells into positive power. Saturn rules the color black. Examples: jet, onyx, obsidian, hematite (silver-black), spinel.

Jet is really fossilized stone, black and glassy looking. Be very careful that you buy from a reputable dealer, because much that is labeled as jet is only glass. The ancient Greeks who worshipped the goddess Cybele wore jet. It is often considered a companion stone to amber and has its static electric properties. Jet increases psychic awareness but also protects against unwanted dreams and nightmares. This protection extends to traveling, especially in foreign countries or strange places.

Onyx gives protection when you must face adversaries in any kind of circumstances. This protection goes beyond physical confrontation to psychic attack, or even subconscious attack by others or your own subconscious programming. Small balls or flat "mirrors" of onyx can be used for divination; these are especially good for past-life work.

Obsidian is formed by volcanic action. The ancient Aztecs used flat mirrors of this substance for divination. It is a grounding and centering stone, protecting you against yourself by making you more balanced. It is also great for protection. Apache tears are really only small globes of obsidian.

Hematite is a fascinating silver-black color and is sometimes called "volcano spit." Hematite is valuable when working to stabilize the life and ground the emotions.

Black spinel is rather rare. It amplifies physical and mental energies during times of stress or crisis. Spinel also draws wealth.

PURPLE
Break bad luck, protection, success in long-range plans, higher spiritual growth. Jupiter and sometimes Neptune rule purple. Examples: amethyst, beryl, quartz, fluorite, spinel, garnet (very dark), dark rhodochrosite, rhodonite (reddish-purple with black lines), kunzite.

Amethyst ranges in color from a blue-green to a very deep purple. It enhances psychic abilities, calms, lifts the vibrations, protects, sharpens mental powers. Amethyst is also known for its healing energies and the ability to attract true love.

Beryl strengthens psychic awareness and helps in divinations of a spiritual nature.

Fluorite of this color reduces any emotional involvement you may have in a reading and enables you to make a clearer contact with other levels of being.

The very darkest, purple-shaded **garnets** are expensive, but also the most beautiful. They break bad luck and protect you by repelling negative energies.

It is very unusual to find a piece of deep, dark **rhodocrosite** for sale. The purplish-pink shade of this stone exudes peace and love of a high spiritual nature.

Very deep-colored **rhodonite** is useful as a centering stone for anyone involved in ritual and magick.

Kunzite is a very expensive stone. It helps a person to become more relaxed but also more disciplined. It appears to be Earth-grounded in vibration.

INDIGO or TURQUOISE

Discovering past lives or karmic problems, balancing out karma, new and unique ideas. This very dark blue or bluish-green color is ruled by Uranus. Examples: turquoise, amethyst, amazonite, aquamarine.

Turquoise, known as *thyites* to the ancient Greeks, is sacred to many Native Americans, especially in the Southwest and Mexico. Although it protects against many things, it also attracts wealth. It is considered a lucky stone. However, working with turquoise is one thing, wearing it another. Some people's vibrations do not mesh well with this stone, so check your feelings carefully before wearing it. Mellie Uyldert *(The Magic of Precious Stones,* Turnstone Press, 1981) says that the sky-blue shades belong to the Sun and Venus, the ice-blue to Saturn, and the green-blue to Uranus.

Blue-green **amethyst** is cheaper than the purple shades, but no less valuable in magickal workings. I have a small scarab of this color of amethyst; it is a powerful little stone when working with past life memories.

Amazonite is of particular value to those who take chances, especially gambling. To magicians, amazonite is an attractant of good luck and success.

The **aquamarine** was once sacred to all sea deities because of its blue-green color. However, I have a beautiful aquamarine that is a clear blue, the color of deep lake water. This stone can be used to purify the aura and soothe emotional problems. When traveling on or over water, it protects. Perhaps its most fascinating power is its ability to break through the conscious mind's fear programming and let the psychic through.

Additional Stones of Value

PYRITE

Also known as fool's gold. Money, prosperity, total success. Ruled by the Sun; especially attractive to the dragons of Light, Mountains, and the Earth.

One can use a flat surface of pyrite as a scrying mirror. Combined with other stones, it intensifies good luck.

MOONSTONE

Gaining occult power, rising above problems. Ruled by the Moon; attractive to all dragons.

I think of all stones, moonstones are my favorites. This is understandable since I was born on the Full Moon near Beltane, and the moonstone is obviously a Moon stone. Its protection powers are of the gentler kind, but very effective. It is good for enhancing the Moon's powers over gardening. Moonstone also strengthens divination abilities. The moonstone is a reflector stone, in that it reflects whatever emotions or vibrations are being given off by the user.

ROCK CRYSTAL

An amplifier of magickal power; psychic work. All dragons are drawn to crystal, but Earth dragons especially.

Crystal quartz has been used in magick and spiritual endeavors in a great many cultures around the world. Clear crystal was known as the star stone in early British cultures. It has been used for scrying, both in its pointed shape and when fashioned into spheres. Pieces hung on a silver chain make excellent pendulums. Chunks, spheres, or points of crystal act as amplifiers of magick when set about the circle. Crystal quartz can also be "programmed" or used as power-sinks of energy, so be very aware of what you are doing when working with this stone.

Crystal quartz are very powerful stones, emitting strong fields of energy. On one occasion, my grandson accidently erased a set of computer disks by leaving several large crystal points on a shelf directly underneath the disk storage boxes. I was fortunate that I had printed out the section of manuscript in question and did not have to try to reconstruct it from memory.

LODESTONE or MAGNET

Drawing-power; ability to attract what you want. Representative of stars and meteorites, which have always been associated with dragons. Genuine lodestone is a fascinating thing, but if you cannot find one, substitute a magnet. Many magicians do not like this substitution; however, I have found it to be satisfactory. Anything magnetic attracts. Lodestone sends out vibrations of attraction according to the type of magickal working you are doing.

EYE STONES

These are represented by hawk's eye, cat's eye, tiger's eye, etc. The pupil in a dragon's eye resembles a cat's eye with its vertical slit. The eye-shimmer of these stones is remarkably similar to those seen in dragon eyes. Any form of eye stone is valuable when working with dragons. Representative of all dragons in general, and the little guardian dragons in a gentler way.

According to Scott Cunningham, the name cat's eye applies to several kinds of stones, usually olive-green quartz. Chrysoberyl is another name for it. In ancient Asia it was a form of chrysoberyl. As with all eye stones, cat's eye has a shimmer down the center. It protects and increases wealth, gives protection and insight into problems or speculations, helps with healing on the emotional and mental planes.

Tiger's eye stone has a golden flash in it. It promotes energy, luck, and courage while helping with protection and the gaining of money. For those magicians who are well balanced and willing to truthfully see themselves as they are, tiger's eye is a great stone for focusing the power and vision of the mind and the inner eye.

HOLED STONES

Stones with a naturally formed hole in them are valuable as a symbol of the hole through time and space through which dragons move back and forth from their realm to ours.

Holed stones, or holey stones, have long been considered to be sacred and magickal. Their particular value to the magician who works with dragon magick is their protection while traveling with dragons and a center focus for returning.

STAUROLITE
These natural stones look like an X or an equal-armed cross and are also called faery crosses. These four arms represent a balance of the four elements known in magick. Protection, balance on all levels, money, good luck.
The staurolite is symbolic of the four elements with which the magician works. A balance of forces protects, something every magician must learn sooner or later. Staurolite also attracts wealth and good health.

FOSSIL STONES
There are a great many kinds of these; any stone having the fossilized remains of a plant or animal would fall within this category. Strangely enough, one of the old names used during the Middle Ages was "draconites." The British know them as snake stones. Protection, balancing with Earth energies, past lives, guide through other worlds.
Fossil stones, with their unique connection to the past, are valuable for working with past lives. There is a slightly different vibration of power in each one that makes them valuable when traversing other worlds or times.

CORAL
Coral is not really a stone, but the skeletal remains of a sea creature. However, it has a long history in magickal workings. It is best if it has not been worked (that is cut, polished, etc.) and comes to you without being harvested.
Coral is helpful because of its protective qualities. It guards against unwanted astral entities, negative magick, accidents, and acts of violence.

GEODE
A geode is a round, rough-looking rock which usually reveals a hollow center lined with crystals when split open. Sometimes intricate

mineral patterns are exposed instead. Either way, geodes are very beautiful and fascinating. Geodes which reveal a crystal-lined cave are excellent stones for magicians working dragon magick, as they resemble the dragon cave of initiation.

LAVA

The formation of lava rock is accomplished by the four elements working together. Although lava is of particular importance when working with dragons of Fire and volcanoes, it is also of interest to all types of dragons, as they all breathe destroying-creating fire.

PETRIFIED WOOD

Ancient trees which slowly had their fiber dissolved by water and replaced by minerals turned into petrified wood. It is actually fossilized wood. Defense, setting up barriers, exploring past lives.

METEORITE

Small meteors that fall from space. Protection, traveling from one plane of existence to another. Meteorites give off vibrations of protection, while also helping the magician to understand any destruction-creation experiences which she/he may be experiencing.

4
Candle Colors

The following list of colors is slightly different from the average lists in most books. But then no two lists on candle colors are ever alike. The colors in parenthesis are a further clarification of the shades. For dragon candle-burning magick, read the ritual called "Dragon Fire" in the chapter on Basic Rituals.

This list of colors can also be used to coordinate colors employed for other ritual purposes. You might decide to use special altar cloths to enhance magickal power, or a robe of a specific color to add to your personal vibrations. This choice of clothing color can extend to the normal, everyday clothes, especially if you find yourself needing to project a specific vibrational atmosphere. Keep to as true a shade of color as possible and avoid the indistinct blends until you become more experienced in the uses of color.

Red is one color to be treated with respect. Everyone is aware of the saying that a certain shade of red car is a ticket-catcher. If you are looking for companionship and attention, I would caution you to be very careful about projecting that vibration while wearing red. You will attract every good, bad, and ugly active libido in the area.

Purple is another color that can easily be overdone. It is a powerful spiritual color that can cross over the line into spiritual fanaticism and dogmatism unless the wearer is in complete control at all times. Even then the experienced magician knows to use purple only for short periods of time.

RED: Physical power, will power, strength, purely physical sex. Dragons of Fire, Mars, Aries, Leo (scarlet), Scorpio (deep), Guardian.

PINK: Love, affection, romance, spiritual awakening, healing of the spirit, togetherness. Dragons of Venus, Taurus, Libra (soft rose).

YELLOW: Intellect, imagination, power of the mind, creativity, confidence, gentle persuasion, action, attraction, concentration, inspiration, sudden changes. Dragons of Air, Leo, Sun, Mercury (pale), Guardian, Fire, Wind, Storm (dark).

ORANGE: Encouragement, adaptability, stimulation, attraction, sudden changes, control, power, to draw good things, change luck. Dragons of Mercury, Leo, Virgo (rust-orange), Aquarius (dark), Guardian, Fire.

GREEN: Abundance, fertility, good fortune, generosity, money, wealth, success, renewal, marriage, balance. Dragons of Venus (pale), Forest, Mountain, Earth, Taurus, Pisces (sea-green), Guardian.

BLUE: Truth, inspiration, wisdom, occult power, protection, understanding, good health, happiness, peace, fidelity, harmony in the home, patience. Dragons of Water, Jupiter, Venus (light), Lakes, Seas, Pisces (dark), Venus (pale), Taurus, Cancer (dark), Virgo (navy), Libra (light or blue-green), Sagittarius (deep), Moon, Aquarius (iridescent), Guardian, Wind, Storm (dark).

PURPLE: Success, idealism, higher psychic ability, wisdom, progress, protection, honors, spirit contact, break bad luck cycle, drive away evil, divination. Dragons of Sagittarius, Jupiter, Moon (lavender), Mercury (violet), Chaos (dark).

BROWN: Attract money and financial success. Concentration, balance, ESP, intuition, study. Dragons of Earth, Mountains, Forest, Virgo, Aquarius (rust) Guardian.

BLACK: Discord, protection from retribution, power, will power, strength, revenge, reversing, uncrossing, binding negative forces, protection, releasing, repel dark magick and negative thoughtforms. Dragons of Saturn, Earth, Dark Spirit, Scorpio, Chaos, Guardian.

WHITE: Purity, spirituality and higher attainments of life, truth, sincerity, power of a higher nature, wholeness. Dragons of Light Spirit, Cancer, Moon, Guardian.

MAGENTA: Very high vibrational frequency that tends to work *fast,* so usually burned with other candles. Quick changes, spiritual healing, exorcism. Dragons of Scorpio, Taurus, Fire, Chaos (dark).

INDIGO or **TURQUOISE:** Meditation, neutralize another's magick; stop gossip, lies or undesirable competition; balance out of karma. Dragons of Venus, Saturn, Taurus, Libra, Aquarius, Guardian, Seas.

GOLD or **VERY CLEAR LIGHT YELLOW:** Great fortune, intuition, understanding, divination, fast luck, financial benefits, attracts higher influences. Dragons of Sun, Leo, Guardian.

SILVER or **VERY CLEAR LIGHT GRAY:** Removes negative powers; victory, stability, meditation, develop psychic abilities. Dragons of Moon, Cancer, Virgo (gray), Guardian, Chaos (pewter, iron).

5
𝔇ragon 𝔖cript

The accompanying chart of Dragon Script or alphabet was taught to me by Fionna, a woman gone for many years from this Earth plane. I have no idea where or with whom it originated, for she never told me.

Fionna is a spiritual entity who appeared, in dreams, in meditations, and during trance, very early in my seeking for spiritual direction along the Pagan path. She says she is of Irish-Celtic origin but has never specified a time period during which she lived. Information from her, both of a magickal and personal nature, has proved to be accurate and helpful on a great many occasions. It was through Fionna and her companions that I first learned to contact dragons as co-magicians during rituals. Before that, I had experience with dragons as friends, but was unaware that they would help in magick. The dragons' not sharing this information is typical; dragons do not volunteer help or information until they have spent considerable time acquainting themselves with a magician. This makes perfect sense when one realizes how unreliable and greedy the average human is.

Dragon Script appears to be similar in many ways to the angelic alphabet obtained by Dr. John Dee, the Theban used by the Wiccan, the Runic, the Ogham, and several other uncommon magickal methods of writing. Dragons are acquainted with all these alphabets and will, depending upon the occasion and temperament of the individual dragon, respond to their use, as they do to ordinary, everyday alphabets in common use around the world. But, in my experiences, dragons seem to pay more attention to something written in this script than they do to anything written in another alphabet.

Dragon Script can be used for writing on tools, candles, or other ritual and spell objects. It is also used when writing out requests to specific dragons. Use of this magickal alphabet, or any magickal alphabet, increases the power placed into an object by the magician because of the concentration needed to write it out. One of the goals of every magician is to fill with as much power as possible all his ritual tools, spellworking objects, etc.

A	B	C, K	D

E	F	G	H

I, J	L	M	N

O, Q	P	R	S

T	U, V	W	X

Y	Z	END OF SENTENCE

Dragon Script

Bibliography

Aima. *Perfume Oils, Candles, Seals & Incense.* Los Angeles: Foibles Publications, 1981.

Barrett, Francis. *The Magus.* London, 1801. Reprint. Secaucus, NJ: Citadel Press, 1980.

Blavatsky, H. P. *Isis Unveiled.* New York, 1877. Reprint. Pasadena, CA: Theosophical University Press, 1976.

Blavatsky, H. P. *The Secret Doctrine.* New York, 1888. Reprint. Wheaton, IL: Theosophical Publishing House, 1978.

Branston, Brian. *Gods & Heroes from Viking Mythology.* New York: Schocken Books, 1982.

Buckland, Raymond. *Anatomy of the Occult.* New York: Samuel Weiser, 1977.

Budge, E. A. Wallis. *Amulets & Superstitions.* London, 1930. Reprint. New York: Dover Publications, 1978.

Byfield, Barbara Ninde. *The Glass Harmonica.* UK: Collier-Macmillan Ltd., 1967.

Campbell, Joseph. *Masks of God,* vol. 2 & 3. New York: Viking Press, 1962 and 1964. Reprint. Penguin Books, 1976.

Campbell, Joseph. *The Power of Myth*. New York: Doubleday, 1988.

Cavendish, Richard. *The Black Arts*. New York: G. P. Putnam's Sons, 1967.

Cavendish, Richard, ed. *Mythology: An Illustrated Encyclopedia*. New York: Rizzoli, 1980.

Cirlot, J. E. *A Dictionary of Symbols*. 2nd ed. 1971. Reprint. New York: New York: Philosophical Library, 1978.

Corrigan, Ian. *The Book of the Dragon: A New Grimoire*. n.p., 1982.

Crossley-Holland, Kevin, ed. *Folk-Tales of the British Isles*. New York: Pantheon, 1985.

Cunningham, Scott. *The Complete Book of Incense, Oils & Brews*. St. Paul, MN: Llewellyn Publications, 1989.

Cunningham, Scott. *Cunningham's Encyclopedia of Crystal, Gem & Metal Magic*. St. Paul, MN: Llewellyn Publications, 1988.

Cunningham, Scott. *Cunningham's Encyclopedia of Magical Herbs*. St. Paul, MN: Llewellyn Publications, 1985.

Cunningham, Scott. *Magical Aromatherapy*. St. Paul, MN: Llewellyn Publications, 1989.

Cunningham, Scott. *Magical Herbalism*. St. Paul, MN: Llewellyn Publications, 1983.

De A'Morelli, Richard and Sharana Reavis. *The Book of Magickal & Occult Rites & Ceremonies*. West Nyack, NY: Parker Publishing, 1980.

Dennys, Rodney. *The Heraldic Imagination*. New York: Clarkson N. Potter, 1975.

Dickinson, Peter. *The Flight of Dragons*. New York: Harper & Row, 1979.

Evans, Ivor H., ed. *Brewer's Dictionary of Phrase & Fable.* New York: Harper & Row, 1981.

Fox-Davies, A. C. *A Complete Guide to Heraldry.* New York: Bonanza Books, 1978.

Gayley, Charles Mills. *The Classic Myth in English Literature & in Art.* New York: Ginn & Co., 1939.

George, Llewellyn. *A to Z Horoscope Maker & Delineator.* 1910. Reprint. St. Paul, MN: Llewellyn Publications, 1974.

Goodavage, Joseph. *Write Your Own Horoscope.* New York: New American Library, 1968.

Gray, William G. *Inner Traditions of Magic.* 1970. Reprint. York Beach, ME: Samuel Weiser, 1984.

Grieve, M. *A Modern Herbal,* 2 vols. New York: Dover Publications, 1971.

Grimal, Pierre, ed. *Larousse Encyclopedia of Mythology.* London, 1959. Reprint. New York: Hamlyn, 1978.

Hall, Manly P. *The Secret Teachings of All Ages.* San Francisco, 1928. Reprint. Los Angeles: Philosophical Research Society, 1977.

Healki, Thomas. *Creative Ritual.* York Beach, ME: Samuel Weiser, 1986.

Herzberg, Max J. *Myths & Their Meaning.* New York: Allyn & Bacon, 1928.

Hogarth, Peter. *Dragons.* New York: Viking Press, 1979.

Hoult, Janet. *Dragons: Their History & Symbolism.* UK: Gothic Image, 1990.

Huxley, Francis. *The Dragon: Nature of Spirit, Spirit of Nature.* UK: Thames & Hudson, 1979.

Jung, C. G. *The Archetypes and the Collective Unconscious.* trans. R. F. C. Hull. 2nd ed. 1968. 9:1 of *The Collected Works of C. G. Jung.* Bollingen Series XX. Princeton, NJ: Princeton University Press, 1990.

Knight, Gareth. *The Secret Tradition in Arthurian Legend.* UK: Aquarian Press, 1983.

Leek, Sybil. *How to Be Your Own Astrologer.* New York: Cowles Book Co., 1970.

Lum, Peter. *Fabulous Beasts.* New York: Pantheon Books, 1951.

Lust, John. *The Herb Book.* New York: Bantam, 1974.

MacKenzie, Donald G. *German Myths & Legends. (Teutonic Myths and Legends,* n.p., n.d.) New York: Avenel, 1985.

Norton, Andre. *Dragon Magic.* New York: Ace Books, 1972.

Page, Michael & Robert Ingpen. *Encyclopedia of Things That Never Were.* New York: Viking Penguin, 1987.

Richardson, Wally & Lenora Huett. *Spiritual Value of Gem Stones.* Marina del Rey, CA: DeVorss & Co., 1983.

Serraillier, Ian. *Beowulf the Warrior.* New York: Scholastic Book Services, 1970.

Sjoo, Monica & Barbara Mor. *The Great Cosmic Mother: Rediscovering the Religion of the Earth.* San Francisco: Harper & Row, 1987.

Talbott, David N. *The Saturn Myth.* New York: Doubleday, 1980.

Taylor, F. Sherwood. *The Alchemists.* New York: Barnes & Noble, 1992.

Tolkien, J. R. R. *The Hobbit, or There and Back Again.* 1937. Rev. ed. Boston: Houghton Mifflin Co., 1966.

Tyl, Noel. *The Principles & Practice of Astrology,* vol. 1 & 4. St. Paul, MN: Llewellyn Publications, 1974.

Uyldert, Mellie. *The Magic of Precious Stones.* UK: Turnstone Press Ltd., 1981.

Walker, Barbara. *The Woman's Dictionary of Symbols & Sacred Objects.* San Francisco: Harper & Row, 1988.

White, T. H. *The Book of Beasts.* New York: G.P. Putnam's Sons, 1954. Reprint. New York: Dover Publications, 1984.

Wright, Elbee. *Book of Legendary Spells.* Minneapolis: Marlar Publishing, 1974.

Index

THE 21 LESSONS OF MERLYN
A Study in Druid Magic & Lore
Douglas Monroe

For those with an inner drive to touch genuine Druidism—or who feel that the lore of King Arthur touches them personally—*The 21 Lessons of Merlyn* will come as an engrossing adventure and psychological journey into history and magic. This is a complete introductory course in Celtic Druidism, packaged within the framework of 21 authentic and expanded folk story/ lessons that read like a novel. These lessons, set in late Celtic Britain A.D. 500, depict the training and initiation of the real King Arthur at the hands of the real Merlyn-the-Druid: one of the last great champions of Paganism within the dawning age of Christianity. As you follow the boy Arthur's apprenticeship from his first encounter with Merlyn in the woods, you can study your own program of Druid apprentiship with the detailed practical ritual applications that follow each story. The 21 folk tales were collected by the author in Britain and Wales during a ten-year period; the Druidic teachings are based on the actual, never-before-published 16th-century manuscript entitled *The Book of Pheryllt*.

0-87542-496-1, 420 pp., 6 x 9, illus., photos, softcover   **$12.95**

ANCIENT MAGICKS FOR A NEW AGE
Rituals from the Merlin Temple,
the Magick of the Dragon Kings
Alan Richardson and Geoff Hughes

With two sets of personal magickal diaries, this book details the work of magicians from two different eras. In it, you can learn what a particular magician is experiencing in this day and age, how to follow a similar path of your own, and discover correlations to the workings of traditional adepti from almost half a century ago.

The first set of diaries are from Christine Hartley and show the magick performed within the Merlin Temple of the Stella Matutina, an offshoot of the Hermetic Order of the Golden Dawn, in the years 1940-42. The second set are from Geoff Hughes and detail his magickal work during 1984-86. Although he was not at that time a member of any formal group, the magick he practiced was under the same aegis as Hartley's. The third section of this book, written by Hughes, shows how you can become your own Priest or Priestess and make contact with Merlin.

The magick of Christine Hartley and Geoff Hughes are like the poles of some hidden battery that lies beneath the Earth and beneath the years. There is a current flowing between them, and the energy is there for you to tap.

0-87542-671-9, 320 pp., 6 x 9, illus., softcover   **$12.95**

MAIDEN, MOTHER, CRONE
The Myth and Reality of the Triple Goddess
D.J. Conway

The Triple Goddess is with every one of us each day of our lives. In our inner journeys toward spiritual evolution, each woman and man goes through the stages of Maiden (infant to puberty), Mother (adult and parent) and Crone (aging elder). *Maiden, Mother, Crone* is a guide to the myths and interpretations of the Great Goddess archetype and her three faces, so that we may better understand and more peacefully accept the cycle of birth and death.

Learning to interpret the symbolic language of the myths is important to spiritual growth, for the symbols are part of the map that guides each of us to the Divine Center. Through learning the true meaning of the ancient symbols, through facing the cycles of life, and by following the meditations and simple rituals provided in this book, women and men alike can translate these ancient teachings into personal revelations.

Not all goddesses can be conveniently divided into the clear aspects of Maiden, Mother and Crone. This book covers these goddesses as well, including the Fates, the Muses, Valkyries and others.

0-87542-171-7, 240 pp., 6 x 9, softcover $12.95

MAGICK OF THE GODS & GODDESSES
World Myth, Magic & Religion
D.J. Conway

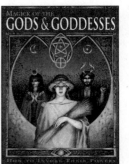

Magick of the Gods & Goddesses is a handy, comprehensive reference guide to the myths and deities from ancient religions around the world. Now you can easily find the information you need to develop your own rituals and worship using the Gods/Goddesses with which you resonate most strongly. More than just a mythological dictionary, *Magick of the Gods & Goddesses* explains the magickal aspects of each deity and explores such practices as Witchcraft, Ceremonial Magick, Shamanism and the Qabala. It also discusses the importance of ritual and magick, and what makes magick work.

Most people are too vague in appealing for help from the Cosmic Beings—they either end up contacting the wrong energy source, or they are unable to make any contact at all, and their petitions go unanswered. In order to touch the power of the universe, we must re-educate ourselves about the Ancient Ones. The ancient pools of energy created and fed by centuries of belief and worship in the deities still exist. Today these energies can bring peace of mind, spiritual illumination and contentment. On a very earthy level, they can produce love, good health, money, protection, and success.

0-56718-179-1, 448 pp., 7 x 10, 300 illus., softcover $17.95

CELTIC MAGIC
D. J. Conway

Many people, not all of Irish descent, have a great interest in the ancient Celts and the Celtic pantheon, and *Celtic Magic* is the map they need for exploring this ancient and fascinating magical culture.

Celtic Magic is for the reader who is either a beginner or intermediate in the field of magic. It provides an extensive "how-to" of practical spell-working. There are many books on the market dealing with the Celts and their beliefs, but none guide the reader to a practical application of magical knowledge for use in everyday life. There is also an in-depth discussion of Celtic deities and the Celtic way of life and worship, so that an intermediate practitioner can expand upon the spell-work to build a series of magical rituals. Presented in an easy-to-understand format, *Celtic Magic* is for anyone searching for new spells that can be worked immediately, without elaborate or rare materials, and with minimal time and preparation.

0-87542-136-9, 240 pp., mass market, illus. $4.99

NORSE MAGIC
D. J. Conway

The Norse: adventurous Viking wanderers, daring warriors, worshippers of the Aesir and the Vanir. Like the Celtic tribes, the Northmen had strong ties with the Earth and Elements, the Gods and the "little people."

Norse Magic is an active magic, only for participants, not bystanders. It is a magic of pride in oneself and the courage to face whatever comes. It interests those who believe in shaping their own future, those who believe that practicing spellwork is preferable to sitting around passively waiting for changes to come.

The book leads the beginner step by step through the spells. The in-depth discussion of Norse deities and the Norse way of life and worship set the intermediate student on the path to developing his or her own active rituals. *Norse Magic* is a compelling and easy-to-read introduction to the Norse religion and Teutonic mythology. The magical techniques given are refreshingly direct and simple, with a strong feminine and goddess orientation.

0-87542-137-7, 240 pp., mass market, illus. $4.99

CUNNINGHAM'S ENCYCLOPEDIA OF CRYSTAL, GEM & METAL MAGIC
Scott Cunningham

Here you will find the most complete information anywhere on the magical qualities of more than 100 crystals and gemstones as well as several metals. The information for each crystal, gem or metal includes: its related energy, planetary rulership, magical element, deities, Tarot Card, and the magical powers that each is believed to possess. Also included is a complete description of their uses for magical purposes. This is the classic on the subject.

0-87542-126-1, 240 pp., 6 x 9, illus., color plates, softcover   **$14.95**

CUNNINGHAM'S ENCYCLOPEDIA OF MAGICAL HERBS
Scott Cunningham

This is the most comprehensive source of herbal data for magical uses ever printed! Almost every one of the over 400 herbs are illustrated, making this a great source for herb identification. For each herb you will also find: magical properties, planetary rulerships, genders, associated deities, folk and Latin names and much more. To make this book even easier to use, it contains a folk name cross reference, and all of the herbs are fully indexed. There is also a large annotated bibliography, and a list of mail order suppliers so you can find the books and herbs you need. Like all of Cunningham's books, this one does not require you to use complicated rituals or expensive magical paraphernalia. Instead, it shares with you the intrinsic powers of the herbs. Thus, you will be able to discover which herbs, by their very nature, can be used for luck, love, success, money, divination, astral projection, safety, psychic self-defense and much more. Besides being interesting and educational it is also fun, and fully illustrated with unusual woodcuts from old herbals. This book has rapidly become the classic in its field. It enhances books such as 777 and is a must for all Wiccans.

0-87542-122-9, 336 pp., 6 x 9, illus., softcover   **$14.95**

THE ONCE UNKNOWN FAMILIAR
Shamanic Paths to Unleash Your Animal Powers
Timothy Roderick

Discover the magical animal of power residing within you! Animal "Familiars" are more than just the friendly animals kept by witches—the animal spirit is an extension of the unconscious mind, which reveals its power to those who seek its help. By using the detailed rituals, meditations, exercises and journaling space provided within this workbook, you will tap into the long-forgotten Northern European heritage of the "Familiar Self," and invoke the untamed, transformative power of these magical beasts.

This book focuses on traditional Northern European shamanic means of raising power—including drumming, dancing and construction of animal "fetiches"—and provides a grimoire of charms, incantations and spells anyone can work with a physical animal presence to enhance love, money, success, peace and more.

This is the first how-to book devoted exclusively to working with physical and spiritual Familiars as an aid to magic. Get in touch with your personal animal power, and connect with the magical forces of nature to effect positive change in your life and the lives of those around you.

0-87542-439-2, 240 pp., 6 x 9, softcover $10.00

ENCHANTMENT OF THE FAERIE REALM
Communicate with Nature Spirits & Elementals
Ted Andrews

Nothing fires the imagination more than the idea of faeries and elves. Folklore research reveals that people from all over the world believe in rare creatures and magickal realms. Unfortunately, in our search for the modern life we have grown insensitive to the nuances of nature. Yet those ancient realms do still exist, though the doorways to them are more obscure. Now, for the first time, here is a book with practical, in-depth methods for recognizing, contacting and working with the faerie world.

Enchantment of the Faerie Realm will help you to remember and realize that faeries and elves still dance in nature and in your heart. With just a little patience, persistence and instruction, you will learn how to recognize the presence of faeries, nature spirits, devas, elves and elementals. You will learn which you can connect with most easily. You will discover the best times and places for faerie approach. And you will develop a new respect and perception of the natural world. By opening to the hidden realms of life and their resources, you open your innate ability to work with energy and life at all levels.

0-87542-002-8, 240 pp., 6 x 9, illus., softcover $10.00

FAERY WICCA
BOOK ONE
Theory & Magick • A Book of Shadows & Lights
Kisma K. Stepanich

Many books have been written on Wicca, but never until now has there been a book on the tradition of Irish Faery Wicca. If you have been drawn to the kingdom of Faery and want to gain a comprehensive understanding of this old folk faith, *Faery Wicca* offers you a very thorough apprenticeship in the beliefs, history and practice of this rich and fulfilling tradition.

First, you'll explore the Irish history of Faery Wicca, its esoteric beliefs and its survival and evolution into its modern form; the Celtic pantheon; the Celtic division of the year; and the fairies of the Tuatha De Danann and their descendants. Each enlightening and informative lesson ends with a journal exercise and list of suggested readings.

The second part of *Faery Wicca* describes in detail magickal applications of the basic material presented in the first half: Faery Wicca ceremonies and rituals; utilizing magickal Faery tools, symbols and alphabets; creating sacred space; contacting and working with Faery allies; and guided visualizations and exercises suitable for beginners.

This fascinating guide will give you a firm foundation in the Faery Wicca tradition, which the upcoming *Faery Wicca, Book Two: The Shamanic Practices of Herbcraft, Spellcraft and Divination* will build upon.

1–56718–694–7, 320 pp., 7 x 10, illus., softcover$19.95

ANIMAL-SPEAK
The Spiritual & Magical Powers of Creatures Great & Small
Ted Andrews

The animal world has much to teach us. Some are experts at survival and adaptation, some never get cancer, some embody strength and courage while others exude playfulness. Animals remind us of the potential we can unfold, but before we can learn from them, we must first be able to speak with them.

Now, for perhaps the first time ever, myth and fact are combined in a manner that will teach you how to speak and understand the language of the animals in your life. *Animal-Speak* helps you meet and work with animals as totems and spirits—by learning the language of their behaviors within the physical world. It provides techniques for reading signs and omens in nature so you can open to higher perceptions and even prophecy. It reveals the many hidden, mythical and realistic roles of 45 animals, 60 birds, 8 insects and 6 reptiles.

0–87542–028–1, 400 pp., 7 x 10, illus., photos, softcover$17.95

MYTHIC ASTROLOGY
Archetypal Powers in the Horoscope
Ariel Guttman & Kenneth Johnson

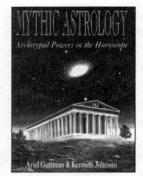

Here is an entirely new dimension of self-discovery based on understanding the mythic archetypes represented in the astrological birth chart. Myth has always been closely linked with astrology; all our planets are named for the Graeco-Roman deities and derive their interpretative meanings from them. To richly experience the myths which lie at the heart of astrology is to gain a deeper and more spiritual perspective on the art of astrology and on life itself.

Mythic Astrology is unique because it allows the reader to explore the connection between astrology and the spirituality of myth in depth, without the necessity of a background in astrology, anthropology or the classics. This book is an important contribution to the continuing study of mythology as a form of New Age spirituality and is also a reference work of enduring value. Students of mythology, the Goddess, art, history, Jungian psychological symbolism and literature—as well as lovers of astrology—will all enjoy the text and numerous illustrations.

0-87542-248-9, 382 pp., 7 x 10, 100 illus., softcover $17.95

MAGICAL AROMATHERAPY
The Power of Scent
Scott Cunningham

Scent magic has a rich, colorful history. Today, in the shadow of the next century, there is much we can learn from the simple plants that grace our planet. Most have been used for countless centuries. The energies still vibrate within their aromas.

Scott Cunningham has now combined the current knowledge of the physiological and psychological effects of natural fragrances with the ancient art of magical perfumery. In writing this book, he drew on extensive experimentation and observation, research into 4,000 years of written records, and the wisdom of respected aromatherapy practitioners. *Magical Aromatherapy* contains a wealth of practical tables of aromas of the seasons, days of the week, the planets, and zodiac; use of essential oils with crystals; synthetic and genuine oils and hazardous essential oils. It also contains a handy appendix of aromatherapy organizations and distributors of essential oils and dried plant products.

0-87542-129-6, 224 pp., mass market, illus. $3.95

THE COMPLETE BOOK OF INCENSE,
OILS AND BREWS
Scott Cunningham

For centuries the composition of incenses, the blending of oils, and the mixing of herbs have been used by people to create positive changes in their lives. With this book, the curtains of secrecy have been drawn back, providing you with practical, easy-to-understand information that will allow you to practice these methods of magical cookery.

Scott Cunningham, world-famous expert on magical herbalism, first published *The Magic of Incense, Oils and Brews* in 1986. *The Complete Book of Incense, Oils and Brews* is a revised and expanded version of that book. Scott took readers' suggestions from the first edition and added more than 100 new formulas. Every page has been clarified and rewritten, and new chapters have been added.

There is no special, costly equipment to buy, and ingredients are usually easy to find. The book includes detailed information on a wide variety of herbs, sources for purchasing ingredients, substitutions for hard-to-find herbs, a glossary, and a chapter on creating your own magical recipes.

0-87542-128-8, 288 pp., 6 x 9, illus., softcover $14.95

MAGICAL HERBALISM
The Secret Craft of the Wise
Scott Cunningham

Certain plants are prized for the special range of energies—the vibrations, or powers—they possess. *Magical Herbalism* unites the powers of plants and man to produce, and direct, change in accord with human will and desire.

This is the Magic of amulets and charms, sachets and herbal pillows, incenses and scented oils, simples and infusions and anointments. It's Magic as old as our knowledge of plants, an art that anyone can learn and practice, and once again enjoy as we look to the Earth to rediscover our roots and make inner connections with the world of Nature.

This is the Magic of Enchantment . . . of word and gesture to shape the images of mind and channel the energies of the herbs. It is a Magic for everyone—for the herbs are easily and readily obtained, the tools are familiar or easily made, and the technology that of home and garden. This book includes step-by-step guidance to the preparation of herbs and to their compounding in incense and oils, sachets and amulets, simples and infusions, with simple rituals and spells for every purpose.

0-87542-120-2, 260 pp., 5¼ x 8, illus., softcover $9.95

THE NEW A TO Z HOROSCOPE MAKER AND DELINEATOR
Llewellyn George

A textbook … encyclopedia … self-study course … and extensive astrological dictionary all in one! More American astrologers have learned their craft from *The New A to Z Horoscope and Delineator* than any other astrology book.

First published in 1910, it is in every sense a complete course in astrology, giving beginners ALL the basic techniques and concepts they need to get off on the right foot. Plus it offers the more advanced astrologer an excellent dictionary and reference work for calculating and analyzing transits, progression, rectifications, and creating locality charts. This new edition has been revised to met the needs of the modern audience.

0-87542-264-0, 592 pp., 6 x 9, softcover $14.95

ARCHETYPES OF THE ZODIAC
Kathleen Burt

The horoscope is probably the most unique tool for personal growth you can ever have. This book will help you understand how the energies in your horoscope manifest. Once you are aware of how your chart operates on an instinctual level, you can work consciously with it to remove obstacles to your growth.

The technique offered in this book is based upon the incorporation of the esoteric rulers of the signs and the integration of their polar opposites. This technique has been very successful in helping the client or reader modify existing negative energies in a horoscope so as to improve the quality of his or her life and the understanding of his or her psyche. There is special focus in this huge comprehensive volume on the myths for each sign. Some signs may have as many as four different myths coming from all parts of the world. All are discussed by the author. There is also emphasis on the Jungian Archetypes involved with each sign.

This book has a depth surprising to the readers of popular astrology books. It has a clarity of expression seldom found in books of the esoteric tradition. It is very easy to understand, even if you know nothing of Jungian philosophy or of mythology. It is intriguing, exciting and very helpful for all levels of astrologers.

0-87542-088-5, 576 pp., 6 x 9, illus., softcover $14.95

SPELL CRAFTS
Creating Magical Objects
Scott Cunningham & David Harrington

Since early times, crafts have been intimately linked with spirituality. When a woman carefully shaped a water jar from the clay she'd gathered from a river bank, she was performing a spiritual practice. When crafts were used to create objects intended for ritual or that symbolized the Divine, the connection between the craftsperson and divinity grew more intense. Today, handcrafts can still be more than a pastime—they can be rites of power and honor; a religious ritual. After all, hands were our first magical tools.

Spell Crafts is a modern guide to creating physical objects for the attainment of specific magical goals. It is far different from magic books that explain how to use purchased magical tools. You will learn how to fashion spell brooms, weave wheat, dip candles, sculpt clay, mix herbs, bead sacred symbols and much more, for a variety of purposes. Whatever your craft, you will experience the natural process of moving energy from within yourself (or within natural objects) to create positive change.

0-87542-185-7, 224 pp., 5¼ x 8, illus., photos $10.00

THE LLEWELLYN PRACTICAL GUIDE TO ASTRAL PROJECTION
The Out-of-Body Experience
Denning & Phillips

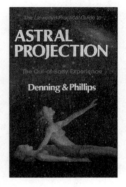

Yes, your consciousness can be sent forth, out of the body, with full awareness and return with full memory. You can travel through time and space, converse with nonphysical entities, obtain knowledge by nonmaterial means, and experience higher dimensions.

Is there life after death? Are we forever shackled by time and space? The ability to go forth by means of the Astral Body, or Body of Light, gives the personal assurance of consciousness (and life) beyond the limitations of the physical body. No other answer to these ageless questions is as meaningful as experienced reality.

The reader is led through the essential stages for the inner growth and development that will culminate in fully conscious projection and return. Not only are the requisite practices set forth in step-by-step procedures, augmented with photographs and visualization aids, but the vital reasons for undertaking them are clearly explained. Beyond this, the great benefits from the various practices themselves are demonstrated in renewed physical and emotional health, mental discipline, spiritual attainment, and the development of extra faculties.

0-87542-181-4, 266 pp., 5¼ x 8, illus., softcover $9.95